3rd

ENGAGING PERFORMANCE

Engaging Performance: Theatre as Call and Response presents a combined analysis and workbook to examine "socially engaged performance." It offers a range of key practical approaches, exercises, and principles for using performance to engage in a variety of social and artistic projects. Author Jan Cohen-Cruz draws on a career of groundbreaking research and work within the fields of political, applied, and community theatre to explore the impact of how differing genres of theatre respond to social "calls."

Areas highlighted include:

- playwrighting and the engaged artist
- theatre of the oppressed
- performance as testimonial
- the place of engaged art in cultural organizing
- the use of local resources in engaged art
- revitalizing cities and neighborhoods through engaged performance
- training of the engaged artist.

Cohen-Cruz also draws on the work of major theoreticians, including Bertolt Brecht, Augusto Boal, and Doreen Massey, as well as analyzing in-depth case studies of the work of US practitioners today to illustrate engaged performance in action.

Jan Cohen-Cruz is director of Imagining America: Artists and Scholars in Public Life. She is the author of *Local Acts: Community-Based Performance in the US*; the editor of *Radical Street Performance*; co-editor, with Mady Schutzman, of *Playing Boal: Theatre, Therapy, Activism* and *A Boal Companion*; and a University Professor at Syracuse University.

ENGAGING PERFORMANCE

Theatre as call and response

Jan Cohen-Cruz

Routledge
Taylor & Francis Group

LONDON AND NEW YORK

First published 2010
by Routledge
2 Park Square, Milton Park, Abingdon, Oxon OX14 4RN

Simultaneously published in the USA and Canada
by Routledge
270 Madison Avenue, New York, NY 10016

Routledge is an imprint of the Taylor & Francis Group, an informa business

© 2010 Jan Cohen-Cruz

Typeset in Goudy by Taylor and Francis Books Ltd
Printed and bound in Great Britain by TJ International Ltd, Padstow,
Cornwall

British Library Cataloguing in Publication Data
A catalogue record for this book is available from the British Library

Library of Congress Cataloging in Publication Data
A catalog record for this book has been requested

ISBN 10: 0-415-47213-X (hbk)
ISBN 10: 0-415-47214-8 (pbk)
ISBN 10: 0-203-84769-5 (ebk)

ISBN 13: 978-0-415-47213-5 (hbk)
ISBN 13: 978-0-415-47214-2 (pbk)
ISBN 13: 978-0-203-84769-5 (ebk)

Dedication: To my departed teachers, on whose insights I build:

Brooks McNamara (1937–2009), for making parallels between US and European forms of popular entertainment like *commedia dell'arte*, bringing the former the respect it so deserves. Brooks taught me that a scholar can change the perception of a cultural practice, so relevant to my own work with engaged theatre.

Barbara Myerhoff (1935–1985), for writing in such a way that both the people at the source of her work and scholars can read and savor it, and for her sense of responsibility to both communities.

MC Richards (1916–1999), for her careful connecting of the inside and the outside of an experience, be it the shaping of a pot or of a community event.

Augusto Boal (1935–2009), whose *Theatre of the Oppressed* I encountered on a remainder shelf at the Strand Bookstore in New York City, opening up a new way of looking at engaged art. And who modeled the inextricability of theory and practice.

CONTENTS

CONTENTS

FIGURES

ACKNOWLEDGEMENTS

Thanks to my long-time writing partner Deborah Mutnick; to my Syracuse writers' group – Margaret Himley, Alison Mountz, and Robin Riley; and to Imagining America staff members Jamie Haft for research assistance, Kevin Bott for conversations, Victoria Del Prato for administrative support, and Robin Goettel for keeping the office running smoothly when I was absorbed with the book. I am grateful for the generous exchange with many of the people I write about and with friends who discussed particular chapters with me, notably Amy Koritz, Bob Vorlicky, and Lucy Winner. Much gratitude to Syracuse University (SU) Provost Eric Spina for allowing me to balance my institutional duties with the completion of this book. Special appreciation to SU Chancellor Nancy Cantor for her fervent commitment to, belief in, and furthering of engaged scholarship and practice nationally. I also want to acknowledge Talia Rodgers, my Routledge champion for this manuscript and three other books I edited (two of them with Mady Schutzman) with this press, for her unflagging confidence in my work and full-hearted commitment to a full range of theatre and performance. Finally, as always, I am beholden to Dionisio for being such a steady and loving presence through it all.

I am grateful for permission to reproduce the following ten photographs:

1.1 Tony Kushner's *Angels in America*. Photo permission, Ann Marie Costa.
1.2 Cornerstone Theater, *Walker Street Chalk Circle*. Photo permission, Cornerstone Theater.
2.1 Mady Schutzman, playwright, *Upset!* Photo permission, CAP Program, CalArts.
2.2 *El Yunque is in the Laundromat*. Photo permission, Arthur Aviles.
3.1 *home land security*. Permission, Marty Pottenger.
4.1–3 *Thousand Kites*, photo permissions, www.thousandkites.org for more.

5.1 *Home, New Orleans?* Youth troupe performance. Photo permission, Jan Cohen-Cruz.

6.1 Open-Hand Theater performing outdoors for new Syracuse University students, Syracuse, New York. Photo courtesy of The Syracuse University photo archive.

INTRODUCTION

This book is about *engaging performance*, in two senses of the word. The one is as a verb, to engage, referring to the act of choosing performance to respond to social controversies. The other is as an adjective, and describes the compelling expressive potential of performance that draws on a broad range of people involved in the social situation in question. Such collaborators encompass those who contribute both through the authority of their lived experience and by virtue of particular professional expertise – the person with a loved one incarcerated or the prison guard, as well as the community organizer able to translate insights about the criminal justice system into political action.

In the pages that follow, I elaborate on a broad range of theatrical methodologies for engagement, drawing on internationally recognized theories that illuminate them – from the German theatre theoretician and playwright Bertolt Brecht, the Brazilian inventor of Theatre for the Oppressed Augusto Boal, the British geographer Doreen Massey, and others – and demonstrated largely through US practitioners whose work resonates beyond their geographical parameters. At the heart of this practice is an ethos and an aesthetics of call and response.

Geneva Smitherman defines call and response as "spontaneous verbal and non-verbal interaction between speaker and listener in which all of the speaker's statements ('calls') are punctuated by expressions ('responses') from the listener" (Smitherman 1977: 104). Translated to engaged performance, call and response foregrounds the many opportunities for interactivity between a theatre artist and the people involved in the situation in question. These exchanges happen at various points along the performance process: the early phases, especially research and devising, or perhaps a workshop not intended to lead to anything else; the duration of the play itself; and the period following, whether a talkback conversation, story circles, or more long-term actions that the production supports or inspires.[1] The process is iterative: the call may be initiated from a community, and the response may come from an artist, who then sets forth a new call directed to an audience. The overall process of such art must be

1

reciprocal and must benefit the people whose lives inform the project, not just promote the artist.

The "call-and-response" dynamic of engaged art brings a community together for both political and spiritual reasons. Political because it provides a way for a group of any status to participate in a public discourse about issues that affect their lives; spiritual because a purpose is embedded in the process and goal of such work that goes beyond material results and our day-to-day existence. Both the political and the spiritual provide models of how we live together, suggesting something bigger than our individual selves. Smitherman explains:

> The traditional African world view conceptualizes a cosmos which is an interacting, interdependent, balanced force field. The community of men and women, the organization of society itself, is thus based on this assumption ... the fundamental requirement is active participation of all individuals.
>
> (Smitherman 1977: 108)

Smitherman cites Robert Farris Thompson, who describes call and response as "perfected social interaction" with everyone performing and everyone listening (Smitherman 1977: 109). "Emphasis," writes Smitherman, "is on group cohesiveness, cooperation, and the collective common good" (Smitherman 1977: 109). An active relationship between actors and community, not only the connection among the actors, is at the heart of the work. Call and response brings the fruits of that relationship to the public sphere: something in our shared life speaks urgently to the artist and the work s/he consequently makes goes beyond personal expression.

To connect art beyond the aesthetic sphere, artists must themselves be engaged in the world around them. Granted, some theatre has had great impact because of the heightened context of a particular time and place. Elsewhere, I have written about this phenomenon as "the motion of the ocean," quoting artist John O'Neal, who was quoting a Detroit deejay: "It's not the ship in the sea that makes the waves, it's the motion of the ocean" (Cohen-Cruz 2004: 35). In the early 1970s, for example, Bread and Puppet Theater could perform anti-Vietnam street parades that helped keep public attention on the human cost of that war, because so many people were already publicly debating US participation there. But generally, engaged performance requires not just theatre craft, but organizing skills as well, in order to make relationships in contexts that take the work beyond the actor and the spectator.

Engaged performance, then, is an inter-sectoral undertaking, calling for art and some other knowledge. Linda Frye Burnham, curator of the Community Arts Network (CAN),[2] which provides the main glue in the USA for what is known, globally, by such terms as community-based art,[3] applied theatre, and theatre for development, elaborates:

> [M]ore and more people are being drawn into the arts from other fields and into other fields from the arts. This kind of crossover goes beyond collaborating with others to reach a common goal. It involves immersion in another train of thought and action, bringing about a synergy that can create paradigmatic change.
> (Linda Burnham, "Can report, again", email, May 25, 2009)

Art that originates interactively in the world does not tend to stick to disciplinary boundaries. Seeking out audiences for their social as much as aesthetic passions, engaged performance frequently takes place in other than traditional theatre spaces. Anthony McCall distinguishes works in public spaces from those in art venues as not having "quote marks" around them (McCall 2009: 5). That is, there is not a built-in buffer in non-specifically art spaces to mediate the effect of an act in the flow of life.

Kinship among engaged performance practices

In this book I resuscitate the term "engaged" with its historical connotation of commitment, but unfettered by assumptions of aesthetic mediocrity and strictly material usefulness such as encumbers its manifestation as community-based or applied art (more on that shortly). The French existential philosopher and writer Jean-Paul Sartre advocated for all art to be "*engagé*," translated as committed. He writes, "The only really committed artist is he who, without refusing to take part in the combat, at least refuses to join the regular armies and remains a free lance" (cited in Charlesworth 1975: 32). Sartre thus suggests taking a stand while maintaining a degree of independence. Albert Camus, also identified as an engaged writer, advocated for the artist to accept his responsibility "to act as a witness" for the persecuted, who "need all those who can speak to communicate their silence and to keep in touch with them" (cited in Charlesworth 1975: 32). In contemporary engaged art we go further, making opportunities for people to speak for themselves in some phase of the process, even while not always in the performance.

The term "engaged" foregrounds the *relationships* at the heart of making art with such aspirations, and dependence on a genuine exchange between artist and community such that the one is changed by the other. Writing about Sartre, Michael Scriven explains the significance of relationships in engaged art:

> The notion of culture as an autonomous aesthetic object was consequently replaced by the idea of culture as a social process

3

engaging writer/artist and "reader" in a mutually rewarding activity ... The aesthetic object was consequently the site of a process of interaction between writer/artist and "reader," the ultimate aim being revelation and disclosure of the world.

(Scriven 1999: 87)

But whereas the artist/writer, in the above description, is the proactive figure in the relationship, engaged performance encompasses an active role for other partners as well.

Writing about an engaged model of visual art, Grant Kester describes this kind of aesthetic experience as "a process of communicative exchange rather than a physical object" (Kester 2004: 90). In performance, the relationship begins between an artist and the people to whom she or he is drawn in order to make the work, continues between actors and spectators, and often reaches fulfillment back in the world beyond the theatre.

I have regularly encountered the parallel notion of engaged *scholarship* since becoming director of Imagining America: Artists and Scholars in Public Life, in summer 2007. Even as engaged art-making requires more social interaction than the solitary garret or distanced rehearsal room can by themselves provide, so engaged scholarship is dependent on relationships with people in other than academic circles, beyond the solitude of the library or separateness of the classroom. The engaged scholar cannot learn all she needs from books, but must also rub up against the situations in which knowledge is tested, in lived experience. Responding to actual situations rather than furthering their work strictly theoretically, engaged scholars seek out expertise not all to be found in one discipline. And they, in turn, bring a range of approaches to such situations.

Engaged but not married,[1] performance models that respond to real-world calls similarly are situated in a range of taxonomies; they do not forsake all other ties. Engagement frequently has been a component of *avant garde* performance, as the mission statement of the experimental art producers, Creative Time, reflects: "to commission, produce and present the most important, ground-breaking, challenging and exceptional art of our times; art that infiltrates the public realm" (www.creativetime.org). "Revolutions in Public Practice," a Creative Time 2009 international gathering, featured artists associated with

social aesthetics, participatory art, dialogic art, political art, "constituting" a type of artistic work that has been growing over the last twenty years and is the most exciting and groundbreaking work happening today ... [It] emphasizes social relationships and the impact of this work stretches into the public realm enough to constitute a sort of political action.

(N. Thompson 2009: 3)

4

The engaged artist embraces rigorous connection and exchange, becoming involved in the issues and people at the source of their work, not assuming the need to keep a critical distance.

Or take devised performance, work emerging directly from an individual or group of people rather than beginning with a written script. Tom Leabhart, who has pursued a life's work in corporeal mime, identifies the ascendency of devised performance in contemporary performance generally. He notes that his teacher (and, briefly, one of mine), the mime master and purist Etienne Decroux, believed theatre had been colonized by the European mind and needed to cast off the playwright, choreographer, and scenic designer to get to the core of the actor standing before the spectator. That is, rather than accept the hierarchy of conventional definitions of expertise, each of us becomes the seed of devised work; it is a bottom-up model. Relatedly, Leabhart further recounts, director Eugenio Barba, who emerged from the experimental performance context of the 1960s and 1970s, has said that the actors in his company perform themselves first, their character second. Devising reflects the belief that all of us can be expressive in ways worthy of attention, gesturing towards the democratic impulse in engaged work.[5]

Engaged performance includes, but is larger than, *applied theatre*, the term of record for many of the case studies in this book, and an important way in which many people identify their practice.[6] Performance scholars Tim Prentki and Sheila Preston describe applied theatre as "a broad set of theatrical practices and creative processes that take participants and audiences beyond the scope of conventional, mainstream theatre into the realm of a theatre that is responsive to ordinary people and their stories, local settings and priorities" (Prentki and Preston 2009: 9). Helen Nicholson also emphasizes applied theatre's otherness – "dramatic activities that primarily exist outside conventional mainstream theatre institutions" – and efficacious nature – "specifically intended to benefit individuals, communities and societies" (Nicholson 2005: 2).

While these formulations are not inaccurate, I argue that such *theatre* is not necessarily "other," but rather some of the *voices* they bring in have been othered and marginalized. I am concerned that we inadvertently limit such performance by foregrounding its difference from other theatrical undertakings. Theatre reproduces the same hierarchies that plague the world at large, the same assumptions of who can speak, who must listen, and who is not even invited into the conversation. While broadly inclusive, those initiating the performances of which I write bring very particular elements of craft to these undertakings as well.

Then, too, there is the unfortunate association of "applied" with the professional who has all the answers and simply bestows (applies) them upon "a community," rather than co-producing work drawing on both parties' strengths. This notion of "applied" is also a drawback of

Ernest Boyer's otherwise exemplary distinction among four kinds of scholarship: discovery, integration, application, and teaching (Boyer 1990). Gregory Jay, professor and director of the Center for Cultures and Community, University of Wisconsin/Milwaukee, points out that Boyer's terms had the utterly useful intention "of trying to separate engagement from service." Service in this sense corresponds to theatre theorist and maker Augusto Boal's critique of artists with liberatory goals imposing their own monologic perspectives rather than engaging dialogically with a community. In an observation equally relevant to applied art as to scholarship, Jay notes:

> [I]nsofar as the "application" category was intended to subsume engagement, it perpetuated a "missionary" model in which knowledge was first created on campus and then "applied" to "problems" off-campus, effectively pathologizing the community and future campus partners.
>
> (Jay 2009: 15)

Theatre-based critiques of "applied" also abound. Judith Ackroyd avows that applied theatre has over-defined itself into a set of exclusionary practices, whereas "Art has for centuries been seen as cathartic, instrumental, instructive" (Ackroyd 2007: 7). I am not advocating abandoning the term "applied theatre," recognizing with colleagues like James Thompson that it is a category that is meaningful to many practitioners and already in place in numerous college and university courses (J. Thompson 2009: 4). I am nevertheless mindful of its need to break free of certain strictures.

The intervention I seek to make to the applied theatre project is framing it as part of a larger project of engagement, and articulating its place in the continuum of art. For applied theatre has gathered some baggage over the years, which it could usefully cast off. This problem was evidenced at what was nevertheless a wonderful applied theatre symposium that I attended in the summer of 2009 in the UK.

A participant is waxing poetic about the value of performance that allows people to bring their story to the public domain, building to the conclusion that the raison d'être *of applied theatre is telling one's story. No, I shriek to myself. Please let's not reduce applied theatre to "one's story." But before I figure out how to protest politely, fellow participant Paul Murray asserts that in the theatre he needs, no one will ask him "his story," as if he only has one. Because the one they mean is about his abusive childhood, and he doesn't want to root his self-expression in that history. Rather, which story shall he tell? And why just his stories, why not emphasize collective stories? And how shall any of these stories be told? Sometimes the emotionally-fragile people with whom he frequently works make performances with no narrative line, but rather feature a series of images and impressions. Whether doing individual experimental work or collaborating,*

Murray wants to be freed of the expectation that working with a particular demographic means working in a particular genre.

Practitioners can interact with a broad range of people and subjects and still draw from the full spectrum of performative approaches. There are frequent examples of challenging performances connecting brilliantly with audiences in a range of circumstances. *Waiting for Godot* utterly resonated with inmates at Sing Sing Prison in the 1950s, while audiences at commercial theatres were clueless in response to the same play. In New Orleans a few years after Hurricane Katrina (which struck in 2005), another production of *Godot* drew the rapt attention of a broad range of people who'd learned – on rooftops, in the immediate aftermath of the storm – what waiting was. Mainstream producers have invited practitioners who engage with local sources, issues, and performers onto regional theatre stages; director Bill Rauch, formerly of Cornerstone Theater, has often been commissioned to such ends and is now executive director of the Oregon Shakespeare Festival, the regional theatre with the largest budget in the USA.

This is not to leave out narrative. Engaged performance sometimes takes the most elemental of forms, what we can say when seemingly nothing we do can affect a terrible situation. Back at the symposium: *Hala is from Palestine and is all about narrative. She tells us a story by way of introduction about a Palestinian killed by an Israeli soldier. The man had requested that his organs be given to others upon his death. His parents receive his body and after some deliberation, bring it to a hospital in Haifa, Israel, where three Israelis and two Palestinians benefit. Hala explains that while many at this symposium make art as part of reconciliation, she is in a situation where the conflict has not abated so such a process is premature. But people need a fuller view of Palestinians, so she is compelled to tell stories like this one about the Palestinian organ donor, and enact narratives to demonstrate that her people are not "terrorists."* Whereas "applied" sometimes carries the totally unrealistic expectation of direct contribution to a large political goal, such as ending the Occupation, this instance of narrative demonstrates engaged performance's more modest but significant capacity to affect our understanding of each other.

For even when theatre can accomplish nothing material, it can fulfill a variety of purposes. *Marina, also from Palestine, expresses the joy of theatre-making with youth. She tells us that surrounded by violence, many young Palestinians feel they must participate in resistance to the Occupation. Marina wants to lighten that burden, wants them to have their childhoods. Theatre-making's effect on them is transformative, she says, providing a context in which they can thrive, be recognized, feel important, and simply play.* In this case, performance is a necessary occasion to *not* be responsible to a larger political frame. Not all of engaged performance's benefits are solutions.

At the symposium, I talk about the dialectics of my own theatrical journey, alternately motivated by opportunities to explore aesthetic forms and to support, through performance, people in difficult circumstances. When I was 17, I went to Paris to study mime with Etienne Decroux. I wanted to apprentice myself to a European master and develop a physically expressive capacity. But it was 1968, that astounding year of questioning top-down political constrictions all over the West. At the same time as I was acquiring an exacting physical discipline, I was experiencing the thrill and immediately relevant content of Bread and Puppet Theater, touring Europe with its beautiful puppets and masks of all sizes and its anti-war plays. Company members stayed in the communal apartment in which I was living. I also got to experience Ariane Mnouchkine's aesthetically astonishing Theatre du Soleil. Mnouchkine's "1789", in solidarity with grassroots movements for genuinely democratic decision-making happening at that same moment, retold the story of the French revolution, putting working-class people in the center of the story and recasting Louis XIV and Marie Antoinette as buffoons.

I am relieved to confess my love of unpredictable performances at an applied theatre conference. I call for a softening of false boundaries that over-polarize theatre as being use-driven on the one end, aesthetically-driven on the other. [See *Performance Affects* (J. Thompson 2009) for a full exploration of this subject.] While embracing the applied field's cultural democracy, creating art by, of, and for a broad population, I don't concur that such theatre is by definition amateurish. I am most satisfied by theatre with a compelling aesthetic language as well as a broad social reach. Nicholson, too, resists over-simplifying applied theatre's purview, even while accepting the term: "I would be very concerned if the convenience of this collective noun reduced a rich diversity of theories and artistic practices to a single homogenous discourse" (Nicholson 2005: 5). I long to see the end of assumptions not only that applied/community-based theatre is necessarily high on the useful end of the spectrum, but also that usefulness is in inverse proportion to aesthetics – that is, that high on the one scale means low on the other.

Engaged art-making practices tend to share *social justice* aspirations: they have been used in the name of, and often in the hands of, people struggling for human rights that have been denied. This is a concept of social justice in philosopher Amartya Sen's sense, as "ultimately connected with the way people's lives go, and not merely with the nature of institutions surrounding them," alluding to John Rawls's framing of justice as "the first virtue of social institutions" at the heart of his analysis (Rawls 1971). Critic Carlin Romano quotes Sen further: "The identification of redressable injustice is not only what animates us to think about justice and injustice, it is also central ... to the theory of justice" (Romano 2009: B4).

Martin Luther King, Jr epitomizes this sense of social justice as redress in the face of historical and structural inequalities. He wrote "Letter from Birmingham Jail" (King 1963) in response to a public statement from eight Alabama clergymen criticizing recent demonstrations he led for civil rights in Birmingham. King responded, "[I]t is even more unfortunate that the white power structure of this city left the Negro community with no other alternative." King adjured that a direct action such as a demonstration ought to be undertaken only when negotiations fail: "It seeks so to drama-tize the issue that it can no longer be ignored." Explaining this political use of the dramatic, King espouses direct action that is expressive, publicly compelling, and critical without being violent. King also points out the necessity of dialogue, which plays a central role in engaged performance generally, writing, "Too long has our beloved Southland been bogged down in the tragic attempt to live in monologue rather than dialogue." He suggests that demonstrations *perform* unwillingness to accept second-class status as a way of entering into dialogue, of critiquing the *status quo* publicly.

Art with social justice underpinnings contains a vision that exceeds what its makers expect to accomplish materially, and that is the space of art, utopia, the imagination. The performance is both useful in some way, and a gesture toward something not attainable any time soon, but what those performing most wish. To embody such aspirations, all the performative drawers must be unlocked, so one can sing or dance the vision, speak it clearly or embellished.

Given the enormity of this goal, the full range of practices that share a similar impulse would do well to claim kinship. Engaged art is still art; it still has the capacity to ask questions rather than tote a party line, through its own particular configuration of language, image, artifice, and actor/spectator interaction. What distinguishes engaged theatre from the main-stream is not lack of technique, which many performances that fit engaged criteria display in abundance, but rather the artists' actively committed relationship to the people most affected by their subject matter.

Purposes of writing this book

The symbolic realm, of which performance is a part, is a tool for those whose vision of a just and capacious world is greater than their material means to make it so. We've seen the symbolic at play when small bands of people occupy and set up peace camps at military installations, such as took place at the British Greenham Common in 1983, very briefly stopping production of weapons of mass destruction (Cook and Kirk 1983). We saw it when mothers of disappeared activists during Argentina's Dirty War of the 1980s circled the central square of Buenos Aires, weekly, with photos of their (adult) children, feared murdered by the government for their pol-itics, carrying signs asking where their children were, symbolically posing a question that the government would never answer (Taylor 1997). In the 1960s, when it seemed that migrant workers in California lettuce fields had no leverage *vis-à-vis* the owners, El Teatro Campesino joined with organi-zers and, through culturally familiar songs, characters, and humor, helped bring masses of people into what became a union. These gestures were initially symbolic – no-one held the illusion that the nuclear plant would suddenly beat its swords into plowshares; or the Argentine state would publicly expose the mass murder it was condoning; or the farm-owners would, on their own, improve workers' housing, work conditions, and pay because of some songs and jokes. But one could focus a public on images and energies of the just and the unjust. One could be active rather than passive, and join with others who felt similarly compelled to resist, and that could lead to other acts that *were* efficacious. And that could be performed.

But such acts could be performed so many different ways. From the acting out of utopia evidenced in turning a military encampment into a peace-loving temporary commune; to the "invisible" theatrics of what Diana Taylor (1997) has framed as acting out the role of motherhood in public as a cover for resisting a state that forbade dissent; to the short, physically expressive, satirical *"actos"* so familiar to the Chicano farm-workers, choosing which theatrics to employ to intervene for justice in a given situation takes analysis. Theatre-makers must identify the intended spectators and appropriate actors, the right tone and the potential impact and risk, knowledge of a range of performative possibilities, and the critical capacity not simply to repeat a methodology, but to shape and adapt it to fit the circumstances.

In what follows, I map out a range of forms that engaged performance takes and a range of methods for making it. I'm motivated by three aspirations. First, I want to demonstrate that such work fits in the continuum of art. Why? So people who do it get the respect they deserve, the public experiences art in its many guises, and young people attracted to a profession in the arts see more options of what that can entail. So work shaped locally is perceived, *a priori*, as no less valuable than work that comes to us from far away. I intend to provide evidence that engaged art is not necessarily less interesting aesthetically than other art; that what distinguishes it is intention to respond to a social call and a relationship with people most implicated. Commenting on visual artists who likewise foreground dialogue and relationship over object produced, Grant Kester addresses their aesthetics:

> Their sense of artistic identity is sufficiently coherent to speak as well as listen, but it remains contingent upon the insights to be derived from their interaction with others and with otherness. They define themselves as artists through their ability to catalyze understanding, to mediate exchange, and to sustain an ongoing process of empathetic identification and critical analysis.
>
> (Kester 2004: 118)

Artists who make theatre with a broad range of participants often struggle to get such work acknowledged as part of art, with aesthetic and other criteria for evaluating it. For like any art, not all socially-engaged work is "good."

Assessing applied art entails revisiting the work's goals, which are themselves often aesthetic and something else. The "something else" in the case of Moises Kaufman's *Laramie Project*, for example, has proven to be education, specifically opening up conversations about tolerance and homosexuality in high school classes. Indeed, over the 25 years when I taught hundreds of drama students at New York University, more entered college having read that play in high-schools all across the USA than those of any other author, including Shakespeare. It is not beside the point that the aesthetic form of theatre, situated between intimacy and distance, is the way some difficult conversations are initiated. Too much intimacy can feel intrusive; too much distance can feel like nothing at all and easily be disregarded.

Second, I aim to point performing artists who want to participate in large issues of our shared social life to a broad palette from which to choose how to make such work, and how to think about choosing. In that regard, the book is a response to practitioners who use only one set of techniques, no matter what the social situation. The idea to take on this task was suggested while presenting at a Pedagogy and Theatre of the Oppressed conference[7] with Dudley Cocke, artistic director of Appalachia's Roadside Theater.

Cocke and I were explaining the differences in how personal story is used by the Brazilian founder of "theatre of the oppressed," Augusto Boal, and Cocke's company. For Boal, storytelling is a strategy for locating social oppression among the individuals participating as a step in seeking collective solutions. For Roadside, personal story is part of a community engagement methodology grounded in local cultural assets, which in Appalachia include the oral tradition and particular music, both to solve community problems and, paraphrasing the rural poet and essayist Wendell Berry, to celebrate "local life aware of itself." While acknowledging Boal's pioneering work, Cocke pointed out that too few of Boal's US practitioners employ his methodologies within the context of their own local culture: "This failure of adaptive imagination in service to local community grounding makes the results less than optimum" (Dudley Cocke, "Roadside, Boal, story", email, June 15, 2009). On the other hand, as I added, working with people who are not necessarily part of the same cultural tradition, Boal's story-sharing quickly connects people around a pressing issue. Someone in the audience said, "I wish you would write a book on a range of socially-engaged performance practices and how one decides which to use when." In this book, I do so, presenting a range of methods that have fruitfully engaged a broad array of voices in understanding the issues of our times. I discuss the fit between each of these methods and provide a case study of the circumstances to which they responded.

This diverse set of possibilities is a reminder that artists can walk and whistle at the same time; they can make any sort of theatre and engage with people in challenging circumstances without compromising either. Paul Murray explains participating in the applied theatre discourse in order to keep it safe for people like him, with roots in theatre and clowning, not social service practice, who have found more satisfaction "making theatre with people and traditions outside of conventional theatrical settings; on the street, in prisons, and in asylums for those regarded as being mentally ill":

> The kind of activities I have been involved in facilitating over the years have become increasingly recognized and advocated by experts as promising epistemological and methodological paradigms with which to try and better understand and even *deal with* serious problems of human existence ... In the face of these new appreciative and appropriating threats, clowns ... need to seek out and play with those experts who seek to take us seriously, otherwise we will perish ... [What] kind of playing ... may be necessary if the uniquely radical artistic, political and socially developmental benefits of our *innocent* activities are to be maintained.
>
> (Murray 2009: 2)

Murray voices a fear I hear repeatedly: that something simple yet fundamental will be lost if applied theatre is over-framed as useful. And that may be the very aesthetics that support serious playing itself.

Third, this book is an example of praxis, incorporating both reflections and doings – the reflections being the description and analysis of diverse approaches to engaged performance; the doings being the workbook component at the end of each chapter, where I elaborate on a technique central to the preceding discussion. I thus seek to model the interplay of reflection and action that characterizes cultural activism. Instructors wishing to use this book as a course framework can try these techniques with students. We interact with and come to understand engaged performance through words and through the body, as outlined in these workbook sections. The chapter narrative is, in effect, a call to which the technique that follows in the workbook is a response.

Throughout the book, I especially address readers seeking to ally idealism with performative techniques that contribute to bringing a more equitable world into being. I have been mindful of the book's adaptability to the college classroom, though it is informative for anyone with such interests, in or out of a formal educational setting. For in order to become the kind of artist who carries out projects such as those described in these pages, one needs an orientation and a craft that includes and goes beyond a general understanding of aesthetics.

The book is not, let me hasten to add, an encyclopedia. Engaged performance includes many forms not detailed in this book, such as political demonstrations, and educational, therapeutic, and child-centered theatre. It may be based in conflict resolution, bringing together people from two sides of large-scale divides; it may involve practitioners from highly-resourced countries working in parts of the world with only the scantest of material wealth, or people from low-resourced countries working in wealthy nations. My intention is to present enough of a picture of engaged performance and its particular place in the constellation of art that practitioners, scholars, and audiences can recognize other examples of such work when they encounter it.

Book organization: centers of gravity of engaged performance

Any problem has five or six good solutions and five or six bad solutions. What I try to get people to do is choose one of the good ways instead of one of the bad ways, but not influence which one, because that depends on how people function, what people's backgrounds are.

(Horton and Freire 1990: 196–97)

This book reflects my experience that art can be committed socially without being dull and programmatic. Engaged art does not have to situate itself *at the service of* a political agenda and simply communicate what is already known. Each chapter of this book presents a different way in which artists participate in the challenges of their times just as surely as do organizers, politicians, and journalists, but through the particular tools of *our* trade. Framed by ideas of internationally respected thinkers, the first six chapters provide analyses and selected techniques of six artistic approaches and methodologies suggesting the breadth of engaged performance, grounded in case studies from US projects I have participated in or observed. The final chapter is about the kind of training that prepares practitioners to take on such work. While none of the artists I feature sees art or culture as single-handedly responsible for social change, they do see their work as capable of playing a significant role. And they extend themselves beyond conventional notions of art in the pursuit of such goals.

The responses to social calls grounding the first two chapters are squarely situated in art-making. With chapter one, "Playwrighting: Putting Plays to Use," I begin where I first recognized engaged performance, in particular instances of dramatic literature, noting variations on that theme. As a child, I did not know that theatre was anything more than the production of plays. Literature has a privileged status in the West, infatuated with the written word over orality. While applied theatre sometimes just reverses that hierarchy, and *a priori* favors the oral over the written, productions generated from both written and oral starting points have the capacity to be engaged. I start with Bertolt Brecht's theories about activating spectators and the rise of Nazism that forced both his exile from Germany and his need to find other ways to dramatize the struggles with which he was allied. I look at the approach to engagement in Tony Kushner's *Angels in America*, produced at the height of the AIDS epidemic in the USA. I also highlight how adapting plays, as exemplified by Cornerstone Theater, draws on the power of individual playwrights while rendering the language and context accessible to a broader range of collaborators and audiences.

I move, in chapter two, "Specta(c)ting: Theatre of the Oppressed, orthodoxy and adaptation," to the spectator sharing the center of engaged performance. Augusto Boal furthered Brecht's notion of the *intellectually* active spectator into strategies for *physical* activation. In Boal's theatre of the oppressed (TO), engagement happens through both workshop exercises and interactive plays, inviting the erstwhile spectator, called spect-actor, to explore scenes of oppression physically. For Boal, like Stanislavski, the senses are a fundamental pathway connecting us to the world so that we see what we look at, listen to what we hear, and feel what we touch. Boal couples these affective tools of the actor with the pedagogy of Paulo Freire, so that the goal of our artistically-heightened consciousness is becoming the subjects of our own lives. I especially focus on TO's adaptation by subsequent practitioners.

The next two chapters feature practices at the nexus of art and organizing, frequently necessary to bring the work into the social realm. In chapter three, "Self-representing: Testimonial Performance," Marty Pottenger draws on her experience from union organizing and from theatre to create work drawn directly from the people whose issues are the precipitant. She built the play *home land security* about a 2004 raid on immigrants and refugees in Portland, Maine, with people most affected representing themselves. Their complex and humane characterization contrasted sharply with Homeland Security portrayals of refugees as criminals to be deported. In addition, the actors developed community among themselves and with other sympathetic Portlanders through coming together to perform publicly what the raids put their communities through. I describe how this testimonial theatre interfaces neatly with ideas of cultural democracy and participatory governance. Pottenger exemplifies the artist–activist, combining her skills in the two arenas to carry out a very deliberate, jointly activist and artistic project, from her office in Portland's town hall.

Chapter four, "Cultural Organizing: Multiple Modes of Communication," takes the art/organizing hybrid to a greater scale. I focus on *Thousand Kites*, a project that uses multiple cultural forms – radio, video, theatre, and the internet – and a range of perspectives – incarcerated people, their families, prison guards and administrators, and their families – to communicate the impact of the criminal justice system on people from all walks of life. I recount how each of the four aesthetic forms was used to gather and disseminate stories and perspectives to an equally broad public. At the same time, this project sought out national prison reform and abolition organizations with which to partner. Both *Thousand Kites* nationally and *home land security* in Maine are examples of cultural projects contributing to political change. Cultural bias reinforced by politically motivated policy against both the incarcerated and refugees is used to justify subjugation; cultural and broadly human identities enacted by both groups are used to fight it.

The next two chapters are about roles for the arts in response to very different crises having a broad impact on two very different cities. Chapter five, "Gathering Assets: The Art of Local Resources," takes place soon after a very immediate disaster, Hurricane Katrina in New Orleans. I look at *Home, New Orleans?*, a project that engaged in rebuilding through the arts in four neighborhoods, drawing on local culture and expertise. I focus most thoroughly on the one situated at the 7th Ward's Porch Cultural Organization, contrasting a grassroots, "bottom-up" approach with a proposal for a more top-down arts project. In the context of a city with great cultural vitality, I recount how a youth theatre company there is contributing to neighborhood needs made more acute since the storm.

Syracuse, New York, a city whose crisis has been happening much more gradually, is the subject of chapter six, "Particularizing Place: Revitalizing Cities and Neighborhoods" Like many rust-belt cities, Syracuse has suffered the slow exodus of manufacturing jobs since the 1950s. The downtown has ceded its role as vital city center as two-fifths of its population have moved to the suburbs and beyond; people come to the city only for occasional visits to the numerous arts and cultural events, restaurants, and smattering of shops. Partnering with municipal government, local businesses, diverse residents, and colleges and universities, artists are adding to the efforts to make the downtown a place people want to come to regularly. Framed by geographer Doreen Massey's conception of cities as non-static places whose particularities can be constructed only through linkage to places beyond – a global sense of the local (Massey 1994) – I look to art and design projects that draw attention to the pleasures of the diversity, history, and energy particular to Syracuse.

In the seventh chapter, "Training: An Engaged Artist Prepares," I propose educational components for engaged performance-making. I draw from The Curriculum Project, an investigation by cultural writer and consultant Arlene Goldbard, Appalachian theatre director and cultural policy consultant Dudley Cocke, and myself. We began with a thesis: that a good education in this field integrates three elements: craft, scholarship, and hands-on community art experience. I elaborate on each component, also discussing underlying values, obstacles, and opportunities that particularly such programs based in higher education face.

In the brief, closing Afterword, "The Centrality of Relationships in Engaging Performance," I consider the pattern that the various chapters together comprise. Through all the variations, the value of the relationships developed through engaging performance comes to the fore, characterized by paying attention to a social call and making a public, collaborative response. Such performances provide the opportunity to see a little utopia, something that doesn't entirely exist in the world except as a possibility. Evoking collective aspirations, engaged performances are situated in semi-imaginary, semi-hyper-real realms, one foot in a utopian nowhere, the other in a very real striving toward somewhere, because the effort does not end when the lights go up.

1

PLAYWRIGHTING

Putting plays to use

(... A sound, like a plummeting meteor, tears down from
very, very far above the earth ... we hear a terrifying CRASH
as something immense strikes ...)
Angel: Greetings, Prophet;
The Great Work begins:
The Messenger has arrived.

(Tony Kushner 1992: 118–19)

I begin with two of my childhood assumptions about theatre. The first was
taking for granted that all theatre takes the form of plays and is at base
dependent on a playwright – The Messenger – to set the terms of the theatrical experience. This was reinforced by the professional summer stock
company near my childhood home in Reading, Pennsylvania. My mother
was on the board, and the many plays I saw each summer were a source of
great pleasure and fascination. I was sure that actors had the best job
possible, as I watched them experience a whole range of circumstances
depending upon the role in which they'd been cast. While I have since
learned about many other ways that theatre comes into creation, in this
chapter I explore under what circumstances the enactment of great dramatic
literature is part of engaged theatre, and in so doing, sets a starting point for
understanding engaged performance as art.

The second assumption is my childhood experience that theatre exists in
a space fully separate from everyday life. This was reinforced by annual
trips to New York City's Broadway theatre. Though for years we were rapt
fans of totally enjoyable musicals, in 1962, when I was 11, my mother took
me to my first theatre experience that I could see nipping at audience
members' consciences and, however obliquely, raising a critique of
a contemporary social situation, the war in Vietnam. The play was the
Royal Shakespeare Company production of Peter Weiss's *Assassination and
Persecution of Jean Paul Marat Performed by the Inmates of the Asylum of
Charenton under the Direction of the Marquis de Sade*, directed by the rising
iconoclastic British director Peter Brook. It was a matinee and the audience
was composed by-and-large of older white women. The horror of the

17

Figure 1.1 Davidson College Theatre Department's production of Tony Kushner's *Angels in America, Part I: The Millennium Approaches*. Production directed by Ann Marie Costa, with scenic design by Joe Gardner. (Photo by Bill Giduz.)

French Revolution filled the stage with literal buckets of blood, and the actors, experimenting with theatre theorist Bertolt Brecht's epic theatre, confronted the spectators eye-to-eye. Well-dressed women with their coats fluttering behind them raced up the aisles, as if fleeing accosters, and out of the building. Each time the door opened, the light of the day broke into the theatre like the production itself, reasserting its connection to the world outside.

In *A Room of One's Own*, Virginia Woolf writes that art needs to be connected to lived experience at all four corners like a spider web. Indeed, some connection between the world beyond and the beguilingly inventive space of the theatre glimmered the day I saw *Marat/Sade* which, while set in a whole different time and place, resonated with the Vietnam War. While the USA had not yet entered the fray, the French were messily entrenched there, blood was flowing, and world opinion was polarized between those for and those against other countries intervening. And while I was too sheltered to know it, Brook and other theatre artists of the time were speaking out against US and European intrusion in "third world" countries, using their platform as public figures to voice their views.

I wrote Peter Brook my first and only fan letter, thanking him for showing me that theatre could galvanize an audience's attention to contemporary events in ways I had never imagined. He wrote me back a postcard, inviting me to visit him when – not if – I found myself on the other side of the Atlantic Ocean, in his neck of the woods. I vowed I would.

In this chapter I examine ways that plays can catalyze spectators to participate in social struggles in their lives outside the theatre, and aesthetic strategies for doing so. I begin with Bertolt Brecht (1898–1956), who as much as a theorist as a playwright, laid a foundation for engaging the spectator critically through the intellect.[1] I move then to playwright Tony Kushner, whose *Angels in America* (Kushner 1992, 1994), in the context of the AIDS crisis, especially intense from the mid-1980s through the 1990s, addressed spectators, some of whom were, and others who were not, part of the efforts to eradicate the disease. Plays by Brecht and Kushner are not typically grouped with the other case studies in this book. I place them here given how immersed Brecht and Kushner were in the struggles about which they write, their intention that their work both entertain and contribute to the respective causes, and the influence they have had on the applied theatre field.

I close with director Bill Rauch, writer Alison Carey, and the Cornerstone Theater Company, which from the mid-1980s to the mid-1990s adapted classical plays through collaborations with people in towns all across the USA, taking up local issues and building community in the process. Cornerstone's practice is a very pronounced form of call and response, adapting plays that integrate local voices in regard to local circumstances in need of public attention.

Brecht's intellectually active spectator

We hereby report to you the story of a journey,
undertaken by one who exploits and two who are exploited
... Observe the smallest action, seeming simple, with distrust
Inquire if a thing be necessary especially if it is common
We particularly ask you – when a thing continually occurs –
Not on that account to find it natural, let anything be called natural
In an age of bloody confusion, ordered disorder, planned caprice,
And dehumanized humanity, lest all things be held unalterable!
(from the prologue to *The Exception and the Rule*, Brecht 1937)

With lines such as these, German playwright and theorist Bertolt Brecht broke the theatre's famous fourth wall and engaged spectators. Though not the first to do so – one obvious precedent is the genre of popular theatre – Brecht's direct exhortations to his audience were apocalyptic calls to heed what was happening around them. Brecht's view was much influenced by Karl Marx, who he first read in 1926, remarking that he had found "the only spectator for my plays" – not because they were so intelligent, but because Marx was (cited in Willett 1964: 23–24). Marxist ideas abound in Brecht's plays; in *Saint Joan of the Stockyards*, a character is described as not bad but hungry, pointing to economics rather than morality as the major shaper of our lives. In contrasting what he called epic theatre with Aristotelean drama, Brecht emphasizes that social situations are in constant flux. He embraced "the classic Marxist view of human consciousness determined by social being" (Willett 1964: 250); that is, how our class determines who we are and what we think. Brecht so embraced dialectics, a core Marxist principle, that he left notes at the end of his life calling his work Dialectical Theater (Willett 1964: 281).

Brecht cajoled audiences to take a critically active look at quintessential power relationships embedded in plays but reflecting the world beyond. In asking spectators to stand back, observe, and challenge unjust norms, Brecht broke with the long-established western dramatic purpose of providing spectators with a cathartic experience, a great emotional release.[2] The cathartic tradition is grounded in Aristotle's *Poetics*, which asserts that spectators of serious dramatic works are meant to experience vicariously the undoing of a great man because of a tragic flaw, be moved by pity and fear, and come out of the theatre emotionally purged.

In sharp contrast, theorizing a role for drama during the dark times of fascism in the 1930s and 1940s, Brecht favored strategies in full view that never caught spectators up in an emotional sweep lest they miss the opportunity to reflect on the play for its application to the political emergencies of the time: "Instead of sharing an experience the audience must come to grips with things" (Brecht 1927 in Willett 1964: 23).

Surrounded by the abuse of emotional spectacle by which the Third Reich "shocked and awed" crowds attending the Nuremberg Party Rallies of the 1920s and 1930s into conformity – with, for example, row upon terrifying row of impeccably uniformed parading soldiers, workers with gleaming shovels, and women in traditional teutonic dresses and aprons – Brecht theorized an approach to keep spectators' critical faculties alive and well.[3] He sought to do so not only in specific plays, but in the theatre as an institution itself, as part of a necessary cultural shift: "the radical transformation of the theatre ... has simply to correspond to the whole radical transformation of our time" (Brecht 1927 in Willett 1964: 23). Brecht desired no less than the triumph of reason over unbridled emotion as a strategy for attaining the concomitant triumph of socialism over Nazism.

Rather than provide cathartic release *within* the drama as the Aristotelean tradition would have, Brecht restrained his spectators from emotion-driven responses, which he saw as impeding critical thinking. Through this aesthetic, which has been translated as the alienation effect but is literally "estrangement," Brecht intended to keep spectators from buying into a fantasy world which, in the most extreme case, was part of the justification for the Final Solution. Those healthy soldiers, workers, and folkloric women marching and dancing in the sun, on display at annual Nuremberg Party Rallies from 1923 to 1938, were represented as a species different from the starved, dirty creatures packed in dark concentration camps, making extermination of the "scourge" of Jews, homosexuals, gypsies, and Marxists that much easier.

So that spectators would not lose the connection between his art and the world beyond the stage, Brecht made careful choices regarding his theatrical palette. He chose white lights that conjoined audience and actors, unfettered by moody colored gels that would only illuminate the stage, so as not to obscure the other spectator/witnesses and the theatrical artifice itself. His texts combined dramatic action and narration, the latter spoken right to audiences through the previously impenetrable fourth wall through which audiences conventionally "eavesdropped" on the insular world of the play. Songs were marked by lighting changes, abrupt breaks with the action, and direct expression of the author's point of view. He sought a dramaturgy full of contradictions that disallowed simple identification with his characters; rather, he positioned spectators to analyze the situation as it unfolded on stage in order to provoke them to take action on the *off-stage* injustices his plays illuminated. These dramaturgical techniques, known as epic theatre, positioned spectators at a critical distance from the play, from whence reasoned reflection might occur.

Epic theatre, Brecht stated, needs to show that outcomes could be different from what they are; that people can make history, rather than be made passively by it. Summations of scenes preceded them, often on placards, and, later, via slides, so that the focus was on *how* and *why* things unfolded as they did, rather than on *what* happened. Brecht emphasized that particular actions are good or bad, and portrayed characters with a choice of which to choose; people are changeable and not fixed.[4] Remembering they were in the theatre kept the outside world relevant, in contrast to aesthetic experiences that transported the audience outside of their everyday lives.

Identifying Brecht and other playwrights with similar goals as revolutionary, Grant Kester asserts that such theatre "leads viewers to actively question the meanings represented onstage and to extend that critical attitude to the values they encounter in daily political life" (Kester 2004: 83). This is a characteristic of an aesthetic of call and response – Kester calls it dialogic – in contrast to a more conventional aesthetic of escape, in which art provides a respite from everyday life, or of abstract reflection, serious contemplation unbridled by the concerns of everyday life. Brecht's is a politically active aesthetic, dependent on a particular desired audience:

> The factory worker, for example, has a much greater stake in challenging the naturalness of the bourgeois worldview portrayed in the mass media than the wealthy banker whose contingent reality it represents.
>
> (Kester 2004: 83)

Kester suggests that the spectator's subject position shapes what they bring to the theatrical experience and, by extension, what they take from it. Here the spectator calls – give me a way to see the world from a working-class perspective – and the playwright responds.

A word of caution: Brecht the theorist must be balanced with Brecht the playwright. There have been too many deadly productions of Brecht's plays, whose directors have faithfully and over-simply applied Brecht's anti-emotion theory with nary a thought to the audience's entertainment. True, in some essays, Brecht besmirched entertainment, calling for a radical revisioning of theatre's role in society:

> We are free to discuss any innovation that doesn't threaten [theatre's] social function – that of providing an evening's entertainment. We are not free to discuss those which threaten to change its function, possibly by fusing it with the education system or with the organs of mass communication.
>
> (Brecht 1930 in Willett 1964: 34)

However, many of Brecht's writings call for a theatre that entertains as it educates. [See, for example, his essay "Theatre for Pleasure or Theatre for Instruction" (Willett 1964: 69–76), which concludes that theatre ought to do both.]

When Brecht directed his own plays, the *homme de théâtre* strategizing audience engagement balanced the upstart intellectual intent on relaying a message. This I realized in the 1970s, when studying with Carl Weber. As a young man in the early 1950s, Weber had been one of Brecht's assistant directors with his re-established, post-World War II company, the Berliner Ensemble, in East Germany. Weber describes watching Brecht direct a scene from one of his plays.

"Speak softer," he instructed the two actors, "we need a more intimate mood." The actors slightly lowered their voices. "No softer, softer!" Again the actors dropped their voices. "No, no, a whisper, you must speak to each other in barely a whisper."

"But Mr. Brecht," implored one of the actors, "if I speak any softer the audience won't hear your words."

"It doesn't matter!" he exploded. "The audience will feel the mood of the moment and that will communicate it all."

Brecht's approach to playwrighting changed with the times and situations in which he found himself, if not always with immediate success. When he began developing epic theatre, he largely relied on a theoretical strategy since he had no permanent group of actors, resident theatre, subscription audience, or government subsidy. Working with large amateur groups in his *Lehrstücke* (learning plays), immediately before Nazism took full control of Germany, Brecht had a minimal opportunity to experiment with what a resistant theatre might actually be in the flesh. As he had suggested in 1927 – that plays become part of the education system – *Lehrstücke* were focused on how engagement in the text and in the process of embodying its ideas could educate the large cast of actors, even more than the audience. But his writing was seen as such a threat to Hitler's regime that, had Brecht not fled Germany in February 1933, he would have been picked up by the SS two days later.

In each phase of Brecht's work, particular conditions and contexts contributed to his plays' ability to engage participants actively in pressing, contemporary issues. Post-World War II, in his newly-established Berliner Ensemble, Brecht participated in the weeding out of Nazi dramatic literature, the only kind of theatre that had been supported in the previous generation. In order to build up a new repertory quickly, Brecht focused on adaptations of classics that addressed issues he felt were worthwhile for his society. By then, Brecht had an East German audience, already identified with the Communist Party, that provided his subscription base.

That prior constitution of a politically-unified audience made a great difference to how his plays were understood. He was in the tradition of political theatre aligned with what scholar Randy Martin calls "that most robust form of political organization, the party" (Martin 2006: 24). Brecht's work then was a cultural wing of a political organization, supporting the hegemony (the dominant societal ideology) rather than opposing it, as he had in the previous era – but not without some static. He was intensely critical of party officials who tried to dictate the kind of work artists should make to align themselves with social rebuilding:

> No painter can paint with hands that tremble for fear of the verdict of some official who may be well-trained politically and very conscious of his political responsibilities yet be badly trained aesthetically and unconscious of his responsibility to the artist.
>
> (Brecht cited in Willett 1964: 269)

Marxism, yes, but all of art is not subsumed by its ideology. Brecht resisted a conformist, predetermined approach to art in favor of a process that was constantly questioning.

Kushner's magical epic theatre

"It's okay if the wires show, and maybe it's good that they do, but the magic should at the same time be thoroughly amazing."
(Kushner 1992: 5, instructing future producers
of *Angels in America, Part I*)

For Tony Kushner, reading Brecht's theory as an undergraduate at Columbia University was "a revelation ... It was the first time I believed that people who are seriously committed political intellectuals could have a home in the theater, the first time that I believed theater, really good theater, had the potential for radical intervention, for effectual analysis" (in Vorlicky 1998: 106). Kushner's theatre has also contributed beyond analysis, bringing emotional and intellectual attention to bear on the AIDS epidemic, when the Reagan administration's homophobia undermined concerted efforts to find a cure for HIV, in the context of federally-funded health research. Kushner's early experience of writing and directing for the small 3P Productions – Poetry, Politics, and Popcorn – suggests his longtime commitment to heightened language, social message, and entertaining playfulness.

Kushner described the personal commitment a director needs to understanding society and history in order to undertake plays like Brecht's *Good Person of Setzuan*. In that play, not only must the director understand the process of rapid modernization "and the devouring of the country by the city," but, he adjures, "you can't do *Setzuan* ... unless you care about money and where the money goes" (in Vorlicky 1998: 115). This personal desire to challenge the status quo leads to a distinctly engaged kind of theatre, be it performed in a community space or one on Broadway.

Kushner calls for the importance of "an ideological space marked 'alternative' [and] how [its] elimination has absolutely forced people into simply

24

accepting as a given all the things that are contrary to their own self-interest" (in Vorlicky 1998: 121). Note the resonance with the words of Brecht that began the previous section, emphasizing resistance to compliance, in Kushner's desire to use theatre to challenge the norm. Kushner asserts that "there are times so reactionary that the best one can do is to serve as a marker for the possibility of alternatives" (Vorlicky 1998: 122). The possibility of alternatives is radiantly present in the last scene of Part II of *Angels in America*, through the unlikely combination of Prior, Louis, Belize, and Hannah, voluntarily taking in a cold sunny day together in New York City's Central Park. Prior, Louis's abandoned lover with AIDS, leaning on a cane but out and about; Belize, the black nurse furious with Louis for leaving his lover in need and for his liberal politics, but still part of this excursion, and still arguing with Louis; and Hannah, the Mormon who left Utah when her Republican son Joe (and Louis's almost-fling) confessed his homosexuality to her over the phone. Now she's here and at ease with three openly homosexual men, "noticeably different – she looks like a New Yorker, and she is reading the *New York Times*" (Kushner 1994: 145). How wonderful that these four people should be able to enjoy each other's company. And, Kushner notes, "The Bethesda Angel" – a well-known statue in that park – "is above them all." They are talking about how stuck the world felt and now, *perestroika*, the thaw. Things can change. Other ways of living together are possible. This ability to imagine a more inclusive world, a world in flux, is part of engaged art, too.

Angels in the context of a social movement

Kushner is also in the tradition of theatre serving as a cultural wing of a social movement. In the USA in the 1960s and early 1970s, for example, a number of theatre companies situated themselves in direct solidarity with social justice efforts. The Free Southern Theater accompanied the civil rights movement in the south, El Teatro Campesino voiced Chicano farm-worker concerns in the California farmlands, the San Francisco Mime Troupe enlivened the free speech movement in the San Francisco Bay area, and Bread and Puppet accompanied anti-Vietnam War rallies and parades from its Vermont base around the USA and the world.

Each of these theatres played a role in strengthening the concomitant movement. The Free Southern Theater brought the civil rights movement to rural areas through touring plays to churches and other grassroots-gathering sites. El Teatro Campesino gave heart to striking Chicanos through biting humor, often performed on the property line of exploitative farms where migrants worked. The San Francisco Mime Troupe challenged those in charge as beyond critique through its broad caricatures that physicalized excesses. Bread and Puppet death masks graphically represented the horror of the Vietnam War. These amplifying aesthetics – the power of performing in spaces directly linked to a struggle, be it positively (churches where civil rights activists gathered) or negatively (migrant camps), larger-than-life acting styles, and visual expressivity like puppets and masks – were means by which alternative theatres of the 1960s and 1970s supported politically progressive movements of their times.[5] These companies are remembered for how closely sutured they were to political activity, strengthening activist communities around these issues. But few of the plays they devised are performed now, or if they are, only as historical, not dramatically-vivid experiences. With less emphasis on the literary quality of the text, such plays were made quickly for immediate use in very current struggles.

While similarly participating in a social movement, advocating for gay rights and significant expansion of efforts to counteract AIDS, Kushner, by contrast, was already writing dramatically compelling plays. He was inspired by Brecht's detailed exploration of dramaturgical means to activate the spectator. Kushner's *Angels in America*, particularly when it was initially performed in the context of the AIDS epidemic and the Reagan administration's denial of the crisis, reflected, honored, and supported such struggles on stage, re-energizing activist spectators to continue the political struggle. But he took the time he needed to craft the plays themselves as dramatic literature intended to endure beyond that moment.

Kushner has taken on themes of contemporary injustice in the most mainstream of venues, such as Broadway in New York City and regional theatres around the USA. At the same time, his *Angels in America* supported many spectators engaged in the AIDS crisis by offering the then-rare opportunity to see their world reflected back in art. According to critic David Roman, and evidenced even in the play's subtitle, *A Gay Fantasia on National Themes*, Kushner especially urged gay men in his audiences to "persevere in locating and claiming our agency in the construction of our histories" (Roman 1997: 42). Indeed, Kushner opened the door for openly gay playwrights to write about their experiences. Beyond emotionally supporting activists, *Angels'* worldwide success contributed to a more sympathetic social environment for AIDS interventions. Kushner, like Brecht, provides a theatre for activated spectators, supporting those fighting the good fight, positioning such efforts as part of a rich history they need to inscribe, and gaining sympathy for the movement as much through poetry as politics.

Kushner and Brecht demonstrate that theatre can disrupt spectators' habitual ways of thinking so that they connect with their own potential empathy and activism. Janelle Reinelt critiques *Angels* for what I see as one of its strengths in this regard: "keeping the discourse personal." She continues: "Nowhere in the play is there any indication of the community organizing, political agitation, liberal church and other organizations involved in fighting AIDS" (Reinelt 1997: 243). Kushner did not have to be so literal in his support of the political community. AIDS activists constituted a significant component of the play's audience; many were surely energized by the centrality of their concerns and sensibilities in the most successful play of the 1990s.

I suspect many experienced what I did, viewing the original New York production of *Angels* at a moment when I was grieving for a dear friend lost to AIDS: deep companionship with strangers, one of the most profound experiences the theatre offers. And the attention the play brought to the AIDS epidemic was a wildly effective way of supporting the movement. Capturing media attention – as *Angels* surely did – brings subject matter into a public discourse. *Angels in America* brought the topic of the AIDS epidemic onto the radar of millions of people who read the newspaper and watch television, through features about, and interviews with, Kushner. While not a direct intervention with the goal of getting more drugs into sick people's bodies at an affordable price – one of the aims of the activist organization ACT UP, the AIDS Coalition to Unleash Power – raising consciousness of the gravity of the issue and a humanized look at its effects supports political action, too.

The play's efficacy relied on the empathic community it built with people at a distance from the AIDS crisis and the actual community it reinforced and to which it gave heart, in context of a very palpable, ongoing struggle. Reinelt describes the relationship between the play and San Francisco, where it was developed at the Eureka Theater (1991), and to which it returned with much hoopla, "foreground[ing] it as something important to San Franciscans, something to be seen, responded to, and assessed from a position of relationship rather than distance" (Reinelt 1997: 238). This she contrasts with the NYC production, on Broadway, in 1993:

> One of the most positive comments on the play was also one of the most damning from the point of view of a seeker after an American epic theater: 'This heretofore almost unknown playwright is such a delightful, luscious, funny writer that, for all the political rage and the scathing unsanitized horror, the hours zip by with the breezy enjoyment of a great page turner or a popcorn movie.' It is not the popular culture comparisons to popcorn movies that chill – after all, old Bert Brecht himself wanted a popular theater in that sense, theater to be like boxing, not opera – it is the notion that a good night out in the theater dishes up politics and genuinely horrible insights in order to accommodate them to the culinary tastes of an audience for whom these things must be rendered palatable.
>
> (Reinelt 1997: 238)

Reinelt accurately suggests that the play as a format can be co-opted, that given the mainstream context, uncomfortable elements can be overlooked if the play successfully entertains.

Various critics have rightly emphasized the timing of the play to attain efficacious as well as entertainment goals. David Roman attended *Angels'* premiere at the Mark Taper Forum in Los Angeles in November 1992, on the eve of a presidential election. AIDS had been woefully under-funded by Reagan and Bush. Would Clinton win the election and do better? (Roman 1997: 52). Would there be a shift in the national AIDS ideology furthered by the election and this play? James Miller saw the Broadway production the day after the 25th anniversary march of the Stonewall riots, which ignited the contemporary gay rights movement.[6] Engagement in the same issues raging outside the theatre set up an incredibly dynamic relationship inside between spectator, collective audience, and production, reminding us that the theatrical event is not just what happens on stage, but in the whole auditorium and beyond.

Time and place notwithstanding, Reinelt underscores the importance of theatre as a place to imagine:

> The subjunctive mode is always an essential part of epic theater. First, the provisional positioning of a different way of organizing social life – what if the world were not like this? Second the conditional – *if* the spectators and the actors and the play form a Brechtian triangle of speculation and critique, aesthetic pleasure, and political engagement, *then* the 'epic' happens.
>
> (Reinelt 1997: 237)

As such, she is identifying a utopian impulse in Brecht's work, referring to no real place but rather one we can be brought to imagine.[7]

Significant, too, is *Angels'* exquisite balance between, on the one hand, aesthetic, intellectual, and sensual nourishment, and on the other, activist, anti-burn-out encouragement and engagement with pressing issues of the day. The first of the two plays that constitute the work ends with an angel crashing through the ceiling of the theatre! What an amazing confluence of the magic of theatre with the message that we need to crack open our art spaces and bring in the world beyond. What a deliberate opening, in contrast to the light of day accidentally seeping in to the theatre as spectators fled the building where I saw *Marat/Sade* in 1962.

The post-social movement life of Angels

While the context of the movement to garner support for people with AIDS inspired and compellingly contextualized *Angels in America*, the quality of the play as dramatic literature and the expansiveness of its themes are reasons it continues to be produced. *Angels* is able to reach a broad audience with enough frequency to have impact. Kushner's juxtaposition of fantasy with reality and complex dramaturgy illuminated not only AIDS, but an understanding of power, conflicts about expectations from friends, family, and society, how we are and are not there for those we love.

Angels has continued to circulate through theatrical networks, such as regional theatres and high schools, in communities in every corner of the USA. While the desire to produce it is frequently controversial and does not always come to pass, the effort occasions an important dialogue about representation of homosexuality and the threat of censorship itself, both valuable conversations. When the play is in fact produced in such resistant contexts, it often serves as a lightning rod for local struggles around sexual diversity.

Other aspects of Kushner's playwrighting contribute to the continued draw of his plays, not least of which is his socialist philosophy and collective way of creating work in the world. Writing about Kushner's "political and aesthetic appreciation for preserving a dialectic," critic Bob Vorlicky notes Kushner's reference to "the value of community, to the vital necessity for discussion and argument between and among people" (Vorlicky 1998: 3). Kushner does not leave out the people struggling with the issue in testing his material – he is one of them, an openly gay man losing friend after friend to AIDS at a time when the Reagan administration was unwilling to aggressively seek a cure. Nor does he leave out compelling counter-views on the part of characters with whom he disagrees.

Take the scene in which Roy Cohn – based on the right-wing protégé of Communist-hunting Senator Joe McCarthy turned power-broking New York lawyer – is told by his doctor (fictionalized and called Henry in the play) that he has AIDS. After listening to Henry diplomatically try to explain the diagnosis, Roy pushes him to say it straight forwardly:

HENRY: Roy Cohn, you are …
    You have had sex with men many times, Roy, and one of them, or any number of them, has made you very sick. You have AIDS.
ROY: AIDS.
    Your problem, Henry, is that you are hung up on words, on labels, that you believe they mean what they seem to mean. AIDS. Homosexual. Gay. Lesbian. You think these are names that tell you who someone sleeps with, but they don't tell you that.
HENRY: No?
ROY: No. Like all labels they tell you one thing and one thing only: where does an individual so identified fit in the pecking order? Not ideology, or sexual taste, but something much simpler: clout. Not who I fuck or who fucks me, but who will pick up the phone when I call, who owes me favors. This is what a label refers to. Now to someone who does

29

not understand this, homosexual is what I am because I have sex with men. But really this is wrong. Homosexuals are not men who sleep with other men. Homosexuals are men who in fifteen years of trying cannot get a pissant antidiscrimination bill through City Council. Homosexuals are men who know nobody and who nobody knows. Who have zero clout. Does this sound like me, Henry?

(Kushner 1992: 45)

The scene brilliantly interprets homophobia as fear and loathing of power-less men. It redefines "nonproductive" from men who have sex that cannot result in the birth of a child, to men who cannot accomplish things in the world because they lack the power. This suggests that the bias around sexual preference is equally about power dynamics. By extension, women choosing to partner with other women implies that men are not necessary to a woman's well-being in the world, and further erodes the patriarchal power structure. It exposes a pervasive idea of masculinity, which Cohn himself buys into in his unwillingness to accept the label of homosexual because it is so marginalizing.

Community-informed adaptations

Plays that transcend the specific moment that gave birth to them are often heralded as universal. A danger of universality for the purpose of engage-ment is its potential to relieve an audience of response-ability – the capacity to respond to the circumstances that the play was created to incite. But sometimes plays find new life in new circumstances, and that, too, is evidence of their universality. Take the example of Lysistrata, which was performed all over the USA as an anti-Iraqi War statement. In that case, a play originally created as a kind of meditation on power became a tool to generate anti-war activity.

Deliberate re-imagining of the classics in light of time-and-place-specific circumstances characterizes much of the work of Cornerstone Theater. In the first ten years of its life, 1985–95, the company travelled across the USA, doing six- to eight-month residencies in a range of large and small towns. Cornerstone's trademark practice of adapting classical plays with significant local input began in the small town of Marmath, North Dakota. As critic Sonja Kuftinec recounts (Kuftinec 2003), the company was invited to Marmath to perform what the mayor thought was dinner theatre.[8] In fact, Cornerstone had in mind a wild west version of Hamlet, to be performed by some of their actors and some local people. But Marmath participants by and large found the language inscrutable, and asked that it be changed to sound "'more like us and less like you'" (Kuftinec 2003: 74). Cornerstone has continued to fit the circumstances and idiom of specific communities in its work, even while commissioning new plays in other situations.

Adaptations in Marmath and subsequent residencies increased community ownership and enjoyment of the productions. Working on a production of Chekhov in West Virginia, for example, a line literally translated as "Thanks to father, I and my sisters know the French, German, and English languages," first became "Dad taught us how to fish, hunt, and hike." Local historian Otis Rice revised it to "bark a squirrel, dig out a ground hog, run a trot line." In Eastport, Maine, "poppycock" became "bilge water" (Kuftinec 2003: 73–74). These rich, new renditions came out of extensive interviewing as well as improvising with casts composed of locals and company members. As classics, most of the plays that Cornerstone adapts are old enough to be in the public domain, and the language can be changed without special permission. Particular character choices also undergo transformation to ground the plays in each locale. Because more women than men auditioned for *Romeo and Juliet* in Port Gibson, Mississippi, the Capulets were reconceived as a matriarchy. In West Virginia, one woman was such a breathtaking clog dancer that a character was added to *Three Sisters* to highlight her skill.

Cornerstone's choices suggest that the most important element in a production is not the play as written by the playwright, but rather the relationship with the people of the community in which it is being presented. Cornerstone is part of engaged theatre in this regard, prioritizing the relationship of the production to local participants, in a radical revisioning of theatre itself. This harkens back to Brecht's grasp of the need to change theatre in Germany of the 1920s, not simply to write an innovative play. Brecht wrote in 1927: "It is not the play's effect on the audience but its effect on the theatre that is decisive at this moment" (cited in Willett 1964: 22). In the late-20th-century USA, most theatre that garnered respect had, by and large, estranged itself from all but a particular class of (largely urban) audiences. Cornerstone is part of the international movement of theatre, whether called engaged, applied, or community-based, to retain and enliven a relationship to people in any location or circumstance.

Cornerstone cofounder (with playwright Alison Carey) and primary director in the early years, Bill Rauch, exemplifies how a director can enhance the social role of a piece of theatre. One valuable skill is the ability to discern the details that honor local culture. Rauch directed company member Amy Brenneman to gut a fish in a performance of *Pier Gynt* in Maine, where that act is familiar but seldom enshrined in art. Under his direction, the emotional peak of *Steelbound* (adapted from *Prometheus Bound*) in Bethlehem, Pennsylvania was former steelworkers gently laying down the tools of their trade as a kind of inventory of a life that ended when the steel industry there was dismantled.

In re-imagining *Prometheus Bound* in Bethlehem, Pennsylvania, and imbuing steelworkers' lives with public significance, Rauch demonstrates that universality is not reliant on plays being set in ancient Greece, but rather on the recognition of core human experiences, wherever they happen. This Kuftinec refers to as "access[ing] the 'universal' through specific local references" as distinguished from "access without the necessity for translation or modification" (Kuftinec 2003: 76). Interestingly, a small theatre in another steel town, in Ohio, produced *Steelbound* some years later. According to playwright Carey,

> It was not as successful because there were still active steel mills operating locally, and this show was written for a community whose plant had closed. I remember writing a program note about the difference, but I don't think it made any difference.
> (Alison Carey, "Steelbound in Ohio," email, December 22, 2009)

Carey suggests that, had the circumstances been truly parallel, the play may have had as great an impact without local references, more in line with Kuftinec's other definition of universal: "access without the necessity for translation or modification." What may have provided that access was the same situation – the closing of the steel plants – not the particulars of one town or another. It was rare enough to see that working-class struggle on stage. This perspective aligns with the role played by *Angels in America* and other works by gay playwrights in the late 1980s and early 1990s in putting gay experiences onto the stage from their various perspectives, which had not frequently been represented there before.

Do Cornerstone's adaptations contribute to social justice, a frequent goal of engaged performance? They bring people in a community together, raise a significant, shared issue, and then leave it to the people themselves to do with it what they will. For those who see social justice as a material change for the better among people without the power to get their due, more steps are necessary. In Bethlehem, for example, former steelworkers did not get new jobs as a result of the *Steelbound* production. But some of them did put the past a little more to rest – they were given the means to mourn a way of life that, however harsh, hot, and repetitive, was meaningful to many. It was how their fathers and grandfathers had lived, how they had achieved middle-class lifestyles, and sent their kids to college, and it constituted a core component of how they knew themselves. Rauch has told me that, as a theatre director, it is not his role to take the play further in the communities they visit. Indeed, such activities lead to a hybrid role of artist–organizer (which I address in chapters 3 and 4).

Some aspects of adapting classic plays are politically controversial. Cornerstone adapted Brecht's *Caucasian Chalk Circle* in the African American Watts neighborhood of Los Angeles. Some people responded that it would have been more important for the community to make a play directly from its own stories. Rauch did not agree:

Figure 1.2 Cornerstone Theater Company's production of *The Walker Street Chalk Circle* in Watts, Los Angeles. Adapted from Bertolt Brecht's *Caucasian Chalk Circle*. (Photo by Cornerstone Theater Company.)

I think it suggests that an adaptation of a German play, which is an adaptation of a Chinese play, is somehow not as good for a community because it's not as direct. I am troubled by those questions but also irritated by them. There are a lot of great stories that get passed around the world through human history.

(cited in Kuftinec 2003: 141)

The point is not to judge Rauch's decision to adapt *Chalk Circle* in Watts, which, given the company's process, also would have had many community collaborators who saw its value, but rather to recognize conflicting points of view about such choices. One difference between making a German play based on a Chinese tale is, given the large body of German dramatic literature already produced, that representation of Germans themselves is less an issue than self-representation of African Americans.

On the other hand, such translation is especially significant when the new cultural context has not been treated with the same level of respect as the old. Kuftinec proposes reversing the "notion that an audience needs to 'rise to the level of the work' by learning the text's language" in favor of what Rauch describes as "'These classic plays … need[ing] to rise to the level of the community'" (Kuftinec 2003: 141). That is, it is not the Watts community that must prove itself capable of grasping Brecht's text, but

Caucasian Chalk Circle, the relevance of which is tested in this particular context.

Commitment to self-representation situates Cornerstone in an American cultural tradition that constitutes a counterpart to our *politically* democratic origins – *culturally* democratic expression of the people, by the people, and for the people. Take, for example, African American social activist W.E.B. Du Bois, who used cultural expression to promote democratic inclusion of African Americans. To that end, Du Bois used his editorship at the magazine *Crisis* to offer literary prizes and encourage playwrights and actors to participate in his KRIGWA (Crisis Guild of Writers and Artists) productions. Moreover, as he wrote in an editorial for *Crisis* in 1922 entitled "Art for Nothing," people of color had to support black artists and writers if they ever were to get cultural recognition (Lewis 2000: 153). The suggestion here is that cultural recognition leads to a political place at the table as well.

Du Bois was clear about art's contribution to the movement for equal rights:

> Thus all Art is propaganda and ever must be, despite the wailing of the purists. I stand in utter shamelessness and say that whatever art I have for writing has been used always for propaganda for gaining the right of black folk to love and enjoy. I do not care a damn for any art that is not used for propaganda. But I do care when propaganda is confined to one side while the other is stripped and silent.
>
> (Du Bois 1926)

Du Bois' use of the word propaganda here suggests advocacy for the under-represented side of a particular cause. Cornerstone, while not focused on a people's liberation like Du Bois, also extends theatre as a platform for those whose voices are otherwise not heard publicly, but without leaving out diverse points of view on the same subject. Both formulations make perfect sense in their respective contexts.

The unfaithful disciple

Brecht's principles are generative not only for play-makers seeking to activate spectators, but also for workshop facilitators seeking to activate spect-*actors*, Augusto Boal's term for audiences that begin by observing but are provided with opportunities to act. The notion of problem-solving so seminal to Boal's work, as explored in the next chapter, also has roots in Brecht. The various aesthetic techniques Brecht developed as his life circumstances permitted – such as epic theatre, *Lehrstücke*, and adaptations of classics to rebuild the repertoire after World War II – helped audiences think through current social struggles without literally and immediately problem-solving as with Boal's work. Janelle Reinelt articulates this idea among other criteria of an epic play:

> The spectators engage the problems and understand the constraints operating on the nation and on themselves as social subjects ... some sense of what must be done next is suggested but not spelled out ... spectators [are not let] off the hook by allowing too much psychological investment in particular characters or too much good feeling of resolution at the end.
>
> (Reinelt 1997: 236)

The notion of theatrical events ending badly, or at least without "too much good feeling," situates them as part of the flow of life, without their own internal closure. That flow, for some, is impeded when plays take place in theatre buildings. Peter Handke, himself a playwright, asserts that presenting plays in institutional theatre spaces works against the possibility of critical spectatorial response (Handke 1998). Such condoned spaces, he theorizes, have a normalizing effect more powerful than any text that is performed there, ultimately reinforcing the socialized self. But I don't believe that theatre buildings were an obstacle to Brecht and Kushner; many activists of the struggles they addressed *were* theater-goers. Some theatre spaces are counter-cultural, identified with the questioning of mainstream socialization. Brecht's audience, opposing fascism, knew that Brecht's theatre was a space for oppositional points of view, as did Kushner's audience, which in effect took over theatres typically identified as mainstream by attracting so many people seeking to press government response to the AIDS epidemic.

A further bias among some activists is devaluation of not just theatre buildings, but also plays themselves as completed products rather than participatory processes, aimed at less needy middle-class audiences. Although he later embraced multiple forms of theatre, the young Boal who wrote *Theatre of the Oppressed* (1974) noted:

> George Ikishawa used to say that the bourgeois theater is the finished theater. The bourgeoisie already know what the world is like, *their* world, and is able to present images of this complete, finished world ... the spectacle. On the other hand, the proletariat and the oppressed classes do not know yet what their world will be like; consequently their theater will be the rehearsal, not the finished spectacle. This is quite true ...
>
> (Boal 1974: 142)

Workshops – referring both to participatory opportunities to explore material theatrically, without the goal of a final production, and opportunities

35

to share works-in-progress – are an alternative to the seamless theatrical production. They are often available at no cost, and take place at sites frequented by people less likely to go to conventional theatre. Workshops are interactive, process-oriented, and never finished. But one does not have to choose between finished productions and workshops. Even as theatre itself is just one component of the effort, as Brecht wrote, to "improve the world; it needs it!," so the participatory workshop and political performance are just two ways of using theatre to such ends.

What's important is to have a basis for deciding what modality of theatre to use when. During the period when Brecht's theatre was aligned with vigorous unions, performance was a way to reach many working-class people quickly. It was surely significant in the years of ever-increasing Nazi hegemony to be in a large group with an opposing point of view. But often theatre, the politics of which are strictly embedded in the text, has no way to stick to a spectator's bones; they see it and then return to their regular lives. Workshops give people an opportunity to engage more actively with the material.

In the right circumstances, both Brecht and Kushner provide dramatic evidence of a *play*'s capacity to adhere an audience tightly to a related struggle beyond the theatre.[9] And certainly resisting Nazism and addressing the AIDS crisis were two sets of circumstances that called for reaching people across all lines of difference. Significantly, they both acknowledge the artifice of the theatre and ask the audience to do so, too, a prerequisite for them to acting in the world beyond the auditorium. But at the same time, they are both masters of the dramatic form and providers of endless delights for audiences.

I want to reinforce the importance of choosing different modes of performance for different circumstances, and hence developing a broad artistic palette. While studying mime with Etienne Decroux in Paris, I wrote my second letter to Peter Brook, telling him I had made it to his side of the Atlantic, and what I was doing. He wrote me back, telling me he was in Paris, too, editing his film of King Lear with the legendary actor Paul Scofield. Would I introduce him to Decroux, who he had always wanted to meet? And would I be interested in visiting the studio where he was editing? Yes, I said, and yes again.

Brook visited Decroux's little, old-fashioned studio, and I visited his immense, modern editing facility. He asked me what I was planning to do, and I explained that I was fascinated with Decroux, with the cross-currents of people from around the world in Paris, but I had to find a job in order to stay longer than anticipated. He introduced me to some people in adjoining film studios dubbing second-rate films into English for distribution in third-world countries where more English than French was spoken. I was a bit shocked; wasn't it awful to work on such bad films? I wanted to be an artist. He told me that one does many things on the way to becoming an artist. There's much to learn from entering these different worlds, just so one doesn't get stuck. Many of the actors I saw at the mikes dubbing the films made a career of it and no longer pursued anything else. If I strive for something else, just remember to keep moving towards it. I then happily accepted dubbing jobs, supporting myself on my own.

After about a year of exacting discipline *chez* Decroux, I became curious about some of my fellow students who were getting antsy there. They invited me to join them surreptitiously – Decroux did not allow his core students to follow another master – at a workshop they were attending several times a week facilitated by Philippe Buisset, just back from a year of working with Polish director Jerzy Grotowski, all the rage in European and US experimental theater circles. Like several others from our group, I soon left Decroux's entirely to work with Buisset's group, grounded in as exacting a physical discipline as Decroux's, but for other purposes, central among them an exploration of "poor theatre" – paring theatre down to the actor and the spectator, given that their live presence together is ultimately what separates theatre from film and television.[10] Towards that end, Grotowski at the time was exploring the release of impulses through a rigorous physicality based in yoga.

What do Brecht and Kushner, plays and workshops, and my two very different training experiences in Paris teach me about the breadth of theatrical possibilities and the fit between a method and a moment? I had some vague idea of becoming an actress. I didn't know how. From Decroux's ultra-exacting techniques, I learned about the very idea of a method. From Grotowski's search for transcendence, I learned about going beyond what a method itself has charted. As Grotowski wrote, sometimes the best disciple is the unfaithful one, who builds upon the spirit rather than the materiality of the master. I don't need to throw out Decroux in order to value Grotowski. Nor must I renounce the dramaturgy and dramas of Brecht and Kushner to appreciate Boal and participatory workshops. People activate and are activated in different ways, at different times, and their actions can have far-reaching consequences for each other. Spectacle in the 1930s Nuremberg party rallies bespoke Nazi coercion. Spectacle in Kushner's 1990s *Angels in America* bespeaks a fierce commitment to joy in the midst of terrible death, and the release of fantasy in the tension of the exhausting battle to confront homophobia and to get possibly life-saving drugs into critically ill bodies.

Some plays are magnificent meditations in themselves, taking on different emphases at different times. For my current students, *Angels* is more about how loved ones respond to a whole array of crises and identity issues than AIDS *per se*. Other plays provide occasions to support an array of political actions. For example, Eve Ensler's *Vagina Monologues*, based on the playwright's experiences and her interviews with other women about their genitalia, is performed widely, especially on Valentine's Day. Ensler grants permission to do the work so long as a percentage of the proceeds support an organization fighting against violence to women.

I am an unfaithful disciple *vis-à-vis* the vision of theatre that first captured me as a child, in productions grounded in dramatic literature and taking place in theatre buildings. But I am not monogamous to either workshops or plays; I do not see either, *a priori*, as the more evolved form of theatrical expression. I have described, in this chapter, a host of different contexts in which plays can be created and performed, engaging social issues in a range of different ways. The critical thinking underlying when to undertake which approach is what we need to practice and see where it directs us. We must be ready with what Boal called an "arsenal" of different theatrics from which to choose the one that can respond most vividly given the time, place, and set of collaborators.

Workbook

Situating plays for social engagement

The purpose of this exercise is to practice strengthening the link between particular plays and specific, timely contexts by bringing in the voices of people affected by the issue. It attempts to actualize the argument I make in the text: that, put to very particular use, plays are extraordinary vehicles of engaged performances, able to provide the three elements that Kushner sought in a play – politics, poetry, and popcorn – at the same time as responding to a social call.

Cornerstone Theater, especially founding playwright Alison Carey, developed methods for adapting classical plays to respond to resonant contemporary issues in specific neighborhoods and towns, exemplified in the emergence of *Steelbound* from *Prometheus Bound*. Typically, Cornerstone suggests several plays as possible starting points when doing adaptations with communities. However, in the case of *Steelbound*, the local Touchstone Theater in Bethlehem, Pennsylvania had already decided to produce *Prometheus Bound* in response to the dismantling of the steel industry there. They wanted to stage it in the empty ironworks as a sort of funeral for the industry that once animated the town. It was only when local readings of the ancient Greek tragedy left people cold that Touchstone's artistic director Mark McKenna approached Rauch and Carey and asked them to collaborate on an adaptation.

Prometheus Bound, by Aeschylus, is about the half-god, half-human who stole fire from the gods and gave it to humans so they would prosper. Epitomizing for some the revolutionary who stands up to injustice, for others the prideful man unwilling to accept limits, Prometheus has been the subject of various works of art. The original play begins with Prometheus being led to a rocky mountain top by two characters called Power and

38

Violence and shackled there by Hephaestus, god of iron, as the punishment ordained by Zeus, king of the gods. In the Bethlehem, PA adaptation, Prometheus is the human being who resists when collective mortal power (the makers of steel) is cut down by those with an extra dimension of power (the plant owners). This Prometheus is punished for his inability and unwillingness to accept the closing of the steelworks. That play begins with the characters of Brutality and Indifference, a wealthy, well-dressed couple, driving into the vast former iron foundry where the production took place. They pop the trunk of the car and deposit Prometheus on the ground. Three riggers – Heffy, Uz, and Festa – weld him high on the top of the enormous iron "ladle," a giant-sized pot, in which molten iron was stirred in the days that the factory was in operation.

Here are the opening monologues of *Prometheus Bound* and *Steelbound*, respectively:

> POWER: Now we have come to the plain at the end of the earth,
> The Scythian tract and an untrodden wilderness.
> And you, Hephaestus, must turn your mind to the orders
> The father gave you – to discipline and pin down
> This outlaw here upon the lofty ragged rocks
> In unbreakable bonds of adamantine chains.
> It was your flower, the gleam of civilizing fire,
> He stole and handed it over to mortals. Therefore
> He must pay the price of such a sin to the gods,
> That he may be taught to bend to the dictatorship
> Of Zeus, and give up his idea of helping men.
> (Aeschylus: *Prometheus Bound*, Lind 1972)

> BRUTALITY: And so we've come to the end of your world.
> An empty mill, dark and quiet, cooled down.
> Heffy, boys, your green slip came through.
> Take this nice, strong chain of Bethlehem Steel
> And weld this whiny son of a bitch to the ladle.
> He got paid for his years of bridges and buildings,
> But seniority don't mean squat in a service economy.
> He's got to like the way things are now and understand
> That an hourly wage doesn't buy you lifelong respect.
> Even a loving parent can't listen to a baby cry forever.
> We've run out of patience with his mewling.
> (Carey, unpublished manuscript, 1999)

The adaptation came out of conversations and interviews that Carey held with people on many sides of the steel controversy. She spoke with union members angry at the loss of jobs; company CEOs adamant about the economic necessity to move factories overseas; family members of former workers glad to see the end of the back-breaking labor but worried about the local economy. The adaptation was not a one-to-one correspondence. Central to the original play is the sharing of fire, through Prometheus's theft, for the good of mankind. In *Steelbound*, Prometheus is a worker who shared the fruits of fire – all the things wrought from the heating of steel in the plant – with consumers. While steel will continue to be produced, Bethlehem workers will not benefit by way of employment.

The following exercise comes from accounts and experiences of Carey's and Cornerstone's work, as exemplified in the above description.

1. Decide where you would produce a play, partly by deciding with whom you would like to collaborate. Identify an issue that has significance to the people there with whom you'd like to work, and with which you also resonate. Think about who you admire and would like to spend time with. For example, I produced a play about community gardeners in New York City out of respect for their tenacity, growing things in dense urban neighborhoods and fighting former Mayor Giuliani, who wanted to dismantle community gardens in order to build middle- and upper-income housing. I could see the value to the gardeners in creating a theatre piece as advocacy, and the value to me in spending time in urban gardens with people so moved.

2. Identify a play that takes on that issue, directly or subtly, and choose a scene in which that connection is particularly pronounced. Look at some of the plays that Cornerstone Theater has adapted (see Appendix), and with whom. For example, Brecht's *Good Person of Setzuan* was re-imagined as *Good Person from New Haven,* an exploration of morality in a money-driven society developed with people in New Haven, Connecticut in association with the local regional Long Wharf Theatre. In Brecht's hands, this was an incisive critique of capitalism, expressed through Shen Te creating a cousin, Shui Ta, to say no to everyone's requests in order to avoid the bankruptcy into which Shen Te's goodness was leading her. In the collaboration with people in New Haven, adapting the play brought people together across race and class to consider and express how to be good in a money-driven world.

3. Come up with two or three plays with the sought-for resonance that might serve as the jumping-off text for your own adaptation. Have a gathering with people interested in participating in the project or, for the purpose of this exercise, convene several colleagues or fellow students. Describe the plays' storyline, setting, characters, and tone. Read at least part of each out loud. Discuss which might best serve the local issue. In my community garden example, both Brecht's *Caucasian Chalk Circle* and Chekhov's *Cherry Orchard* resonate interestingly with

the issue of land use and its meaning to people in different economic and social strata.

4. Interview people from the community about the issue the play addresses. If you have the personnel to transcribe, you can tape the interviews; if you don't, take notes and write up everything you remember immediately following each interview or outing. That is, sometimes you might go somewhere like a bar or a laundromat and speak briefly to a number of people. Other times you'll set up one-on-one interviews. For the purpose of this exercise, include colleagues or fellow students among those you interview.

5. Back at your desk, look for where local details and data gathered by talking with people can substitute for the play's particulars. Pay attention to central metaphors in classical plays you seek to adapt, and to large themes. For example, in the case of *Steelbound* emerging from *Prometheus Bound*, these included polarization of the powerful (gods translate to factory owners) against the powerless (mortals translate to workers).

6. Do a reading of the excerpt you have developed, discussing where, with what actors, for what audience, and in what context such a production might be situated locally to further efforts around that issue. That is, how could the production be aligned with an ongoing effort so as to contribute to that goal?

2

SPECTA(C)TING

Theatre of the oppressed, orthodoxy and adaptation

> One of the main functions of our art is to make people sensi-
> tive to the "spectacles" of daily life in which the actors are
> their own spectators, performances in which the stage and the
> stalls coincide. We are all artists. By doing theater, we learn to
> see what is obvious but what we usually can't see because we
> are only used to looking at it. What is familiar to us becomes
> unseen: doing theater throws light on the stage of daily life.
>
> (Boal 2009)

Augusto Boal's *Theatre of the Oppressed* (Boal 1974) is a textbook example
of engaged theatre, transforming spect*ators* into spect-*actors*, be they collaborators in creating work or participants in interactive performances.
Boal extends Brecht's audience members from engaging intellectually to
participating *physically*, through techniques for solving problems.[1] Boal's
spect-*actors* literally intervene in performances and workshops, rehearsing
alternatives to apply to their struggles outside theatrical contexts.

Like Nazi Germany for Brecht, the political context of Brazil's military
dictatorship in the 1960s catalyzed Boal to find ways of using theatre for
popular resistance. In his first book, *Theatre of the Oppressed*, he applies the
language of class struggle to the theatrical context. He begins that seminal
text with the idea, reflecting his Marxist ideology, that theatre is "a very
efficient weapon ... The ruling classes strive to take permanent hold of
the theater and utilize it as a tool for domination" (Boal 1974: ix). He
fervently sought, in the Latin America of the early 1970s, "the destruction
of the barriers created by the ruling class" (Boal 1974: x). Indeed, the
38-year-old Boal who wrote *Theatre of the Oppressed* was directly aligning
theatre with the long-term, utopian goal of creating a classless, equitable
society, adapting Marxist precepts to cultural contexts in ideas such as
"the conquest of the means of theatrical production" (Boal 1974: x). For the
theatre of the oppressed (TO) initially responded to the dire situation
of the majority of Brazilians. The oppressed, people who seemingly had
nothing, Boal recognized, could still draw on their collective power. He thus

42

came up with theatrical techniques for rehearsing solutions to shared struggles.[2]

Boal was equally inspired by his fellow countryman, the great liberatory educator Paulo Freire. Years ago, when I asked Boal the genesis of the name "theatre of the oppressed," he told me he wanted to call it "theatre of liberation" but the publisher preferred "theatre of the oppressed," which more transparently tips its hat to the influence of *Pedagogy of the Oppressed* (Freire 1970). In it, Freire propounds an educational philosophy that calls for a shift from a "banking method" of depositing information in passive learners' heads to problem-solving with them and co-advancing knowledge through dialogue. Like Freire, Boal's approach offers transitive, two-way learning and collective empowerment; specific to Boal is embodying these practices in dramatic techniques.

In the years since Boal began inventing the set of tools that constitute TO, he expanded its reach to include people of any class with the will to fight both social and personal oppression. At the same time, Boal continued to follow both Freire's model of joining forces with those having the least power, and Brecht's principle of activating the spectator, seeking out spect-actors further afield than theatre auditoriums – in community centers, union halls, schools, poor neighborhoods, and other spaces where a broad range of people congregate. Boal left behind a broad and diverse network extending TO around the world when he died in May 2009.

The system of theatre of the oppressed

"Art is the search for truths by means of our sensory equipment."
(Boal 2006: 5)

Boal emphasizes that TO

> is always seeking the transformation of society in the direction of the liberation of the oppressed. It is both action in itself, and a preparation for future actions. ... [I]t is not enough to interpret reality: it is necessary to transform it!
>
> (Boal 1974: 6)

Whereas normally I am skeptical about the claim of theatre's transformative capacity, Boal invented techniques that do precisely that – theatrical methods through which people with no apparent power achieve some degree of agency.

Boal's techniques are used most often in the participatory workshop format. TO workshops begin with games, physical structures that follow rules while relying on individual and collective creativity.[3] They enhance the senses, break habits, energize, and connect people to themselves and others. As Boal writes, "Games facilitate and oblige this de-mechanisa-tion, being, as they are, sensory dialogues where, within the necessary discipline, they demand the creativity which is their essence" (Boal 2006: 5). For example, in The Hand Shake, a group breaks into pairs who shake hands and freeze. Then one person steps out, looks freshly at the other person's body language, and completes the image through a new physical configuration, inspired by an alternate reading of their partner's body language. Then the other steps out, observes the new physical shape of their partner, and once again completes a fresh image. This goes on for a few minutes, building the capacity to see ever-shifting body language in new ways and to recognize multiple interpretations of any one image.

TO is in the Stanislavski aesthetic tradition of knowing the world through the senses. Like Brecht's goal of providing audiences with a critical perspective on the everyday world, Boal's goal, through the games, is to

> help enable the de-mechanisation of the body and the mind alie-nated by the repetitive tasks of the day-to-day, particularly those related to work and to the economic, environmental and social conditions of those who take part in them.
>
> (Boal 1974: 5)

But whereas Stanislavski's exercises prepare actors to live truthfully in the imaginary circumstances of the playwright, Boal very deliberately uses the awakened senses beyond the stage, as tools for interpreting the world for oneself rather than accepting what we've been taught.

Boal's dialogic aesthetics call for face-to-face exchange between actors and specta(c)tors through an ever-expanding set of techniques, which are inten-ded to probe more deeply than games.[4] As early as 1970, Boal catalogued methods of demystifying news articles in what he dubbed "newspaper theatre," a body of theatrical strategies for expressing critical perspectives on current events (Boal 2006: 4). One example is the cross-reading of news articles linked not thematically but through juxtaposition, such as a piece about budget cuts to education next to one about increases for a war, through which useful connections are made. Another exercise invites the participant to set the article to music, all the better to hear it. Boal devised a dozen such tools for theatricalizing current events.

Invited to participate in a national literacy campaign in Peru in 1973, Boal developed image theatre, a wordless set of exercises through which partici-pants express their feelings, ideas, and experiences about a particular subject through the body. A group might choose a theme such as the family, say, and silently sculpt three or four colleagues into their image of the oppression they experience in the context of family, entering the picture as where they are in it. Once an image has been created, Boal offers a series of dynamizations to explore it. Other spect-actors, observing the image, then describe what they literally see, for example, three people standing, one lying down, no eye contact, etc. The next step is projecting their interpretation of that image. (The person who made the image, who Boal calls the protagonist, never says what she had in mind.) In one dynamization, calling this first image the "real," Boal invites the protagonist to sculpt a second, "ideal" image of the same situation. That, too, is described and interpreted. Then, in a third step, the protagonist sculpts a transitional image, suggesting how to get from the real to the ideal. Note that the ideal is sculpted before the transitional, as it is often easier to move forward when one has a vision of where one wishes to go.

Boal's best-known technique, forum theatre, developed in response to the limitations he experienced when performing agit prop (agitation propaganda). In such plays, the actors rile up an audience about a particular situation (agitate) and then show what they should do (propagandize). In an early version of forum theatre, Boal directed a company of professional actors who performed scenes, with words, around social issues meaningful to particular audiences – for example, a play about deteriorating schools for an audience of teachers, students, and parents. These short plays always end badly for the "protagonist," Boal's term for the person struggling against oppression. Then the spectators would suggest alternatives, which the actors would immediately enact as possible ways to improve the situation. Boal called this follow-up exercise "simultaneous dramaturgy," and the proposing and performing of alternatives, "interventions."

This aesthetic shift to spect-actors presenting their own solutions marks a political shift as well. Boal was acknowledging that he and his educated actors did not have the answers for another group of people; more important was posing the problem clearly, and creating a space where people could decide for themselves what to do. He was thus providing a tool for liberation: a physical space literally to act out alternatives before applying them to the real world.

Boal's moment of revelation leading to *physically* activating spectators to enact interventions, rather than make suggestions that the actors perform, is instructive. One day, during the intervention phase of a forum theatre performance, a spectator protested that the actors did not understand her suggestion. After several tries explaining it and still being unsatisfied with the actors' interpretation, Boal, exasperated, asked her to step into the scene and show them. She eagerly did. A new phase of forum theatre was born, premised on spect-actors enacting alternatives themselves, which communicated their ideas more fully than just explaining them. The doing was also more instructive for the spect-actor, who encountered insights in simulation that were not evident in observation. Thus, as Boal described TO, while not making revolution, it provides a rehearsal for it (Boal 1974: 155).

Yet another technique, invisible theatre, masquerades as everyday life. It takes place in public venues such as the subway, a restaurant, the beach, the street, the supermarket, a department store, or waiting in line for a bus. It brings attention to inequities in everyday life by enacting them in the midst of people who do not know it is being staged. So for example, after eating a meal at a restaurant, a diner, not letting on that he is performing, proclaims that he is out of work and unable to pay his bill. This apparently real situation becomes an occasion to involve other patrons in a conversation about social responsibility to the unemployed, especially at times when jobs are tight. Unbeknownst to the regular diners, a number of the people adding comments from other tables are also pre-rehearsed actors. Created in the repressive context of Argentina in the early 1980s, invisible theatre was a way to deliberate publicly and critically about important issues without risking arrest.

Whereas the techniques cited above focus on *social* oppression, Boal's rainbow of desire is a set of exercises that uses words and images to give form to *individual internalized* oppressions (see *The Rainbow of Desire*: Boal 1995). Boal developed it in the 1980s in response to middle-class participants at TO workshops – especially in Europe, the USA, and Canada – seeking relief from loneliness, despair, alienation, and other personal manifestations of social malaise. Individuals prepare and enact such scenes but rather than other people replacing them in interventions, the protagonist engages with the oppression as given physical form by others. For example, after seeing a scene in which a boss takes advantage of a protagonist and while she could protest, she doesn't, the facilitator has spect-actors create physicalizations of what they see psychologically impeding the person – perhaps a moralistic figure imposing a restrictive sense of goodness, or a threatening authority figure, or a coercive parental figure trading love for obedience. The protagonist re-enacts the scene, this time trying to prevail in relationship to the now obvious, externalized versions of the inner "cops," as Boal dubbed them.

Politically, recognizing internal conflict as another form of oppression, no matter what a person's class, moved Boal further from classical Marxism. The great hope is that unearthing how we stop *ourselves* will naturally lead all of us to acting more justly in the world. Boal also explored the linkage between the therapeutic and the activist. He sometimes combined cop in the head (an early name for rainbow of desire) with forum techniques, demonstrating that the internal is the other side of the coin of external oppression.

In the early 1990s, when a democratic government was back in control in Brazil, Boal returned to Rio de Janeiro. No longer needing to create theatrics resistant to a hostile government, he became interested in what one could do within the context of a supportive government. Active in the Workers Party, he accepted their request to run for office and won a city council seat in Rio de Janeiro from 1992 to 1996, installing his theatre troupe as staff. He then developed legislative theatre, which picks up where forum theatre leaves off, and collective wisdom cannot solve the problem. For example, teachers, school workers, and students often themselves needed a place to take care of their young children when they were at school. When enacting the problem as forum theatre yielded no solutions, Boal used his position as a city councilman to get a law passed requiring public schools to provide nursery facilities for those employed or attending school there. Following this method, Boal initiated thirteen laws during his term of office (see *Legislative Theatre*: Boal 1998: 102–5).

As Boal writes in *The Aesthetics of the Oppressed* (Boal 2006), "In TO, reality is conjugated in the Subjunctive Mode ... What if I were to do this?" He links the subjunctive to legislative theatre, "so that the knowledge acquired during the theatrical work can be extrapolated into laws and juridical actions, or by invisible theatre, to intervene directly in reality" (Boal 2006: 40–41). Note that the mature Boal of this 2006 text adheres less to Marxism, or any system, for answers to social problems, but rather looks to the people who are experiencing those challenges.

In the Appendix of *Theatre of the Oppressed*, Boal describes one other technique, the Joker System, that pre-dates his systemized TO methodology. He created the Joker System while working with actors at the Arena Stage in São Paulo in the 1960s and early 1970s. In response to the prevailing sense that most great plays came from Europe and the USA, Boal initiated a series of experiments to generate a theatricality of their own, including adaptations of world classics to Brazilian contexts, a playwrights' lab for the development of new Latin American work, and the Joker System (Boal 1974: 159–72). He also created the Joker, referencing the figure in a deck of cards that can stand in for any other card. The Joker moves freely through workshops and performances in the role of facilitator/interlocutor and/or emcee.

The Joker System is a way of writing and performing a play to present multiple points of view, and alternative ideas and feelings, in contrast to official accounts of historical characters or incidents. The Joker inserts supplementary information about the characters, as commentators do at sporting events, filling in background about the players. The system embraces a range of theatrical genres (melodrama, circus, musical comedy) in order to break the hold of realism that Boal inherited from Western theatre conventions in the 1960s (Boal 1974: 169–70). Actors rotate through the various roles, each bringing their own twist, thus separating them from the characters and giving each an interpretive voice. The cast also develops a collective interpretation.[5] This principle of both presenting one's own point of view and collectively communicating what the group sees runs through Boal's work. In the same spirit, Boal once told me that the collective strength of the Arena was part of a cultural moment in Brazil that also produced a winning soccer team featuring individually superb players working equally well as a team.

The multiplicity of perspectives within plays created through the Joker System means that spectators have to decide what they think for themselves. The Joker System shows Brecht's influence: the activation of the spectator is intellectual. Note the contrast between the Joker System's goal of raising questions and forum theatre's goal of finding solutions. The former invites complexities, while the latter depends on simplification. Both are equally valuable so long as participants know when simplification will best serve a project's goals, and when a more complex performance will be illuminating.

Note that Boal's arsenal of social intervention also draws from other cultural sources. Forum theatre builds on the practice of Latin American audiences calling for forums after plays, occasions to discuss collectively the issues the plays embody. Boal borrowed freely from popular theatre; remnants of circus and carnival abound in his work, notably the three-ring circus nature of the Joker System. And while Boal is best known for TO, he was fascinated by theatre of every sort. Under the auspices of New York University, I brought him to the USA in the late 1980s. Discussing theatre-going options with him, I suggested Pregones, a terrific Puerto Rican theatre company based in the Bronx. He requested rather we go see *Cats*, an Andrew Lloyd Webber extravaganza on Broadway, that while British in origin, seemed to Boal to capture the centrality of spectacle he identified with quintessentially US theatre. This fascination with particularized cultural expression is also evident in Boal's adaptations of classics, for example turning the opera *Carmen* into a Brazilian, samba-driven musical style he called samb-opera. Appreciating theatrics that engage the spectator directly does not mean rejecting other forms of theatre, but rather selecting different forms as dictated by the purpose and context.

Adapting Boal

The embrace of Theatre of the Oppressed is worldwide – Boal's first book, by the same name, has been translated into at least 35 languages. TO is remarkably adaptable to a range of cultures and situations. Encountering scores of TO practitioners over the years, I'm struck by the number of people who read *Theatre of the Oppressed* and use the techniques exactly as Boal describes them, often with great success. But TO sometimes fits awkwardly, feels imposed, and is critiqued for its relentless emphasis on oppression. As TO techniques have circulated around the globe, they are sometimes applied whole cloth, without enough thought to the particulars of the situation. Boal himself has remarked that the techniques, though about oppression, are not meant to be oppressive, recognizing the pall to the spirit such emphasis can produce.

Indeed, I remember a gloom coming over a group of recently-incarcerated women for whom I was facilitating a workshop using Boal techniques.

Spirited and upbeat during warm-ups, which followed the participants' lead and took the form of impromptu singing, dancing, and spoken word at which they excelled, the atmosphere became unbearably pessimistic when we turned to the oppressive issues of their lives. Then we got the idea to set up forum scenes with "girl group" singers and dancers backing up the struggling protagonist, still building to audience intervention as in forum theatre. We were using theatre to problem-solve, but the women's skill, pride, and pleasure in movement and song was equally center stage, and helped solve a different sort of problem – their need for pleasurable release.

In the same spirit, I saw an inventive adaptation of forum theatre at a TO conference some years ago, which incorporated culturally meaningful forms into Boal's problem-solving structure. In a break from orthodox TO, the actors, from Burkina Faso, used drumming as the lead-in to a story with a narrator. When the scene ended badly – the pregnant wife was given all the work as the family undertook a long journey on foot – the actors turned the event into forum theatre, stopping the performance and inviting people to intervene so as to brainstorm how the wife could deal with her husband's (and culture's) inequity around gender roles. The aesthetics remaining in sync with popular forms, not the more pared-down style most typical of TO, accounted for much of its success.

There's something contradictory in taking a system built on critical thinking and applying it without reflection to any situation. Collaborating with Mady Schutzman, with whom I've facilitated workshops and co-edited two volumes on Boal's work, I have come to see the key to meaningful uses of TO as returning to Boal's underlying principles, analyzing the situation, and assessing the available assets. The following three examples evidence in more detail how adapting TO is itself generative of creativity, and thus even truer to Boal than importing his exercises directly. After all, Boal premises his work on everyone's capacity to make theatre – to be the one doing and the one watching herself doing, the spect-actor rather than spectator – not on following him letter and book.

The three experiments that follow evidence "multipliers" who have taken Boal's work in their own directions. They are artists and thinkers in their own right, thereby adding a new generation of invention to what Augusto made. For teaching and facilitating are themselves capable of being elevated to art. There's a place for reproducing TO exactly as Boal made it, and also a great value in exploring new permutations, thereby keeping the body of work alive and growing.

Semi-invisible theatre: magic that mystifies and reveals

I believe it is politically, pedagogically, and psychologically important that teachers/directors/parents not hide the fact that they often exercise power over their class/actors/offspring. Attempts to pretend that the audience and actors (students and teachers/children and parents?) are on equal footing is a mystification with real, though often hidden, dangers of oppression. And yet, if one is a magician, isn't this mystification necessary for the "trick" to work? Is it possible to, at once, exercise the power of theater and show the exercise?

(Steve Wangh, "Semi-invisible theatre," email, January 14, 2008)

Reminiscent of Tony Kushner's emphasis on magic while letting the wires show (chapter 1), acting teacher Steve Wangh attributes to several sources his attraction to a version of Boal's invisible theatre that reveals itself as theatre. One is the unforgettable experience, at age 14, of seeing the Living Theater's production of *The Connection* (1960), unfolding in real time, about a group of junkies waiting for the person who is bringing their fix. Wangh especially remembers company co-director and lead actor Julian Beck, as the house manager, coming from the back of the audience to stop the performance. Wangh loved being challenged to wonder what aspects of the event were real. Similarly, a William Ball production of Pirandello's *Six Characters in Search of an Author* made Wangh think deeply about the very nature of theatre. In that play, a family of characters from an unfinished play interrupts the rehearsal of another play by Pirandello and begs the director and cast to enact their story. In the same spirit, Wangh recounts that as a child, what drew him to theatre in the first place was something about reality and play. He remembers crying into his pillow as a small child thinking: "Isn't this an interesting sound I'm making?" (Steve Wangh, email, 2008, *op. cit.*).

While drawn to ambiguity between art and life, Wangh and others have voiced some misgivings about invisible theatre. Is it ethically questionable to present a rehearsed action unmarked as theatre as if it were occurring spontaneously? Is that duping people? In the 1960s, Wangh directed a play with his street theatre company in which an actor came out of the audience and drew a gun on another actor. Then they turned to the audience, many of whom thought the gunner was real, and asked them which should die. Wangh later came to distrust representing theatrics as real as a kind of vanguardism, a mistreatment of the audience: "in the name of progressive politics, one was tempted to engage in oppressive activities" (Steve Wangh, email, 2008, *op. cit.*).

Wangh has increasingly been drawn to a theatrics of transparency. In the late 1990s, he and some of his acting students explored *semi*-invisible theatre as a way to explore the line between life and art with the audience's knowledge. While beginning with a spectacle that pretended to be "real life," they would gradually reveal it as theatre to their audience. A number of their experiments took place on the New York City subway, at times when the subway cars had a good number of riders but were not so full that semi-invisible theatre would get lost in the crowd.

In one piece, a number of rider–actors, reading their newspapers, performed a choreography of legs crossing and uncrossing, pages turning, heads peering out and back, side-to-side, that began in a random way and little by little was performed in unison. Riders noticed at different times that what had seemed to be everyday life was in fact a planned performance. The reminder of the beauty of everyday life, with the chorus line of subway newspaper readers a sort of dance, was a joy to behold. It had the effect of tuning spectators in to the quirky, interesting, and artful moments that occur around us every day, often without our noticing. Wangh's subway dance was in effect a piece *about* seeing one's surroundings.

The semi-invisible scenario Wangh liked best was a love affair which began totally invisibly as performance. A young man and a young woman, on opposite sides of a subway car, were struck with love at first sight. Each was with a few friends who mocked and yet encouraged them to approach the other, in the process getting the attention of the unknowing spectators sitting in the subway car. Part of the trick in such veiled performances is to get people's attention without annoying them, a feat accomplished in this case by unfolding the scene with the joy of intense and shy attraction.

As the two moved across the car to each other, a boom box began playing the theme from *Love Story* (1970), the familiar title song of an old romantic movie about two college students who fall in love and then discover that one has a terminal illness. The music let everyone in on the trick. They knew that what was unfolding had been planned, and allowed themselves to enjoy the encounter in a different way. The deliberate intervention into a space of public comings and goings was a way of saying to the spect-actors, imagine the world you want and enact it in everyday life. Wangh describes the pedagogical idea here as, "Yes, we (actors) are so magical that we can fool you into believing in make-believe realities ... but this is how we do it, so you can see that it is not really 'magic,' it is something you could do, too."

Wangh thus calls for a Brechtian invisible theatre, in which the seams show, but not right away. He encourages spect-actors to not just look at, but to really see their surroundings, while eventually revealing the theatrical prompts he inserted into everyday life in order to do so. As such he is true to Boal's core, anti-oppressive values without giving up the fun. Wangh recognizes the role of hidden knowledge in holding onto power. On the extreme end of the spectrum, some regimes forbid their subjects to learn how to read. On the benign side are theatre-makers who stage scenes in public without letting on that the people in those scenes will not be held accountable for their actions in the same way that ordinary mortals would. Wangh also recognizes the pleasure in first experiencing the magic of something extraordinary happening before discovering how it worked. Moreover, by exploring and adapting Boal's methods within the context of an acting course in the New York University Drama Department, Wangh was also affirming that engaged theatre can be complex, professional, and boundary-pushing.

The Joker System as Pedagogy and Performance

Though TO often unfolds in the spaces of workshops or everyday life, the rehearsal hall and theatre auditorium are the venues of the Joker System. Mady Schutzman, professor at California Institute of the Arts and longtime Boal practitioner, writer, and thinker, explored the Joker System by writing the annual play for the Plaza de la Raza Youth Theatre Program, working with a group of Latino/a teenagers. According to its website, La Plaza is "the only multidisciplinary cultural arts center serving Latinos in Los Angeles ... Through the arts, La Plaza provides a vital human resource service, bridging geographic, social, artistic and cultural boundaries of Los Angeles and beyond." By basing the play she devised on a rich technique created by the Brazilian Boal, Schutzman both affirmed the richness of Latino/Latin American cultures and engaged the youth with a complex aesthetic enhancing their budding acting and critical thinking skills.

Whereas Boal's troupe of professional actors developed the Joker System as an experiment in theatrical form geared to an audience, Schutzman used it for performance *and* pedagogy: to provide the young actors with a Freirean model of education, the opportunity to focus their learning on subjects of their choice, and to explore contradictions rather than simply absorb what they were taught – in this case, the story of civil rights. Schutzman asked, "How were these young people processing the murders of so many black people whose acts of resistance constituted the civil rights movement? What connections were they making between these seemingly remote historical characters of the past and their current lives as Latinos in Los Angeles?" (Schutzman 2009: 76) The young people co-devising the piece were at the same time actors and activated learners, previously largely passive in the face of their own education.

In keeping with a Freirean, dialogic approach to learning, Schutzman invited the young actors to choose historical characters they wanted to know more about or celebrate. She taught them about the nominated characters they didn't all know, and then they voted, with Rodney King and Claudette Colvin gaining the most support (Schutzman 2009: 74). Rodney King was the African American man whose beating by four white Los Angeles Police Department officers in 1991 was captured on a bystander's videotape. The officers' acquittal, a year later, set off widespread rioting in Los Angeles. Claudette Colvin was the 15-year-old African American who, in 1955 in Montgomery, Alabama, refused to give up her seat on a bus to a white passenger. Yet she received no recognition for this same act of resistance that catapulted Rosa Parks to fame some months later. Schutzman urged the students to question every aspect of the historical record, providing them with the facts they needed to do so, such as the laws at the time reserving seats at the front of public buses for whites, at the back for blacks, and in the middle for whites unless they did not require all of them. The students' questions informed the spirit and the content of the play (Schutzman 2009: 74).

The play, directed by BJ Dodge and entitled *Upset!*, has a rough-and-tumble quality, in keeping with both Boal and Schutzman's interest in filling pleasurable popular forms with critical, complex content. (Indeed, Schutzman has also written for the gender-bending circus-theatre company Circus Amok.[6]) In *Upset!*, a spotlight follows the main action, and lots of rowdy cheering punctuates events. The large cast – 37 names appear on the program – are all on stage for most of the show, which runs just over an hour and a half. As represented in the performance, King and Colvin's unfolding stories are at once history lessons; a commentary on how people are represented publicly to fulfill a role, be it shaped by the media or by the movement; and an occasion for the young actors to insert themselves into the history of civil rights by reflecting on its meaning personally and claiming it as their legacy.[7]

The Joker (a Boalian facilitator/master of ceremonies) in *Upset!*, a self-possessed teen wearing a large jester hat, directly addresses the audience. His tone is conversational with a touch of magic; he carries a scepter with which he starts and stops action. Rather than a character in the conventional enclosed world of a play, he closely parallels the ringmaster of a circus in his direct address to the audience, from his very first words: "Ladies and gentlemen, boys and girls of all ages … ." He ambles casually around the stage; indeed, that informality characterizes the entire production. Little by little I see the stage as a space the youth have come to own. What's important is that they see themselves as the next link in a great chain of people of color resisting an oppressive history, a history largely written by others. And that's accomplished by making the stage a kind of club house where they hang out, cheer, step in and out of the spotlight, watch the other scenes, argue, muse, make jokes, and listen to the music and to each other.

The world of this play also communicates a degree of skepticism. The central image is the taped silhouette associated with a crime scene where someone has recently died, dominating the floor at the center of the stage. There's graffiti on a wall – "No Justice, No Peace" – right alongside "Post No Bills," suggesting both are equally unexceptional, everyday sentiments. Across the back of the stage is a ramp of a freeway. "Are there any cars in this show?" one of the kids asks early on. "Of course," the Joker answers. "We're in Los Angeles." The central metaphor of the play is in fact a bus, both the ones we get on and the ones we don't, including the buses on which both Colvin and Parks resisted unjust laws, what Schutzman calls in the play "sitting down to stand up."

Figure 2.1 Gabriel Torres, youth participant in the CalArts Community Arts Partnership (CAP) program with Plaza de la Raza in East Los Angeles, playing the role of the Joker in the play *Upset!* written by CalArts School of Critical Studies faculty member Mady Schutzman with the CAP youth participants in May 2006. (Photo by Rachel Slowinski.)

The forward movement of the narrative opens up now and again through several strategies. One is the kids' personalizing of some of the ideas about the historical characters. For example, the protagonists of the play, Claudette Colvin and Rodney King, introduce themselves and the roles they inadvertently did or did not play in history: Colvin, whose act of resistance preceded Parks's but was not recognized; King, who never meant to be a civil rights symbol. Reflecting on the way we may be unsuccessful in assuming the role we crave, or be cast in roles not of our own making, the young actors all repeat the line "Someone who'd meet me for the first time would think I'm … " and fill it in for themselves: "Someone meeting me for the first time would think I'm lazy," says one; "outgoing," says another; "white," "so cool," and "crazy," say a third, fourth, and fifth. "Harry Potter," says one more, keeping a dose of irreverence in the mix.

The actors provide an overview of major civil rights cases. We hear about Plessy v. Ferguson, 1892, in an early challenge to segregation, in that case on a New Orleans street car; Emmet Till, 1955, a black teenager kidnapped, beaten, and killed for whistling at a white girl, his murderers acquitted; Fannie Lou Hamer, 1963, who struggled for the right to register to vote; Medger Evans, 1963, civil rights worker murdered, and the 30 years it took to convict his killers; JFK, 1963, assassinated according to this history for supporting civil rights; Malcolm X, 1965, assassinated; Dr Martin Luther King, Jr, 1968, assassinated. The youth also try on key ideas from the historical figures. After Fanny Lou Hamer is introduced as the person who said, "I'm sick and tired of being sick and tired," several of the young actors tell us what makes *them* sick and tired.

In Joker System spirit, we experience a range of performative genres. Two girls in gowns, reminiscent of TV game shows, do game show activities such as spinning a giant wheel. At the trial of the policemen who beat Rodney King, very loud, flowery music turns the scene into melodrama, communicating the sense that the public was manipulated to accept their acquittal. At yet another moment, the gowned girls become back-up singers for a Motown number featuring Claudette Colvin. Is this the acclaim she never got before, or is this, sadly, the most attention a "girl" can hope for – a solo in a pop song?

The first of the two central stories in the play is the 1991 beating of Rodney King, the subsequent Los Angeles riots, and the acquittal of the police who did the beating. It's good to see the kids wrestle with this terrible thing that happened to a person of color. They count off the 56 blows to Rodney King's body, freezing while each says how they, in the character of a police person carrying out the violence, feel about it: "I don't know why I'm doing this but my buddies aren't stopping me so it must be okay;" "I'm so confused;" "I'm sick and tired;" "I don't get paid to do street fighting." King lays in the taped silhouette center stage, communicating that a serious crime has been committed. At another point, the actor playing

Rodney King gets up and takes the baton, imagining himself as one of the perpetrators. This scene leads into personal stories of racial profiling.

The young man playing Rodney King delivers a monologue expressing his desire not to be constantly the person of color receiving other people's gifts. He questions who gets to be in the giving position and why, linking it to white privilege. Later, the cast acknowledges that while Rodney King "wasn't exactly a model citizen," he nevertheless has the right to be protected by the law. It feels as though the youth are asserting basic human rights that they are ready to claim for themselves, and may not have thought through without this play experience.

In the scene of the trial of the four police caught on videotape beating Rodney King, the opinion of the cast is uniform: the trial was unfair. It was held in Simi Valley, which they describe as "police heaven," with no blacks on the jury. The Joker asks if this is an ordinary town or is it bizarre; is it safe or not? The message I get is that what's normal and safe for some is bizarre and dangerous for others, based on one's social position, largely determined by race.

We soon get to the most despairing and powerful scene in the play, in which four white supremacists mock Rodney King's statement from the time "I felt like a crushed can," and rant proudly about crushing cans – "Afro-*cans*, Jamai-*cans*, Domini-*cans*" – as a Ku Klux Klan member dressed in full KKK regalia performs a wild staccato dance, literally crushing aluminum cans scattered across the stage. At the end of the scene, the Joker invites the cast onto the bus, but they do not want to get on. It's as if the often-losing struggle of the just in history makes cowards of us all:

JOKER: How tragic! The bus of the past, the bus of the future, the bus we
    have been waiting for, is an empty bus, stuck between then and now,
    between as-always and what-if, a real Could-Have-Been-A-Great bus but
    instead just sitting here with nowhere to go and no one to get it there.
    (*Everyone looks at each other, no one moves.*)
CLAUDETTE: I'll get on the bus!
CHORUS: YEAH!!

Colvin gets on the bus, and her scene is enacted; the young actors wearing black or white masks play the other characters. She sits near the front of the bus. The actor playing the driver tells her to move back. When she refuses, policemen enter and take her off the bus. The actors reflect on the moment for themselves:

CHORUS: If I were on that bus, where would I have to sit?

So Colvin finally gets some public respect, on this stage. She is poor, black, 15 years old, and pregnant. The civil rights movement leadership did not think they could successfully challenge segregation in public buses with Colvin as the test case, so instead recruited the lighter-skinned, upstanding citizen, seamstress Rosa Parks. Colvin resentfully refers to Parks as the superstar.

Near the end of the play we meet one more group struggling for civil rights: South Central Los Angeles farmers going to court to keep their land. They participate in non-violent civil disobedience, a relief to include as a form of resistance after the violence we have witnessed. The play ends on a note of how mixed the world is, "good and ghastly," filled with people who are "upbeat" and those who are "upstagers." We hear what happened to each of the main characters after they left the limelight. The play suggests that people's real lives are not just different from the public versions, but also a lot more complicated.

Using the Joker System to educate the cast first, and only later the audience, Schutzman's work echoes Brecht's *Lehrstücke* (learning plays), developed to engage large numbers of people in a play the process of which is as important as the product. Schutzman is a reminder to pay attention to what draws you into a body of work, even if it is not the component immediately popularized. Indeed, although Schutzman made the request, Boal never facilitated a workshop on the Joker System in the USA, despite the fact that she set up numerous other workshops for him over the years. So she explored it on her own, the only person I have ever known to do so.

The Spirit of Boal in the Bronx

> Arts residencies to be developed in Hunts Point. A strong proposal will address issues of importance to the residents and will involve the participation of one or several segments of the community – students, children, seniors, professionals, etc. At the end of the year, all individual projects will be integrated into a community-based pageant.
>
> (Action Lab, public announcement produced jointly by The Point Community Development Corporation and the Bronx Museum, Hunts Point, the Bronx, spring 2004)

Action Lab was a two-year project supporting artists' work with community residents through workshops, exhibitions, and performances in Hunts Point, a neighborhood in the Bronx. Boal was Action Lab's theoretical touchstone, particularly the idea of using the arts to both problem-solve and activate segments of the community – groups of residents with some collective identity – who had few material resources. Action Lab asked applicants to articulate how they would incorporate Boal into their work, and what community partnership they would establish. Most interesting to me about Action Lab was its openness to the ways an artist might adhere to Boal's principles while making very different-looking work.

Initially, eight projects were funded. Only one of the grantees, George Sanchez, carried out an orthodox TO workshop, specifically with local teachers, both to use forum theatre to brainstorm classroom problems, and to re-energize participants through the creative pleasure of the work and contact among peers. Another grantee, Erin Dunleavy, adapted TO with a troupe of teenagers, juxtaposing Shakespearean monologues with interviews of incarcerated youth set against personal images of oppression generated through Boal image-theatre techniques.

One of Dunleavy's pieces, for example, interwove an interview with a young girl raised in foster homes, trying to find her own rules to live by, with Portia's "The quality of mercy is not strained" monologue from *The Merchant of Venice*. The young actors also stretched their horizons through working with interviews with incarcerated youth. Locating Shakespearean texts in relationship to the struggles of both sets of young people demonstrated the profundity of their experience through its resonance with *The Merchant of Venice*. A theatrical event that might have been pigeonholed as merely good for the young participants was, instead, seen as an expression of the human experience to which attention must be paid.

The Action Lab artist who drew most from the spirit rather than the letter of Boal was the choreographer Arthur Aviles, who began the project unclear about what TO brings to political art. He considers his company's frequent partnering of men and men, and women and women, to be political; the delicacy of dance, which he has sometimes explored in public parks in the Bronx to mutterings by passers-by of "faggot," is political. For Aviles, art is political, indeed art is art, whenever it generates heated discussion: "If a piece you do doesn't elicit some kind of discussion outside and inside of what you've presented then you haven't really presented art or made a statement."[8]

Aviles left the acclaimed choreographer Bill T. Jones's company to return to the Bronx,

> because I need to be a part of my community. I have an affinity for Latino people so my departure from them had been very scary. At the same time I'm apprehensive because I'm building something that is different. I came back to take a stand. My come-back is very defiant.
>
> (Arthur Aviles, unpublished interview with the author, the Bronx, New York, September 10, 2005)

He set up a space called BAAD! – Bronx Academy of Art and Dance – especially for gays, lesbians, bisexuals, transsexuals, women, and people of color.

Aviles addresses the difficulty of being a minority voice in his community:

> Whenever I am surrounded by the Latino culture and homo-
> sexuality comes up, it's very difficult to get my point-of-view across
> in a way that is about taking a stand rather than coming from
> underneath and saying, "Would you allow me to say this please?"
> So that's the little bit of positioning that I'd like to take within the
> really wonderful influence of Boal in Action Lab. Because I find that
> a lot of the voices of "the community" that get heard are from the
> status quo. I want to push against that. All voices need to be heard.
>
> (Aviles, interview, 2005, *op. cit.*)

Aviles makes an important case for the element of difference within communities, which are in fact never entirely monolithic.

For his artistic contribution to Action Lab, Aviles responded to Boal by
creating *El Yunque is in the Laundromat*, whose central image is the Puerto
Rican rain forest (El Yunque). The performance took place in a large laundromat on Hunts Point Avenue, the main street of his Bronx neighborhood, as Aviles wanted to connect the ritual of washing as it takes place in
ancestral natural settings with the way he and his neighbors wash their
clothes now. His idea was to juxtapose elements of shared Puerto Rican
identity like El Yunque, familiar music, and an everyday site, with less-
known movement forms. Aviles intended to put *Animal Planet* on a VCR
to contrast with the talk shows typically played there. He wanted the whole
laundromat engulfed in tropical plants and animal sounds through collaboration with a horticulturalist and a sound designer.

The performance took place on a Saturday afternoon when the laundromat was bustling. Evocatively, the dancers performed in front of a long
row of washing machines, some with water splashing away on the clothes
inside. Aviles choreographed the piece to the song "Always and Forever,"
by a group from the 1970s called Heatwave, because it is romantic and well-
known in the neighborhood, often played at Latino weddings and *Quince-
neros* (the Latino version of Sweet 16s).

The six dancers were costumed as animals, two of which were rather
Disneyesque – a chicken with a plastic mask and a generic fur bunny – and
the other four more free-form, featuring cloth scale-like fringes, feathers,
wings, and a green unitard, respectively. Aviles chose them because, he said,

> forests and animals go well together, and animals ease the tension
> of performance in an unusual space. I tried to make them familiar
> benevolent animals. I think the children might remember real ani-
> mals weaving in and out of each other in harmony.
>
> (Aviles, interview, 2005, *op. cit.*)

59

Figure 2.2 Arthur Aviles Typical Theatre, *El Yunque is in the Laundromat*, 2005, part of an exploration of Boal in Hunt's Point, the Bronx. (Photo by Charles Rice-Gonzalez.)

Aviles saw the Disneyesque costumes as humorous, valuable to amuse an audience that was not watching a dance piece by choice, but he agreed with me that the other costumes were more aesthetically pleasing. The bottom line was that he needed to use costumes the company had from past pieces, given financial restraints (Arthur Aviles, "Action Lab", email, August 2, 2005).

The performance caused a bit of a stir among the 30 or 40 people, of all ages, there doing their wash. Many paused to see what was happening; kids sat at the edge of the impromptu performance space. But the laundromat, with the addition of only a few plants, had not been transformed into a rain forest due to lack of time and money. Way in the upper corner of the space, a television screen showed a tree in the wind, a far cry from the video of a rain forest with which Aviles wanted to replace the talk shows that usually played there. While Aviles feels the performance achieved his goal of creating "a surreal, quiet, zen-like atmosphere," he also commented that *El Yunque is in the Laundromat* had a pretty rocky birth. I agree that the performance temporarily changed and softened the atmosphere. But overall, audience response seemed to be low-level curiosity and momentary puzzlement. When it ended and the artists danced back into the street, people inside went back to the talk shows and their laundry. It's unlikely that audience members saw a connection between the rain forest and the laundromat.

But Aviles took a long view, knowing the project was huge and multi-faceted. In what he sees as the first of several attempts, he chose to focus this time on the relationship with the laundromat owners, to gain access to the space, and to get the dancers comfortable performing there:

> It felt like a mini-Christo project.[9] In the future I imagine all the same elements – plants, a TV, music, and live performance – but ten-fold. Given what I know now, we can take the next step to a more realized transformation of the laundromat into a rainforest, a true and complete space where cleaning one's clothes and the experience of performance could be possible.
>
> (Aviles, interview, 2005, *op. cit.*)

While *El Yunque is in the Laundromat* in no way looked like TO, the every-day setting of the laundromat, and the desire to juxtapose the real and the imagined, reflects a core Boalian principle called metaxis. Boal describes it as the image of reality becoming the reality of the image. That is, instead of performing a dance in a theatre, which is set in the Puerto Rican rain forest, with dancers pretending to wash clothes, Aviles inserted dancers into a venue where contemporary NYC Puerto Ricans really wash clothes. The churning water in the row of activated washing machines is at once a poignant reminder of how far urbanites have come from washing their clothes in a stream, and a pleasurable moment of noticing the beauty of the movement of water, even in a washing machine. Aviles's layering produc-tively complicates expression of how far his Nuyorican[10] neighbors have strayed from their roots without denying the audience aesthetic pleasure. It is a utopian gesture towards the nowhere of a village stream on a noisy Bronx avenue, that Aviles brings into being and then magically makes dis-appear as the dancers melt back into the crowd.

However, while Aviles was in no way obliged to use Boal's *approach*, he *was* meant to take up Action Lab's mandate to problem-solve and activate segments of the community. Aviles did not clearly address the problem of cultural deracination, and the audience was never given the means to do more than watch the show. On the one hand, to fully take up the challenge Boal represents, *El Yunque is in the Laundromat* would have to be developed with direct engagement of that community. On the other hand, as a Latino living in Hunts Point, Aviles avows that he is part of the community being engaged. But either way, he did not take up the challenge to create a pro-blem-solving situation. Still, the groundwork is in place to explore aspects of Puerto Rican culture that have been lost, others that have been trans-formed, still others that have been retained, and those that are hanging in the balance and require collective energy if they are to continue to be part of shared Puerto Rican life in Hunts Point. *El Yunque is in the Laundromat* was more an exploration of a blurred line between art and life than a full exploration of metaxis – the image of reality becoming the reality of the image. That would entail Aviles making real his poignant longing for the elemental beauty of lush plants and a village stream as an everyday venue for people doing their wash. That setting has a special cultural meaning for Puerto Ricans, even living in the Bronx, as part of a collective memory and history.

El Yunque is in the Laundromat most captured the spirit of Boal's commitment to art in everyday life; Aviles connected most with Boal through artistic attentiveness to the senses. As suggested in the opening epigram, Boal's philosophy encourages us to see what we look at, feel what we touch, and hear what we listen to. Using his own artistic language to manifest that vision in a way that the community could have understood, Aviles points the direction to another fruitful building on Boal.

Activating the specta(c)tor

Boal's premise for activating the specta(c)tor represents a meeting of politics and aesthetics: people with the least amount of power, joined together, may find solutions that one could neither imagine nor, in most cases, carry out alone. The results bring rarely seen perspectives into public view, which can be emotionally compelling. While not everyone might choose to get actively involved, Boal's techniques provide the option to do so; hence one can say there are no spectators in TO. There are other theatrical techniques that likewise serve a problem-solving function, and likewise exist in a context without an audience. Role-play is a not uncommon component of preparing a group for a political action, particularly one that might lead to arrest; or, in the context of drama therapy, of working through emotional knots. By practicing for the future or unpacking the past, options for action or interpretation open up.

Invisible theatre was initially invisible not to fool the observer, but because of the danger political manifestations would have caused the actors in 1980s Argentina, when and where Boal was developing it, in exile from Brazil. Given that making a political statement in public is not forbidden in most English-speaking countries, one would have to think long and hard to justify invisible theatre in such contexts. While invisible theatre's appearance of spontaneity has an immediacy that overt theatre often lacks, one can begin a piece as if it's spontaneous and, little by little, reveal the artifice, as in Wangh's semi-invisible theatre. Realizing that the subways skits were planned did not take away from the sense that the assumption of distrust on the train was an over-reaction. These actions were in the spirit of problem-solving: how do we dispel the deep-seated distrust on the subway, a caution that may have been an appropriate response in the more crime-ridden 1970s, but was not a big problem by the mid-1990s, when Wangh's students performed it. Wangh's scenarios were designed to be recognized as theatre, which made them more conducive, not less, to fulfilling their task as the revealed actors created a ready context for talking with spectactors about what happened and why.

With an equal emphasis on the here-and-now, Boal came up with the Joker System as a way to break with the tradition of simply importing the great theatre from the capitals of the Western world (Boal 1974: 174). The Joker System was a playful way to put responsibility on the spectator for interpretation, rather than passively absorb the playwright and director's point of view. In Schutzman's hands, it put equal emphasis on the actors, in rehearsal, to figure out their perspective as well. The pleasure of *Upset!* for an audience is as much watching the youth express themselves as watching a play *per se*. How often does the public get to hear 37 Latino teens respond to the history of civil rights in the USA?

Boal's influence on Aviles is most captured in the quote with which I began this chapter, "doing theater throws light on the stage of daily life," which Aviles did and did not accomplish. In the same spirit as invisible theatre, inserting performance into everyday life seeks to "cleanse the windows of perception" and bring two realities, one imagined and one concretely lived, in proximity to one another. It's in the Artaudian tradition of theatre as experience rather than representation, by making it something of which the spectator is part.[11] But if the performance was a call to remember shared cultural roots, it lacked a mechanism for the audience to respond.

While Boal's techniques never force anyone to interact, the danger of activating spectators is that of coercively disturbing someone who does not want to get involved. I once attended a performance set during the Nazi era and, to my chagrin, the actors pointed the spotlight into the audience and asked all the Jews to stand up. I didn't want to set myself up for the unknown ramifications that were bound to follow, nor was I comfortable keeping silent when asked if I were a Jew. While I don't think all theatre has to be comfortable, I do think the audience needs to feel it is in good hands, and in that case I most emphatically did not. Boal's rule of thumb, that activation of the spectator involves making opportunities for engagement which the audience may accept or reject, strikes me as a good base for pursuing such explorations.

Boal died in May 2009. The man was endlessly inventive, with a phenomenal capacity to organize theatrical techniques into what he called the arsenal of TO, and to add to it as he traveled the world. He also had an extraordinary presence. Amy Goodman, host of a daily news/radio program called *Democracy Now*, called him "legendary … tireless" (May 6, 2009). Bruce Weber of *The New York Times* described him as "an affable intellectual and effervescent teacher" (May 9, 2009). The announcement of his death emailed out by the US-based Center of Pedagogy and Theatre of the Oppressed referred to him as a "giant" and a "visionary" (May 4, 2009).

Canadian TO practitioner David Diamond evoked his "passionately theatrical spirit and his uncompromising commitment to human rights, combined with an infectious sense of play" (David Diamond, email, May 4, 2009).

When Boal ran for city councilman in Rio in the 1990s, his campaign slogan was "the courage to be happy." At the time I was disappointed; why such a sappy message from such a deep man who knew how so many people suffer? But with his passing, I am reminded of Hamlet's line, "I could be bounded in a nut shell and count myself a king of infinite space, were it not that I have bad dreams" (*Hamlet*, scene ii). Boal was king of infinite space, able to open up possibilities through the act of collaboration in spaces where seemingly nothing could move forward. I think he was motivated by good dreams, and was himself the quintessence of metaxis – the reality he perceived with all his senses always infused with what he could imagine at the very same time.

Workbook

Boal's theatre of the oppressed techniques

In order to adapt Boal, one first must know the basics. Ideally, people teaching this material will have participated in a TO workshop at some point; it helps to have done these exercises before facilitating a workshop. The Pedagogy and Theatre of the Oppressed organization in the USA has a website through which one can connect with a network of practitioners. That said, many people have read Boal's various exercise descriptions and then tried them without formal training first.

Even a 2-hour workshop – two class periods, or one 2-hour slot – is a valuable introduction. But a five-hour workshop, perhaps on a weekend, is even better.

Games for Actors and Non-Actors (Boal 1992) documents many of the games and techniques described here. I recommend spending a bare minimum of 20 minutes for games, 45 minutes for image theatre, and 1 hour for forum theatre. A longer workshop could devote more time to forum and include more games and techniques described earlier in the chapter, specifically rainbow of desire, invisible theatre, the Joker System, or legislative theatre. Ideally what follows would nevertheless be a basis for proceeding with any of the other techniques because they viscerally introduce Boal's physical vocabulary and principles.

TO workshops generally begin with a few games. They are intended to warm up the participants individually and as a group, as well as to demonstrate the principles of TO. A good energizing exercise is Afraid of/Protect. Everyone moves around the room. The facilitator then asks each person subtly to choose someone in the room, other than the facilitator, who they'll think of as their protector for the duration of the game. Don't let on to the person that you have so designated them, but as you continue moving around the room, try to stay close to them. After a minute or two, the facilitator asks everyone additionally to designate someone who, for the duration of the exercise, they fear. Without letting on who that is, try to keep your protector between you and the person you are afraid of, at all times. This exercise provides a palpable experience of the contagiousness of emotion. The "Afraid of" step has a feeling of mass hysteria, as each person's movements around the room cause the whole group to shift constantly. When the game is over, reflecting on who one chose as one's threat and protector is also instructive (5–8 minutes).

Move next to image theatre. The experience of the body's expressivity is fundamental in Boal's system. While he knows well that some people are more physically expressive than others, image theatre goes a way towards leveling the playing field regarding some people's greater verbal propensity. While image theatre has many variations, one that allows everyone to fully participate is "Groups of Four." Working wordlessly, simultaneously, in groups of four or five, everyone gets a chance to sculpt their group into an image of their own oppression, with the last step being to enter the image as oneself. The image might embody an unequal power dynamic in one's family or workplace, for example. "Sculpting" means either gently putting the people's bodies into the positions you need in order to communicate the oppression, or working through mimicry, showing them how you want them to pose. Understand that you will never be asked to tell the group anything about your image. Only after each person has composed an image do the group members talk together, not to discuss the content of the images, but to choose one image to share with everyone, based on identification, or at least resonance, with what each person understands it to signify.

Each group gets a turn to remount that one image in the center of the work space. Everyone else stands in a circle around them, first identifying, out loud, what they literally see: two people standing with perfectly straight legs, a fist on one person's heart, no eye contact, etc. The second level of response is "how do you interpret what you see?" That's when comments such as "the parents disagree about how to handle what the son is telling them"; "someone is mocking someone else"; are invited. Again, people experience that their interpretation is not the only possibility. This can be especially insightful for the person who first made the image.

The last step is dynamization. The Joker asks each group to dynamize the image by, for example:

1 Thinking of this as the "real" image, have the person who created it (known as the protagonist) sculpt the "ideal" image. Discuss it with the group. Then have the protagonist sculpt a transitional image, somewhere between the two.

2   The facilitator puts her hand on the shoulder of each person in the image, the protagonist last. The person who is touched speaks streams of consciousness, informed by a sense of who s/he is in the image. Discuss.

3   The facilitator claps three times, each time leaving a moment for the people in the image to move towards where it feels their characters are going.

Which brings us to forum theatre. The participants identify issues of oppression (or unequal power dynamics) in their lives that they recognize as social – not only their individual struggles, but part of an unequal *status quo*. Then groups are formed around each. Typical themes are racism, sexism, class inequities, family oppressions. To be in a group, each person must be willing to share a story recounting a concrete manifestation of the oppression they experienced. Each group creates a scene in which a protagonist tries, unsuccessfully, to overcome that oppression in a concrete scenario built out of the shared stories. Each group shows their scene to everyone, then at least one is chosen, based on its resonance for the people in the room, to be brought to forum. The scene is replayed, with a facilitator (the Joker) inviting the spect-actors to replace the protagonist at any point in the scene when they can imagine an alternative action that could lead to a solution. The scene is replayed numerous times with different interventions. This results in a dialogue about the oppression, an examination of alternatives, and what Boal calls a "rehearsal" for real situations.

If you are working with a group that already knows these basic exercises, you may want to break into groups and invent adaptations for particular workshop contexts.

3

SELF-REPRESENTING

Testimonial performance

(A different version of this essay appears in *The Applied Theatre Reader*, Prentki and Preston 2009.)

> Ubuntu botho ... speaks about humanness, gentleness, hospitality, putting yourself out on the behalf of others, being vulnerable. It recognizes that my humanity is bound in yours, for we can only be human together.
>
> (Archbishop Desmond Tutu)

In the aftermath of the September 11, 2001 attack on the World Trade Center, countless numbers of people sought fellowship as they processed sorrow, outrage, confusion, and fear. In New York City, many found their way to Union Square Park, traditionally a public gathering place for protest and political rallies. Throughout that fall, the Square overflowed with informal gatherings, spontaneous acts of comfort, story exchanges, chalked messages, and the ubiquitous photos of loved ones not seen since the attack.

Others were drawn to an empty clothing store in New York City's upscale Soho neighborhood. The store's owner, Michael Shulan, temporarily refitted it as "Here is New York: A Democracy of Photos," a space for anyone to display photos they'd taken related to 9/11. The $25 charged per image went to charities for the offspring of people killed that day. Not until you got to the checkout counter did you know if you'd chosen an image by a famous photographer worth a great deal more than $25 in the art market, or a work by someone who'd never sold an image before.

Here's how Shulan describes that space:

> Not an art exhibition in the conventional sense, partly an impromptu memorial, partly a rescue effort, and partly a testimonial of support for those who were actually doing the rescuing ... In order to come to grips with all of this imagery which was

haunting us, it was essential, we thought, to reclaim it from the media and stare at it without flinching.

(Shulan *et al.* 2004)

The photos became a way to start to integrate and interrogate the act we had witnessed so suddenly. The space was important, both for the conversations it invited around the images, and for the money raised for offspring of people killed that day.

New York City was not the only place where people sought public spaces for dealing with the enormity of 9/11. Well after most of us had returned to our routines, people all across the country continued to feel its reverberations through subsequent political changes, such as passage of the Patriot Act. This is the story of a role for art in responding to the excesses of one particular situation that the Patriot Act made possible. Directed by playwright Marty Pottenger, the project, called *home land security* (*hls*), reflects her belief that art serves social justice best through what Archbishop Desmond Tutu calls *ubuntu botho*: a way of being human that recognizes equally the humanity of others. The technique Pottenger and others have used to that end involves listening to testimonials of people living through such crises and, as in her case, making something of them.

Social call, cultural response

In February 2004, US Border Patrollers on the Maine/Canada frontier traveled several hundred miles south to Portland, Maine, to carry out raids targeting immigrants and refugees. Made legal by the Patriot Act, the raids incensed many Mainers and became the impetus for Bau Graves, director of Portland's Center for Cultural Exchange, to invite Pottenger to come there and use art to create a public response. Known for making performances out of interviews and Story Circles with under-represented people who have first-hand experience of the subject at hand, Pottenger on this occasion shaped and directed *hls* in this tradition of "first-voice" art-making.

The notion of "first voice" contrasts with much radical theatre of the 1960s and early 1970s, which, while a viable form of political activism, frequently entailed middle-class actors speaking *for* the poor and oppressed. In contrast, Pottenger and other grassroots artists incorporate storytelling to facilitate a process whereby people with stakes in a topic respond publicly for themselves. The act of communicating their own challenges becomes a step toward resolving them. In *hls* workshops, Pottenger also included city political and educational leaders who make decisions affecting immigrants and refugees. This model of art aims concretely to better the lives of people most adversely affected, both through their own efforts and through the shared experience, from story to performance, of people with the power to affect policy directly.

The Border Patrol agents staked out a Latino grocery store, a Hallal meat market, an interstate bus station, the international jetport, and a homeless resource center, demanding to see people's identification papers. Ten people were jailed for alleged immigration violations and then sent either back to their country of origin, or to out-of-state Department of Homeland Security detention facilities. The Border Patrol withheld the names of detainees, but reports confirmed that they did not come from countries associated with contemporary terrorism (Albright 2004).

With a population of some 66,000 people in the city proper and a quarter of a million in the metropolitan area, Portland is not only the largest city in Maine but also the state's cultural, economic, and social center. In the decade following the Vietnam War, Portland saw itself as a welcoming town, where Vietnamese and Cambodian refugees were supported in their quest for a new home and a new life. After the Vietnam War, largely in the 1970s, thousands of Southeast Asian refugees were resettled in the USA, with the relatively liberal city of Portland one of the destinations (Graves 2005: 1–2). Global tragedies and quests for economic opportunities resulted in waves of refugees from Afghanistan, Russia, and several African nations since the 1980s; the fratricidal war in the former Yugoslavia in the mid-1990s brought more people fleeing violent attacks from Bosnia; and for an even longer period, both economic and political strife have resulted in the northern migration of scores of Mexicans and Latin Americans.

Staff of Portland's Center for Cultural Exchange (CCE) interacted regularly with local immigrants and refugees. Established in 1982, its mission was

> promoting a broad appreciation of the interplay between culture and artistic expression ... by acting as a forum for artists who best exemplify world traditions, reflect contemporary trends and explore artistic frontiers, and by nurturing the artistic and cultural life of its own community in greater Portland and in the state of Maine.

Before closing in 2006, the CCE typically raised money and collaborated with local ethnic communities to design culturally specific artists' residencies, multicultural performances, and educational programs. The CCE hosted over 200 events annually, focusing on both traditional ethnic arts and a wide range of innovative performance genres. Audiences mainly attended events from their own culture.

The Portland City Council passed a resolution condemning the Border Patrol's action; state officials, including Governor Baldacci, called for balance between security against terrorism and protection of individual rights.

Nevertheless, as a result of the February raid, many immigrants and refugees barely left their homes; parents feared that if they went to work, they might be snatched by the Border Patrol and their children would return from school not knowing where they were. They also avoided contact with anyone official, including doctors even when they were ill or needed prenatal care, and police even when they were victims of crime.

The circumstances that led to the raids evolve from 9/11, the subsequent passage of the US Patriot Act, and the doubling of Border Patrol agents at US international borders. The CCE director, ethnomusicologist Bau Graves, was skeptical about the increase of Border Patrollers in the north. People illegally crossing the US–Mexico borders – though largely unrelated to 9/11 – probably provide enough work to keep even the expanded forces busy. But in Maine, says Graves, such agents

> didn't have enough work to do already and all of a sudden there were twice as many of them with not enough work. Since Portland is the biggest population hub in the state, that's where they came looking for illegal residents.
>
> (James Bau Graves, interview with the author,
Portland, Maine, 2005)

By the time of the Portland attacks, Graves estimated that 2,500 Latinos and 2,000 Somalis resided in greater Portland. Graves and his wife and partner Phyllis O'Neill attested, "Twenty years ago, people of color were rarely seen on the streets; today students at Portland High School speak 57 native languages" (Graves and O'Neill 2004: 7).

The CCE staff wanted to respond as an institution to the raids, as Graves explained:

> We wanted to artfully address some of the issues. The main point that was sticking in my mind was that we'd adopted the US Patriot Act because some Islamic fundamentalists attacked the WTC; well, none of the Somalis or Latinos in Portland had anything to do with that. It felt like unintended consequences of the Patriot Act, or maybe opportunism.
>
> (Graves, interview, 2005, *op. cit.*)

Indeed, the Border Patrol raids were made possible by a climate of fear, just under the surface of US life since 9/11, which reframes such transgressive acts as protective of the USA. Graves avows that laws meant to be anti-terrorist have in fact become anti-immigrant.

The kind of response the CCE staff deemed necessary lay beyond their aesthetic vocabulary. But Graves met award-winning playwright–performer Marty Pottenger through the Animating Democracy Initiative (ADI), a program that "fosters arts and cultural activity that encourages and enhances civic engagement and dialogue" (www.artsusa.org/animatingdemocracy). ADI had funded Pottenger's *Abundance* (2003), for which she traveled across the USA gathering stories and convening "civic dialogues" – facilitated conversations in which a broad spectrum of participants express a range of views about a contemporary concern. Meeting with people all along the economic spectrum, from multi-millionaires to welfare recipients to undocumented workers, Pottenger made a play about the role of money in people's lives, asking "How much is enough?" Recognizing an aesthetic model befitting Portland's situation after the raids, Graves invited Pottenger to the Center.

Why, almost a year later, make a theatre piece about the raids, for and with Portlanders? Although local politicians spoke sympathetically on their behalf, no platform was provided for people from targeted groups to speak for themselves or process what had happened with each other. In *hls*, a diverse cast of six epitomizes the richness of widely divergent cultural experiences and points of view. Immigrants and refugees speak for themselves; first-person storytelling is a fitting technique for such projects. Art's ability to bring people together can contribute slowly to *culture* change, without which *policy* change has limited effect. That is, while politicians condemned the border raids and sought protections through local policies, the cultural discomfort many immigrants and refugees continued to feel could be addressed better through their very visibility and speaking out.

Pottenger emphasizes how rarely people have the chance, such as *hls* provided, to converse about subjects – both listening and speaking – on which they hold various opinions, citing her own experience:

> I have always been intrigued by how people of various points-of-view find common cause. For most of my life I have worked on progressive causes, yet always mindful of the honest questions citizens ask on all sides. But where are the opportunities to converse civilly across these differences? At our annual family reunion, my sister, a Rear Admiral, greets my brother who runs a Legal Aid clinic. My other brother, a born-again Christian, breaks bread with my French Socialist brother-in-law as my radically-Conservative Republican father sits down with his second wife, a died-in-the-wool Southern Democrat. Yet we as a culture don't have ways to take on the topics that stir our passions and sense of justice.
>
> (Marty Pottenger, "Portland project," email, June 23, 2005)

Pottenger's call for multiple perspectives aligns itself with Boal's Joker System and, indeed, the very principle of broad participation, through whatever the technique. We thus increasingly see the outlines of an aesthetics of engaged performance, in which listening is a prerequisite for speaking, involving first project participants and then audiences in an exploration of a relevant topic and the articulation of many points of view about it.

The testimonial process

Pottenger spent a week each month in Portland from January through October 2005, conducting individual interviews. From the interviewees, she brought potential performers together for group Story Circles – formal gatherings in which an artist/convener poses questions, and each person answers by recounting relevant personal experiences. I joined her for the July trip. The 2-hour circle that I attended revolved around engrossing stories related to their lives post-9/11, the US war in Iraq, and the Portland raids. Participants in that session included an 82-year-old French Canadian retiree, a conservative leader of the local Sudanese community, a homeless man, a Cambodian classical dancer, a Chicano contractor with ties to the labor movement, a middle-aged Afghan businessman, a politically active African American working-class Muslim, and the president of Portland's chapter of the National Association for the Advancement of Colored People (NAACP). Pottenger integrated components of the stories they shared that evening in the script, which is cited later in this chapter.

Like the photos in the former clothing store immediately after 9/11, the act of sharing responses and, eventually, the performance itself were ways art provides of coming to terms with enormous acts. Art includes a combination of distance and intimacy: distance because in the rehearsal room or performance space one is safe from the horrific act and can mull it over, not merely react; intimate because one is among a community of people who are deeply affected and struggling to come to terms with it. By extending the circle beyond a therapeutic session but rather open to a whole public, one must more specifically frame it, not knowing who will be part of the audience and how much they know; and in so doing, expanding understanding of how people in various positions were affected.

Pottenger relentlessly tracked down individuals with unique perspectives on the raids. She went to the Canadian border and, after much effort, befriended one US and one Canadian Border Patrol agent, who gave her insight into their work. Unsuccessful at setting up interviews over the telephone and via email with two others with important dimensions to add, she persisted until she found ways to sit down with each. I accompanied Pottenger in seeking out one of them, a woman who worked at a drop-in center where undocumented immigrants and refugees could get a meal. The woman was scared for herself and her clients, and did not want to draw more attention to the center, but wanted the opportunity to share the injustices she'd witnessed. Pottenger timed a visit to a half hour before closing, a time of day when the center was nearly empty, allowing the woman to share her experience unobtrusively.

Several promising phone conversations with the second, former Maine Governor King, who'd been in office on 9/11, had not yet led to an in-person interview. Although sounding like he, too, wanted to describe his 9/11 experience, King didn't know Pottenger and seemed concerned about his lack of control over how he might end up represented in the play. But Pottenger was not to be stopped. Direct and unassuming, dressed casually, no make-up, simple haircut, she is not a media queen swooping in and swooping out. She is utterly engaging, and with her warm eyes and boundless attention, Pottenger listens in a relaxed yet concentrated way. She is patient, friendly, and relentless when she's on the scent of a significant story. The strategy that resulted in a three-hour conversation on the deck of King's home, about 90 minutes north of Portland, began with this phone call:

> "Hello Governor King, it's Marty Pottenger, hoping to meet with you about the events of 9/11 in Maine."
> "Yes, yes, hello. Gee, I'm sorry, I'm going out of town tomorrow afternoon and I need to schedule a conference call in the morning. Why don't you call me at 9 am and I'll see if I can fit you in?"
> "Great, Governor, thanks."

That night Pottenger set the alarm for 6:30 am, so by 7:15 we were on the road to his home up the coast. When she called at 9 am, we were about three minutes away. So when he told her that he had to be on the phone at 10 am and she was too far away in Portland to get to him before then, she responded that in fact she was just down the road. And *voila*, he let us come over. Once he started talking, he didn't want to stop; maybe it was that he missed the attention he'd had as governor, maybe it was that 9/11 was of a magnitude that talking about it helped him to continue to process it. Whatever the reason, other than leaving us on the deck for about ten minutes at 10 am while he took his call, he spoke for three hours about how he, as governor of a state with entries from the sea to the east and through an international border to the north, responded to the attack and prepared for what aftermath it might signal.

At the heart of Pottenger's aesthetics are three components:

1 questions and deciding which questions to ask – Pottenger states, "To ask a better question moves things forward and gets to the next question and then the question after that."
2 listening – Being listened to actively, she asserts, is so rare and deep as to affect us "physiologically."
3 creativity – Having people make art as another way of responding to the questions.

In making art together, she finds, "a different part of our intelligence gets engaged; a lot of confusion drops away" (Marty Pottenger, interview with the author, New York, December 12, 2005). So, for example, in a workshop she might ask participants to respond to her questions through short poems expressing what they remember about an experience relating to the topic. These artifacts are often more eloquent than what people are likely to say, conversationally, in response, and deepen the dialogue that follows.

Between the Portland visits, Pottenger began writing a script back home in New York City, looking for a structure and a series of metaphors to tell the tale in a more condensed and artful way. She stayed in phone contact with the people she'd met with, and continued to pursue possible leads for further interviews, to engage people with additional perspectives and those with the ability to affect policies and practices in Portland.

Cultural democracy and self-representation

Performance theorist Dwight Conquergood asserts that marginalized people need spaces "for 'public discussion' of vital issues central to their communities, as well as arena[s] for gaining visibility and staging their identity" (Conquergood 2006: 360). Self-representation frequently contrasts with mainstream images, such as those of dangerous aliens propagated by the Border Patrol raids. To understand the efficacy of self-expression on the part of people who generally lack access to political decision-making, I turn first to the concept of cultural democracy.

Cultural democracy – collective expression of the people, by the people, and for the people – recurs through some of the strongest articulation of art's social purpose in US history. Evoking a "pageant of negro history" that was staged in New York City in 1913, on the 50th anniversary of emancipation, and repeated in other cities, renowned thinker and writer W.E.B. Du Bois defines the role of a cultural group's self-expression in a movement for civil rights:

> I was on these occasions trying for something more than mere spectacle; I was seeking for self-expression on the part of a group of people who, quite beyond the fact of their physical likeness and biological descent, have a cultural and spiritual unity which comes from a long history of oppression and repression; and which called for expression to benefit human progress.
>
> (Du Bois 1946: 1–2)

In the same spirit, Du Bois sought to make a theatre in Harlem "about, for, and by" the African American people who lived there.

We see the expression of cultural democracy based on class commonality in 1915, honoring the workers who lost their lives fighting for fair employment conditions at a silk factory strike in Paterson, New Jersey. The Paterson Strike Pageant recreated the mass action of the strikers juxtaposed against passionate speeches redelivered by the original speakers. The large-scale performance represented the battle between labor and the forces of capital generally at the same time as helping to deal with the grief over those specific losses.

And in an expression of cultural democracy based in national identity, Hallie Flanagan, from 1935 to 1939, directed the Federal Theatre Project, employing 7,900 artists of all kinds and in every corner of the USA as part of the Works Progress Administration in the depths of the Depression. Their artistic expression reflected a great range of aesthetics; the Living Newspaper, for example, took on issues of social justice, whereas other forms, such as puppet shows and ethnically grounded performance, reflected values of equity simply in their cultural diversity and accessibility to broad audiences for free or very modest cost.[1]

The idea of cultural democracy reasserts itself in the work of political theorists, oral historians, and trauma specialists. Political theorists Lani Guinier and Gerard Torres emphasize the value democracy places on "groups that form around common concerns and participate in an ongoing conversation" (Guinier and Torres 2002: 170). Democracy, they elaborate, relies on citizen engagement beyond the act of voting, and opportunities for representatives to meet with their constituencies beyond election season. Guinier and Torres admiringly recount theatre-maker and political activist Augusto Boal's use of first-person storytelling to engage people usually left out of the identification of social problems that need political solutions. Basing discussion on concrete incidents from people's lives, which can be communicated simply in the form of personal stories, is a viable way to increase political participation.

Political theorists Archon Fung and Erik Olin Wright's idea of empowered participatory governance can be applied to Pottenger's art to show how it could function as a site of participatory democracy. The first of three principles of empowered participatory governance, practical orientation, refers to gearing democratic efforts around concrete concerns that are narrowly enough defined to be achievable. Pottenger focused concretely on the Border Patrol's human rights abuses in Portland's February 2004 raids as a local instance of a larger situation, post-9/11 USA. Citizens' stories revealed the seismic changes internally and externally.

The second principle of empowered participatory governance is bottom-up participation, including "establish[ing] new channels for those most directly affected by targeted problems – typically ordinary citizens and officials in the field – to apply their knowledge, intelligence, and interest to the formulation of solutions" (Fung and Wright 2003: 16). Pottenger provided a context for immigrants and refugees who suffered human rights abuses to communicate publicly and be part of the solution by modeling the value of their social integration in Maine life. Fung and Wright argue that the broad base of experience this population encompasses more than makes up for a chief criticism against such participation, namely lay people's lack of technical expertise. While advocates of empowered participatory governance still see a role for technical experts, they point out that grassroots participation wears down the capacity of patronage and corruption to undermine democratic decision-making (Fung and Wright 2003: 17).

The third value of empowered participatory governance is deliberation – a process of decision-making that requires people to listen to each other "and generate group choices after due consideration" (Fung and Wright 2003: 17). The Story Circle, inclusive of many points of view, is a useful tactic for achieving this goal. Sociologist Gianpaolo Baiocchi, writing about empowered participatory governance, attests to the value of Augusto Boal's first-voice theatrical processes, similar to the Story Circles Pottenger conducts, in grounding social issues in people's personal experiences – in Baiocchi's case, collective budget-making in Porto Alegre, Brazil (Baiocchi 2006).

Another way of understanding the efficacy of first-person storytelling comes from the oral history field. Numerous historians seeking to expand who is included in the historical record have turned to personal story as a means of expanding that base. Sometimes called oral history, sometimes popular memory, the objective is including voices that might otherwise be "hidden" from history. Mary Marshall Clark describes oral history's mission as "to restore the individual human subject to history" (Clark 2002: 89). Clark asserts that "stories unleash power, connecting memory and the imagination to the world, and encourage a dynamic organization of forces to combat situations of inequality and justice" (Clark 2002: 103). This is especially important for those with the least public access, such as the immigrants, refugees, and Native American people in *hls*, and the working-class, female, and African heritage subjects of early oral history projects.

First-person storytelling can also be therapeutic. As both a therapist and a historian who has been called upon to assess Holocaust testimony, Dr Dori Laub distinguishes between the ways in which practitioners of the two professions listen to stories. In his experience, historians are more involved in the literal truth of a story. Psychologists, on the other hand, listen for the personal truth a person has come to tell, even if some factual inaccuracies are present. Take the survivor who remembered four chimneys blowing up at Auschwitz as part of an act of resistance, when in fact the historical record evidences only one exploding chimney. Laub's psychological training led him to recognize that "the survivor had come, indeed, to testify, not to the empirical number of the chimneys, but to resistance, to affirmation of survival; to the breakage of the frame of death" in that act of rebellion against the Nazis (Laub 1992: 62). Laub further explains that a listener who neither over- nor under-identifies with the story is essential to the act of "re-externalizing the event," which "can occur and take effect only when one can articulate and *transmit* the story, literally transfer it to another outside oneself and then take it back in, inside" (Laub 1992: 69). To that extent, the act of performance completes the circle by facilitating the teller's movement away from the traumatic event.

Thinking of *hls* in this way, the culminating public event is less theatre *per se* than what anthropologist Victor Turner calls cultural performance, the public expression of group meaning. Indeed, the first words the *hls* actors say are, "This is not a play. Or a concert. It's more like snapshots – of a journey. A scavenger hunt. To discover Portland, Maine, 2005."

home land security as a testimonial performance

A core cast of six people who had participated in interviews and Story Circles performed *hls* three times, in November 2005, as readers' theatre, in which actors are on-script but nevertheless rehearsed and emotionally engaged. I sat in CCE's modest auditorium at one of those performances, surrounded largely by people who had lived through the Border Patrol sweeps in Portland, whether or not they knew anyone directly involved. That, too, shifted the event from pure theatre to something more ritualistic in the sense of efficacy – *doing* something in addition to entertaining. Most of the spectators were personally implicated by what happened insofar as it happened in their home town, and they thus had some agency and emotional investment in affecting what might come next.

Part I, "Home," begins with the sounds of moose, wolves, crows, birds, and wind, abruptly muted by the roar of a chainsaw. Lights come up on the core cast wearing hunter caps with earflaps. Three musicians stage right – a fiddler with deep roots in Maine, a Bolivian guitarist, and a Somalian drummer – intersperse richly diverse music throughout the production, supporting the performers' words. A seventh performer plays the radio announcer, reporting high state productivity in areas that rely on immigrant labor, such as toothpicks, sardine tins, lobsters, and low-bush blueberries. The Department of Homeland Security has declared an "orange" alert for the third month in a row. The temperature, she tells us, is dropping.

Native American Heather Augustine, a college student and member of the Micmac Nation, steps forward and articulates a feeling about home: "We have lived on this land for tens of thousands of years. Our biggest battle was a half mile down the hill ... I struggle not to be ashamed of the half of me that's white." Sudanese Oliver Albino shares a sobering view of his old and new homes:

> When we came to the United States in the mid-1990s, we expected
> a welcome from black people. You must not be teaching history

77

very well. Some of them said to us, "You are the ones who sold us to them." I replied with the truth: "We are still running away ourselves." Today in Sudan, my people are being killed, captured, and sold as slaves.

(Marty Pottenger, home land security, unpublished script, 2005)

After each core actor talks about home, Rachel Talbot Ross, president of the Maine NAACP chapter and Portland's Director of Equal Opportunity and Multicultural Affairs, appears (the first of three different cameos). Relating stories of the astounding nine generations of her family in Maine, she gets to her father, the first African American to serve in the Maine State Legislature:

One of his greatest legislative legacies was removing all geographical markers, place names, titles, and landmarks in the state that had the word 'Nigger' in their name: Nigger Bridge, Nigger Lane, Nigger Lake, Nigger Ridge, Nigger Mountain. If I remember correctly, there were twenty-four instances.

(Pottenger, home land security, 2005, op. cit.)

Overcome with emotion, Ross is horrified to be crying in public. For civic leaders, making complicated personal feelings public is taboo. But the audience is riveted. Ross describes what she loves about Maine but adds, "I don't necessarily feel like a Mainer." The ninth generation in this state and she feels like an outsider? Another actor, Reverend Virginia Marie Rincon, a Mexican/Mayan/Aztec Episcopalian priest who works with undocumented Latinos, spontaneously brings Ross a tissue and stands beside her. In that act, Ross perhaps experiences the possibility that she is not a solitary outsider.

The cast paints a broad picture of Maine, "a working man's state" with the highest percentage of home ownership in the nation, which, in the 1920s, also had the largest Ku Klux Klan chapter and the smallest population of African-heritage people. It is a state where Protestants once ostracized Catholics, forbidding French to be spoken in public, including in the schools. French-Canadian retiree Lucien Mathieu adds, "Teachers pulled your ear if they caught you speaking French; I have the pulled ears to prove it."

The second cameo performer, State Senate President Beth Edmonds, who is also a librarian, takes the stage. She reads the audience one of her favorite children's books, Click Clack Moo, pausing to show us the pictures. The cows in a drafty barn use an old typewriter to ask the farmer for some electric blankets. At first the farmer refuses to comply, so the cows stop giving milk. Soon the chickens, also refused blankets, join the cows and stop providing eggs. Finally, a duck intercedes and an agreement is reached: the cows and chickens will get blankets. The book ends with the ducks' letter to the farmer – click, clack, quack – about how boring the pond is and their request for a diving board. The reading is interspersed with Edmonds' comments and questions about leading and following, building on the book's recognition of class conflict and the power of the strike. Edmonds then shows us the last picture in the book: a duck gleefully leaping off the tip of a diving board.

Act II, "Land," opens with the radio announcer reporting on traffic (so backed up by bicycles that the Portland High principal was late to school), economics (skyrocketing bankruptcies), and agriculture (about the state insect, the honeybee). We're warned, "Wind picking up tonight as heavy rains head this way. Get ready to hunker down, cover your woodpiles, close all your windows, and pull in the laundry."

Now we hear the sounds of the airplanes hitting the twin towers. Billy Woolverton, a homeless man and budding writer/actor, describes where he was and how he learned about the attack. The others tell fragments of their 9/11 stories, too, ending with a sobering reminder of how a few people's actions typecast whole groups in the popular imagination:

> Lucien: All I thought was, "Dear God, don't let it be a Vietnam vet."
> Jill Duson (the African American mayor of Portland): A black man.
> Oliver: A Sudanese.
> Rev. Virginia Marie: An undocumented Mexican.
> Billy: Some poor person.
> Heather: An Indian.
>
> (Pottenger, *home land security*, 2005, *op. cit.*)

The actors share their divergent opinions about, and experiences with, war. This leads to the story of the Portland "border" patrol raid itself, and the fear that followed. The auditorium goes dead silent, as Portlanders listen to what their neighbors experienced and continue to go through.

Act III, "Security." The actors are dressed for a storm, with yellow rain hats. The radio announcer reports that "Temperatures continue to fall as Mainers prepare to welcome another long winter." The musicians, holding flashlights and wearing baseball caps, portray Maine Border Patrol agents. We hear a range of views, from discomfort to pride in dealing with "criminal activity": "You think you know where you're living but believe me – it's a whole new ball game."

The final cameo performer is Fred LaMontagne, Portland Fire Chief and director of Maine's Emergency Preparedness Team. He tells us that at least once a week, he's woken by a middle-of-the-night call about possible danger. He describes how Mainers would be notified about evacuation in case of emergency. He lays out Portland's vulnerability with its "100PSI gas

Figure 3.1 home land security musicians Greg Boardman, Juan Condori, and Peng Kem
stand in as Border Patrol agents. Center for Cultural Exchange, Portland,
ME, May 2006. (Photo by Marty Pottenger.)

lines, an electrical grid, major arteries and institutions; it's the largest
port in the country for oil, gasoline, and liquid propane ... We have a
choice to either be a greater police state or a state that is more vulnerable."
Then he describes the personal toll his position takes: thinking about
his kids' school as the location of a hostage crisis; "looking around my
church in the middle of a prayer wondering where a terrorist might
place a bomb." The core actors then speak their fears – someone will blow
up a small quiet town, Bush will start another war, social security will
go bust.

The cast articulates where they find hope: for Jill Duson, making a difference as a black female mayor; for the Reverend, in her faith and from
the people to whom she ministers. The radio announcer marks the seventh
anniversary of a terrible ice storm during which tens of thousands of
Mainers came south to Portland for shelter. Jill sings a stark acapella ren-
dition of "America the Beautiful," with Lucien joining in for the final
stanza. The play ends with:

Jill: You meet Lucien, you meet Maine.
Lucien: You meet the Mayor, you meet Maine.
Oliver: You meet Reverend Virginia Marie, you meet Maine.
Reverend: You meet Oliver, you meet Maine.

Billy: You meet Heather, you meet Maine.
Heather: You meet Billy, you meet Maine.
(Pottenger, *home land security*, 2005, *op. cit.*)

Some of the strongest moments in the play are the unexpected juxtapositions. Augustine expresses pride in her Native American father and, in the same monologue, thanks her white mother for getting her out of the reservation, rescuing her from pervasive drugs and alcohol, and possibly saving her life. The cast members themselves are an unlikely combination – seemingly so dissimilar but, as the play unfolds, clearly linked in deep ways. For example, Augustine, Woolverton, and Duson speak with equal passion about their relationship to nature. And all the cast members are joined by their bravery as first-time actors, vulnerably standing on a stage just a foot above the spectators. As witness/spectators, it's sobering to see so much about each person in a real reality show, not set in some other place and time but here and now; about a struggle that is not over. So the jury is not in, and we who watch may intercede in the very events as they continue to unfold, off-stage. But to do so requires an artist who also sees herself as an activist.

From self-representation to community action

Returning to the notion of cultural performance, Victor Turner saw the potential of such group expression as an active agent of change, a form for communal reflection, and a space in which to imagine a better way of living together. The emphasis on follow-up as being equal to, or more important than, performance positions audiences as witnesses rather than spectators *per se*, with an invitation to participate in local efforts to protect civil liberties. Seeing their activation as a goal of such projects further underscores the notion of cultural performance rather than "play." The actors rejoin the community, also expected to build on the performance experience to work towards the larger goal that exceeds aesthetics.

hls has required an unabashedly activist follow-up phase to achieve its potential – assisting in the protection of civil liberties – not an easy task, given the habit of seeing art and politics as separate and self-contained. Not even all theatre practitioners approve of art-making that morphs into activism. After all, their training is typically in art, not politics. But Pottenger is one of a number of interdisciplinary (what I call hyphenated), engaged theatre artists, in her case combining training and experience in community organizing and performance to engage around a social problem.

Such performances might be compared with political speeches, which also seek to activate and persuade. But first-person accounts affect audiences differently than political speeches. In *hls*, Albino epitomizes and thus reminds us of how much immigrants contribute to the USA. Homelessness is personalized through Billy's gentle, gaunt face and soft Texan drawl.

Even well-positioned African Americans like NAACP leader Ross are seen to experience isolation because of race. While Conquergood emphasizes that such performance brings people on the edge of society, denied access to public conversations, into our shared life, it just as significantly creates a space for political figures to say what they do not usually have license to make public.

The project also provided informal leadership training for the cast. For example, during the *hls* process, a search was being conducted for a new police chief. The city's Acting Chief and Florida's police captain, an African American, were the short-listed candidates. *hls* cast member Mayor Duson, deciding along with city council members, was the only one supporting the Floridian and the only African American voting. Although Duson's choice for police chief was defeated, she contends that participation in *hls* emboldened her to speak her mind and also jump-started conversations about instituting diversity training for city councilmen.

Part of leadership training is educational, and *hls* was certainly a mini-course on the changed legal status of refugees and immigrants post-9/11. An example of how this played out took place when Reverend Rincon was called to the apartment of a recently-deceased undocumented person, where family and friends were grieving. Police arrived, demanding to see people's papers. Rincon told them that this was illegal harassment according to Portland's resolution following the Border Patrol raids. She got the police to leave, and later told the cast that her ability to be firm was the result of what she described as "getting her voice back" through participation in *hls*.

Leadership is also about coalition-building, another by-product of *hls*, grounded in cross-culture *personal* relationships. For example, hearing Rincon's critique of the new police chief led Albino to endorse her point of view. Other cast members reported that before *hls*, he was unlikely to have listened so openly to a woman, let alone a Latina. Albino's – and, through him, the Sudanese community's – embrace of Mayor Duson was manifested at an event in her honor sponsored by the NAACP, at which he was asked to present her with a bouquet of flowers. Another example of public results of the personal experience of *hls*, Albino's first-voice account of the Sudanese situation led state senator Beth Edmonds to vote for the economic sanction of Sudan.

Pottenger deliberately used the play to further tolerance for different points of view. Given *hls*'s theme of civil liberties, she invited the local library to display banned books in the lobby at each performance and sign people up for library cards on the spot. The initiative was so successful that the library instituted mobile registration, providing library cards at other events where people congregate. At a benefit performance on their behalf, the NAACP also invited lobby displays, particularly from local activist groups. The materials of one group, the National Organization of Women (NOW), included their pro-choice stance. NOW's inclusion was difficult for one of the participating librarians, who is strongly anti-abortion. Pottenger visited her in the library, explaining the initiative and encouraging her to participate. Just co-existing side by side demonstrated more willingness to live with difference.

Although under 400 people in total attended *hls* performances, they included two of the four local high school principals, who, along with NAACP director Rachel Ross, asked Pottenger to expand the initiative. Ross saw the process that built *hls* as a way to move forward the city's stalled dialogue around race and class. Pottenger devised a larger frame, the Arts and Equity Initiative (AEI), for the next phase of the work. AEI uses highly structured facilitated dialogue and art-making activities, incorporating story-sharing and other forms of creativity, to address issues of racial, economic, and gender equity. AEI builds on Pottenger's experiments exploring money and equity in the workshops leading to her production of *Abundance*. She adapted the *Abundance* process, focusing on human rights and equity, in the building of *hls*. She then got to thinking about where in society such a process might be most needed. She figured that unions and municipal governments are two such sites, as organizations/institutions that have the opportunity to play an important role regarding greater equity. So giving this resource to municipal governments made good sense.

In March 2007, Pottenger moved to Portland as director of the Arts and Equity Initiative, with the intention of staying three years. The city of Portland is providing her with an office in City Hall and paying her benefits; the Nathan Cummings Foundation is covering her salary. She's once again using a first-voice, story-driven process, this time with the 15 or so city government department heads from the police, fire, parks, etc., to improve their relationship with diverse Portlanders and raise their multicultural awareness.

The first step was getting to know people in the various government sectors and doing what she calls a creativity assessment: finding out who makes art in each department, be it singing, telling stories, writing, or playing music. Then she hired a handful of artists from different media to facilitate workshops with the department with that corresponding interest, focusing on self-expression about local concerns. After some months, they will pick a community they don't know well, get to know the residents, and make art about them. The fire department website has video clips already, so they may be ripe for working with a video artist. The police include some whimsical poets, so will go with Pottenger herself as the writing workshop facilitator. At the same time, these artists will make their own art from their experiences of the business of the city. The idea is that all these efforts will raise multicultural consciousness and appreciation, making Portland more congenial for a broadly diverse population.

Pottenger names *ubuntu botho*, described by Archbishop Desmond Tutu in the epigram to this chapter, as the term that resonates most strongly

83

for how her art-making contributes to equity. For Pottenger, that phrase, rather than social justice or social change (the latter of which could be for better or worse), captures the kind of interhuman relationships that she feels art-making together can stimulate, and that could lead to more equity as a result of people deeply relating to each other across differences (Marty Pottenger, phone interview with the author, New York, May 8, 2009). Pottenger sees art's capacity to work through our differences as based on everyone's potential creativity. She continued:

> To reclaim creativity and foster it in ourselves and each other is deeply corrective in terms of what being human is. It's so clear that we become smarter in the context of making art, more connected to our feelings about various issues and more interested in those of others. Art-making leads naturally to speaking from the heart.
>
> (Pottenger, phone interview, 2009, *op. cit.*)

In the context of arts workshops on topics of deep interest, Pottenger has witnessed bottomless connection among participants around what each other is saying. She's seen people in such situations able to hold contradictions and show the full spectrum of who they are. She avows that "nothing makes you as smart as making art about meaningful things. The good news is that we are facing global problems that require global solutions so we'll *have to* all work together."

That's what she's doing now in Portland, in art workshops with police and fire department employees, combining stories of the job with creative expression. For example, negativity about the police union, including among many of its own members, became clear in the poetry workshops Pottenger facilitated with police. Marty recognized that was a topic that needed addressing. Over the course of the year, she has seen the union leadership working more cooperatively, giving more press conferences, and challenging city management decisions, and they all say this is a first. While Pottenger cannot prove that the creative writing sessions led to an improved union, she can avow that police both expressed and heard more concerns about the union that they said had ever been aired previously, and in more depth than occasional complaints. Pottenger attributes the contribution of the art-making process to its capacity to open up people's thoughts and feeling about an issue and converse civilly about it.

The school superintendent signed on to the idea of a joint city/ schools partnership with AEI, addressing issues of race, racism, and multi-culturalism. In response, Pottenger has embarked on a related process with high school teachers. Teachers at one local high school want to bring a Cambodian drummer to start a drumming corps with some of them. After a series of workshops sessions, they will each choose a local neighborhood where some of their students come from, and learn a drum rhythm from that student's culture, flipping the paradigm so students are teaching teachers. The drumming corps will perform all the rhythms in a concert at the end of the school year. Pottenger has agreed to do a play based on interviews and story-gathering with youth from all the high schools together, to be performed for all the schools. The first-voice story gathering that began as a process to create *hls* is now being used to create a more multiculturally-aware and appreciative government and school system.

This initiative can be measured against Fung and Wright's model of empowered participatory governance. They emphasize three important properties for the instigation of democratic principles to take hold. The first, devolution, means the local unit of political power must be strong enough to respond to the localized nature of this approach. That is certainly the case with Pottenger, who chose to develop her model in Portland because of a city government that had already proved responsive to her approach and is one of her principal supporters. The second characteristic, centralized supervision and coordination, calls for linkage of multiple local units. This is an important idea for Pottenger's consideration, and a clear challenge to the efficacy of her theatrical approach to social justice. That is, she has not yet completed the phase involving work with separate government offices to have sought to coordinate them centrally, but that will be a test of the usefulness of her work. The third design element is that such efforts be state-centered and non-volunteeristic. While efforts outside of the state, such as Pottenger's own, may apply useful pressure, "they leave intact the basic institutions of state government" (Fung and Wright 2003: 22). This, too, is a challenging arena for an arts-based social justice initiative. Will she be able to institutionalize her efforts in Maine's state government?

On December 24, 2005, nearly two years after the border raids, the front page of *The New York Times* featured an article about Representative Tom Tancredo, Republican of Colorado. Though previously even the Bush administration considered his efforts to curtail immigration too right-wing, Tancredo had become the Republican Party's rallying point in the production of the most restrictive immigration legislation in more than a decade. *hls* expresses the belief that only by knowing and caring for each other, expressed through participation in the struggle for social and economic justice, will there be any real security for any of us. At the end of the play, the radio announcer warns that we may be headed for more snow and ice, "making this as good a time as any to get your storm windows in, load up on supplies, call a friend or neighbor." But *hls* does not end with first-voice storytelling. Through AEI, Pottenger integrates empowered participatory governance techniques. The combination of the two bode well as concerns increased resistance affectively and effectively to the Patriot Act in Maine and beyond.

Workbook

Interviewing and Story Circles

Interviewing

I typically take a class period first to discuss an essay about interview, such as Bruce Jackson's (1987), for both the in-class exercise and subsequent interviewing beyond. I then put students in pairs to practice interviewing each other. I make sure to have enough tape recorders for them to practice taping their classroom interview as well. Depending on the course goals, this may be followed up by having them, singly or in pairs, interview someone in the world beyond the classroom.

Interviewing can be broken down into five steps:

1   Identifying and contacting an interview subject

Be aware that many of the subjects of interviews for the kind of performances this book describes are not well-known and are usually flattered to be asked to talk about something they know a lot about. Make sure to set up a convenient time and place to carry out the interview. Be clear about the purpose of the interview, and offer to share the transcript with them if, indeed, you intend to transcribe it.

2   Coming prepared

Do whatever background research is available, which may be simply what you learn from a mutual acquaintance; but if more is in the public domain, make sure you've perused the internet and found out about them. Come to the interview with a list of questions but don't hesitate to improvise, adding questions as you see fit. Remember to ask questions that require more than a yes or no answer, and that neither "lead" the interviewee to your point of view nor assume a judgement of their opinion (for example, avoid comments such as, "Don't you think that was a racist act?"). As Marty Pottenger states, remember that holding an interview is a way of making a relationship and needs to be satisfying to both parties.

3   Taping your interview … or not

I strongly recommend taping your interviews. That frees you up to make eye contact with the interviewee and focus on content, noting topics to follow up with, rather than just trying to get down what they are saying. Make sure to check your tape recorder and insert new batteries before you meet with the person. Take a moment at the beginning of the interview to state the date and ask the person to say their name. Thus the exchange has a clear beginning. As Bruce Jackson counsels in his essay on the subject, keep the tape recorder on for the entire interview unless the interviewee asks to go off the record at some point. Otherwise you may seem to be weighing some comments as more important than others. Jackson also warns against over reliance on the tape recorder that could make you lazy (Jackson 1987: 102). Be an attentive, engaged listener. Talk neither too much nor too little. Make the subject comfortable and be present with them, but remember you are largely trying to find out what s/he thinks, not hold a conversation.

On the other hand, some interviewers have remarkable memories and would rather listen closely, without a tape recorder, maybe taking very few notes, but doing serious journaling of what they remember after the interview is over.

4   Listening

Interviews are not just for "the facts." Often you are trying to understand different points of view on the same subject. If you will be performing a character based on an interviewee, you'll garner much-needed information besides content – what was the speaker's rhythm? When did s/he take long pauses, or increase the pace, or become agitated? What was communicated besides the literal meaning of the words, and how did that communication take place?

5   Interview record

I encourage you to log the interview, noting the order of topics and the counter number when a new section begins, even if you do not have the capacity to transcribe the whole thing. If you have not recorded the session, make notes in a journal as soon as possible after the interview is over. Whether or not you use a tape recorder, and whether or not you transcribe, it's beneficial to review the interview in a timely manner so you can get back to the person with any follow-up questions that emerge while the exchange is still fresh.

The Story Circle

This technique is easily emulated in class before students strike out on their own. Get into groups of 7–15. If there are too many students for you to include in one circle in which you participate, either bring in someone with Story Circle experience to facilitate the other circle(s), or divide into groups of 7–15 and facilitate the steps from outside any one circle. I assign Roadside Theater's short description of Story Circles (see Appendix) and review it with students before they participate in a Story Circle.

1   Gathering a group

Gather approximately 7–15 people with something to say about a given subject. For *home land security*, Marty Pottenger wanted to hear about experiences of immigrants and refugees in post-9/11 Maine. In 2006, for *Thousand Kites*, Roadside Theater wanted to initiate dialogue about the US prison system, beginning with the people closest to it in any position, be they guards, inmates, or family members. In 2007, the historical society of Bethlehem, PA wanted to gather oral histories of life in Lehigh Valley for people of African descent.

2   Setting it up

Assuming that two to three hours is as long as people can be asked to participate at one sitting, everyone gets about three to four minutes to tell a story on the given subject. Maybe the facilitator is the timekeeper, or maybe each person times the person who tells the story after theirs. Story Circles are usually intended to generate material for the creation of a play. Pottenger often starts with the question, what is your earliest memory connected with whatever the topic is – money in *Abundance*; homeland in *hls*. A Story Circle is largely about listening. There is no cross-talk; the way to respond to a story is through the story you tell. Frequently, other than the first teller, everyone is encouraged to let the story they tell be elicited by others they've heard. If someone can't think of a story when it gets to them, they can pass and tell theirs later. A story is not a speech or a set of general observations on a topic. It is often an incident with a beginning, middle, and end, with characters, a plot, and a setting. Something happens in a story.

3   After the tellings

After everyone has told a story, there is general discussion. Often a more specific topic, reflecting where the energy was the first time around, is chosen for another round. So what begins as stories on, say, family secrets, may be followed by a second round on intergenerational alliances.

4   Variations and follow-up

Cornerstone Theater often begins with questions that elicit short answers rather than stories. "What smells, sights, and sounds do you associate with the Lower East Side?" were the initiating questions for the first three rounds of one of their circles in which I participated.

Pottenger often intersperses Story Circle rounds with simple art-making activities. One format she likes is what she calls refrigerator poems. A refrigerator poem is five or six words that you distill from what you've said on a given topic, and that you remember but don't write down. She gives participants time to rehearse the poem, and is clear that it's fine if you forget. It's important to her to have performative standards, such as working with participants so they don't mumble. To leave them with an inaudible piece fractures the group challenge they're taking on, even at the risk of temporary embarrassment. Pottenger decides who presents their poem to the group first, to ensure strong but unintimidating examples, including someone likely to be among the most oppressed, unless they are struggling the most. But she does not start with someone likely to inhibit others. She looks for who can be themselves, free of pretense, capable but not obviously trained to flourish at such activities.

A follow-up exercise Pottenger inserts later in some of her Story Circles is to ask for a gesture of something they loved to do/play, without identifying a link to the topic on which they've been focused. She then has them rehearse making the gesture. Next, she asks them to combine the gesture with the poem, in any order – maybe the gesture first, at the same time, or after reciting the poem. They rehearse for a few minutes, with Pottenger's reminder to think about volume (speaking loudly enough and varying levels to emphasize their points), focus (awareness of the main point and shaping the recitation accordingly), diction (speaking clearly enough to be understood), and intention to perform in front of people, not to be too inwardly focused unless that's the strategy for an effective presentation.

A variation that performer and teacher Peggy Pettitt employs is to follow a Story Circle with a partner exercise. Each pair chooses one story, or section of a story, that particularly engrossed them from a group Story Circle, which they rehearse and then present to the group.

4

CULTURAL ORGANIZING
Multiple modes of communication

We believe that positive change in the criminal justice system will occur when people from all walks of life can connect to the prison story; therefore, communication is both the means and the end of the project.
(Dudley Cocke, "Thousand Kites," email, September 12, 2007)

We accomplished a lot with radio and film, but we still needed a communication tool with a low cost threshold, great accessibility, and the capacity for participation at the level of the art-making itself. So we went to Roadside Theater.
(Nick Szuberla, conversation with the author)

If the[ir] opinion is right, they are deprived of the opportunity of exchanging error for truth; if wrong, they lose what is almost as great a benefit, the clearer perception and livelier impression of truth produced by its collision with error.
(John Stuart Mill 1859; 1956)

I direct attention here to various forms of artistic communication that provide a cultural dimension to community organizing in order to expand and humanize a social movement. My case study is *Thousand Kites*, which inserts radio, video, theatre, and internet resources into a campaign whose long-term goal is to end the damage the US prison industry causes. *Thousand Kites* is grounded in the voices of prisoners, guards, and their respective families who experience the system's dysfunction daily.[1]

A kite is prison slang for a message sent out from behind the wall. Advocates of prison change also send out messages, which they hope will affect public consciousness. *Thousand Kites* casts a wide net as concerns the forms such messages take, audiences to whom they are addressed, and ensuing actions. It offers its multiple communication strategies to prison reform organizers committed to a public conversation. Its goal is to reduce the unprecedented rates of incarceration in the USA, reform drug policy, and frame prison as a human and civil rights issue. According to a 2008 Pew Charitable Trusts report, more than one adult American out of every 100 is now behind bars. For black males between 20 and 34 years of age, the figure is one out of every nine (Warren 2008: 3). The USA has 5% of the world's population but 25% of its prisoners. In 2007 the USA spent $49 billion to lock people up. (For regularly updated US prison statistics, see the Human Rights Watch website, www. hrw.org.)

My interest in *Kites* is at once professional and personal. Professionally, I'm impressed by this project's effective integration of art in political organizing. *Kites* uses the whole gamut of expressive forms, each with access to people in different situations and a focus on different communicative purposes. Radio, in this project, gathers a public unable to connect face-to-face. Video condenses information and disseminates it far and wide in an emotionally-gripping way. Participatory theatre accommodates personal exchange through storytelling and the live experience of putting oneself in the shoes of characters with various points of view. Websites collect ever-expandable and accessible tools and techniques. The *Kites* team uses these tools to create access and foster connection among stakeholders, who could be just about anyone: most of us are only a degree or two away from someone entrenched in the criminal justice system.

Personally, I am one degree from the criminal justice system. At the age of 21, I co-facilitated a theatre workshop in a men's maximum security prison. The experience shook me to the core. Until then I thought of prisoners as "bad", if I thought of them at all. But almost all the men I met inside who had committed violent crimes were themselves victims of terrible violence, often at the hands of a family member. While this does not condone striking out at others, it suggests that if violence begets violence, humane treatment of inmates might lead to those incarcerated treating others humanely. How long such behavior modification takes with adults is a tough question. And it's important to remember that the great majority of inmates have not committed violent crimes.

Creating cultural organizing tools

Thousand Kites is a collaboration of diverse artists from Appalshop, a 40-year-old arts, activism, and education center in what used to be described as the coalfields of eastern Kentucky, in the Appalachian Mountains town of Whitesburg. Appalshop began as an Office of Economic Opportunity (OEO) site, teaching film-making. It quickly shifted from film to video in the early 1970s and expanded into music, theatre, and radio, all from the impulse to tell the Appalachian story from inside out, under one roof. It didn't lead to jobs in the established film industry, as the OEO had intended, but rather created jobs right there. So it did accomplish the goal of creating jobs and stimulating the economy, but not according to the method the people from Washington had in mind.

Appalshop staff embrace an open-door policy to people who want to work with them to solve community problems; the center as a whole embraces a practice of social call, aesthetic response. An example was the man who brought in a vial of water that was nearly pure black sludge. "This is our water because of the coal industry," he said, helping initiate Appalshop's campaign to hold coal companies accountable for the ramifications of their industry for local people and the environment.

Amelia Kirby, an Appalshop film-maker and Appalachian native, explains that until 20 years ago, when mechanization began replacing jobs, the coal industry controlled the economic life of the region. In the late 1990s, the closing of local mines accompanied the opening of two "supermax" prisons – maximum security institutions built to accommodate inmates referred to as "the worst of the worst" from overcrowded institutions all over the USA. Kirby recalls that 750 people in Wise County lost their mining jobs the same day the two new supermaxes posted 800 corrections jobs. Kirby had just got back from college, and people she knew were suddenly working in prisons. She found it difficult to protest in the face of the region's lack of other employment opportunities (Amelia Kirby, phone interview with the author, November 1, 2007). As writer Arlene Goldbard describes, these workers went from mining that abused *their* bodies, to prison jobs that placed them in a position to abuse the bodies of others (Goldbard 2008).

Now prisons are a major industry in Appalachia, and the voice of need around that industry is entering Appalshop in a way that is different from the sludge that community members brought in: through hundreds of letters from people incarcerated in the region. The messages initially found their way to Appalshop because of a hip hop radio show broadcast by Appalshop's radio station WMMT FM (self-described as "mountain community radio"), created and deejayed by Kirby and fellow Appalshop film-maker and staffer Nick Szuberla. Called *Holler to the Hood* (H2H), the program, featuring hip hop music in its many variations, is the duo's voluntary contribution to Appalshop's radio station. Given radio's unique ability to permeate physical barriers and hip hop's city roots, *H2H* quickly developed a large audience of urban men incarcerated in the burgeoning maximum security prison industry in the region. Soon the show became a two-way communication device. Although it was culturally familiar music that brought Appalshop to the inmates' attention, hundreds of listeners have since written letters to Kirby and Szuberla denouncing prison conditions.[2]

Moved by the letters, Kirby and Szuberla developed another communicative dimension to their program: connecting inmates and their families, who often live at too great a distance to visit, through on-air song dedications. Inmates in the two large maximum-security prisons in the county, Wallens Ridge and Red Onion, are locked down 23 hours a day.

This weekly program provides the possibility of hearing family or friends call in, dedicate a song or a reading to them, or just send a greeting. Lilly Branch Kennedy – aka Miss K, who organizes families of inmates in the Richmond, Virginia area – described her son in Wallens Ridge meticulously adjusting the antenna this way and that, holding it carefully in place, and waiting for Miss K to get through, just to hear her voice. Pulled in to the personal struggles of families of incarcerated people, Kirby and Szuberla instituted another program, *Calls from Home*, a live Christmas show broadcasting families dedicating songs and sending holiday greetings to their incarcerated loved ones over a free 800 number.

The precipitant that moved Szuberla and Kirby from videographers and radio volunteers, albeit socially-conscious ones, to cultural activists occurred one day in 1999. Szuberla was at Appalshop when a press release came in over the wire, announcing the opening that day of nearby "supermax" Wallens Ridge Prison. He grabbed a camera and was off, unhampered as he filmed nearly everything because he blended in with the media assembled for the opening. A prison tee-shirt for opening day read "the ultimate bed and breakfast." People laughed. Officials proudly showed off what amounts to a warehouse for what is not, as advertised, the "worst of the worst," given that the number of inmates with serious crimes that officials were able to ship from across the country was insufficient to fill the 2,400 new beds. Rather, people with prison sentences from states with overcrowded facilities, who need to be incarcerated *somewhere*, have been stuck there as well, not necessarily because of the severity of their crime.

Szuberla and Kirby went on to make a film, *Up the Ridge: A US Prison Story*, about the burgeoning national prison industry, grounded in abuses at their local maximum facilities. One of the most sobering sections of the film depicts two of the tragic consequences resulting from arbitrary use of these facilities. David Tracy was sentenced to Wallens Ridge despite committing only a minor drug infraction and being just a day over 20, the age minimum for that facility. He had a history of mental problems, exacerbated by being far away from his psychiatrist and family. Tracy couldn't take the brutality of the supermax and killed himself. Another man, shipped there from Connecticut, went into diabetic shock, was put into five-point restraint, and left alone. When guards returned to his cell they found him dead. He had serious burns from a stun gun. The governor of Connecticut denied the potency of the gun, saying it was like a bee sting. Nevertheless, in 2004, Connecticut, under pressure, removed its prisoners from Wallens Ridge and the entire state of Virginia.

Up the Ridge shows these stories and contends that such injustices are not limited to Wallens Ridge, but characterize much of the US prison industry, which incarcerates hundreds of thousands of inner-city minority offenders in regions distant from friends and family. We learn that more than half of crimes are victimless (other than the incarcerated and

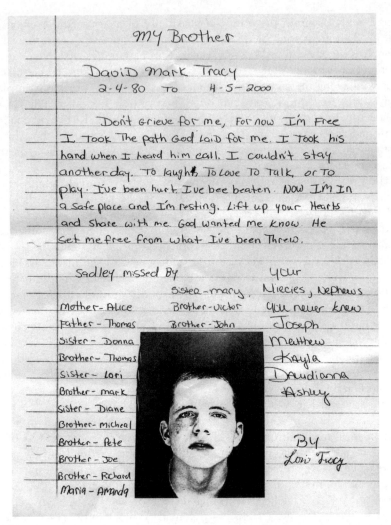

Figure 4.1 Text in memory of David Tracy, featured in video component of *Thousand Kites*. (Photo by *Thousand Kites*.)

their families) – drugs, mostly. In prison, pay can be as low as five cents an hour. Viewers also see the toll on guards, many who worked in the mines before they closed, now spending at least eight hours a day, one-third of their lives, in prisons.

Szuberla and Kirby not only made the film, but also sought ways to insert it into the anti-supermax movement, which has been gaining popular support for a variety of reasons. One is the financial burden of prisons on taxpayers. When *Up the Ridge* was released, George Allen was a candidate for the Virginia senate. People learned he'd spent billions of dollars on new prison facilities. Miss K thinks Allen's identification with building those prisons hurt him, even if, as she suspects, more people objected to the financial cost than to the inhumane conditions. But whatever the reason, Allen lost the election by 7,000 votes. Organizers have shown *Up the Ridge* to legislators across the USA, so they know what they are signing on to by allowing the transport of inmates to other state facilities, and have no illusion that rehabilitation is part of the supermax agenda.

Up the Ridge, and *Kites* generally, evidence an atypical balance of personal expression and political usefulness for artistic projects. While most artists strive to create work that is utterly unique, Szuberla and Kirby want their work to be replicable, adaptable, and cut-up-and-put-back-togetherable. For example, Szuberla and Kirby passed on their *H2H* radio methods to communities all over the USA, many of which now offer similar holiday call-ins at Christmas. It's an easy strategy to replicate, since one needs only to inform families to call in and prisoners to listen. According to Keith DeBlasio, a prison activist in Virginia, attaching prison advocacy to a religious holiday makes it more complicated for people to get angry at what some perceive as coddling offenders.

For some families, especially those with loved ones in distant states, such radio shows are the first opportunity to reconnect since incarceration began. In the intense isolation many experience in prison, radio is one of the few links to the world beyond. It's nevertheless often hard for prisoners to call in. They can only call collect. They are frequently discouraged from calling in themselves; one man who rapped over the radio was placed in solitary confinement for six months as punishment. The shows are also moving for people without direct connections inside, making the case for inmates' basic rights. They put a human face on incarcerated people, and remind listeners that most have families on the outside who are suffering, too, because of the incarceration. Dudley Cocke, artistic director of Roadside Theater, also at Appalshop and part of the *Kites* team, notes that young people, too, get involved in the direct stories they hear in these exchanges, which are more real than the now omnipresent reality TV shows.

Nora Calahan of the November Coalition, an organization seeking to make the prison system more humane, has further mobilized the *Thousand Kites* project. Recognizing that the radio show helps inmates and families get through the holidays (which she refers to as hellidays), she emailed community radio stations all across Michigan to air *Calls from Home*. They got so many downloads – 3,000 – that their website crashed, but Calahan got *Calls from Home* on practically every public radio station in Michigan. To extend the radio shows' usefulness, Kirby and Szuberla made tapes of the calls for house party fund raising for grassroots groups.

Calahan urged Kirby and Szuberla to do more to raise consciousness about the prison system. So they reached out to Appalshop's Roadside

Theater to add a face-to-face theatre piece to *Kites'* repertory. It's fairly typical for collaborations to develop between different Appalshop programs, where like-minded colleagues are working side by side. And so it was that *H2H* and Roadside joined together to make *Thousand Kites*, the play, based on story-sharing with people involved in any way in the criminal justice system. The story-gathering facilitates exchange of experience and provides the basis for a very simple and portable theatre production, which itself leads to audience discussion. It thus adds theatre's ability to facilitate physical interaction at low cost and high accessibility to the *Kites* repertoire of cultural forms.

Donna Porterfield of Roadside wrote the *Thousand Kites* play using the method the company has developed over its 30-year history. The playwright conducts research that, depending on the project, includes such sources as interviews, Story Circles, historical documents, and personal letters. In the case of *Thousand Kites*, Porterfield facilitated Story Circles with an organization called Virginia Cure, composed of families of prisoners and ex-parolees, ex-correction officers, career path correction officers and their families, and anyone else living in communities that house prisons. Story Circles typically involve from five to 25 people who choose a theme and then, one by one, tell a related tale. Participants focus on listening to the other stories and only decide what to tell in response to what they have heard. Telling personal stories in this sense is a way to have a conversation, an exchange, a relationship to others. (See Story Circle details in the Workbook section of chapter three.)

Gathering material for such projects requires casting a wide net. Families of correction officers were often scared that if they talked with Porterfield, their family members would lose their jobs. Lacking direct access to prisoners, Porterfield used *H2H*'s huge archive of materials that prisoners sent to them. Communities may adapt the play by inserting their own stories. Throughout the script creation process, the director typically functions as dramaturge or editor. The actors further shape the work through rehearsals. After public readings, the people who told the stories are invited to participate in Story Circles, which furnish still more material for ever-evolving scripts. Cocke explains, "By the time we produce the play, we've built a circle of stakeholders who recognize the roots of the play in their own lives and culture" (Cocke, email, 2007, *op. cit.*).

The play features a prisoner, a guard, and five community members. It takes place over one day, with the monotony and rigid structure of the 24 hours clearly marked. Within that structure, we hear a range of views about experiences emanating from incarceration. Structurally, the written text is the first act of the play. The second act is the audience's spontaneous response and testimony, that is, an on-the-spot dialogue; and the third act is a call to action, in which the people assembled come up with action steps.

The readings serve a range of purposes. Easily adapted to whoever plays the parts, it gets a range of perspectives in the room and seamlessly leads to public dialogue. It can be inserted into many contexts, such as at conferences to bring together families, communities, and activists, and come out with action plans. A play is more engaging than the "talking heads" model of conferences. The play can be cast on the spot, or can be preceded by modest rehearsal time, as much for connecting the actors to each other and the issues more deeply as for preparing the reading more fully for an audience. There's also been one full production of the play, to date, at University of North Carolina/Asheville, with costumes, set, lighting, and memorized text rather than staged reading.

Cocke asserts that effective grassroots organizing around issues of social justice invariably begins small. He sees the basic unit of such organizing as the individual discovering through experience, reflection, and study his or her own truth about the issue, then testing and developing that truth in dialogue with others, who also have knowledge. Others see the beginning of organizing as the act of looking out at the world. Aggregate and organize this knowledge about an issue, and a movement for change can develop. Cocke believes that organizing can lead to change when those who directly experience a problem make up the generative base for devising and enacting the solution.

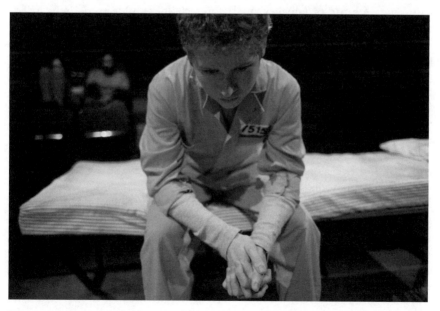

Figure 4.2 Thousand Kites performance in Asheville, NC. (Photo by *Thousand Kites.*)

After the play was up and running, *Thousand Kites* hired Free Range Graphics to develop communication strategies for online outreach. They include a web-based tool kit, outreach guide, the film, 24/7 radio access, the play, and information about *Thousand Kites* events. People may call an 800 number with a digital answering machine and their information will be added to the *Kites* website. The call-in feature provides access to people who don't necessarily have strong writing skills or internet access. The *Kites* team has been databasing as many categories as there are stakeholders, such as criminal justice writers, publishers, and issue-oriented radio personnel, allowing them to shape messages to very specific audiences. They have been learning about embedding their material in YouTube, Facebook, and MySpace. This includes viral strategies – methods of spreading the message easily beyond merely posting it on a website, relying on each person who hears about it passing it on like a contagious disease. Poets who work in prisons, for example, will get a letter targeted to them by a writer they might know, which they can then email to their list of contacts. A different message would be sent by, say, a community radio person, addressing others with a general interest in high-access radio, and spreading the message among them. This leaves the challenge of stitching these various constituencies together into a social movement, which organizations such as *Kites'* new partner (as of this writing in 2009), the Citizen Engagement Lab,[3] is taking on.

The internet component aspires to make *Thousand Kites* interactive and to provide a sense of (albeit virtual) connectedness. One tactic is to insert numerous bubbles on a map. Click on one and get a story about a prison issue in that geographical location. Such a technique is also being used to get audiences to *Kites* events. Because of the isolation experienced by many people who have someone behind bars, the internet provides a sense of connectedness, even globally, around these issues. It also raises the question as to whether the internet can provide a sense of community, or only a website. Perhaps it will have the capacity to show who else is on the site at any given moment.

In sum, *Kites* offers prison activists a menu of artistic dishes for a range of tastes and occasions. Radio has the capacity to overcome distance and scale the prison walls. Radio programs, such as Appalshop's *Holler to the Hood*, can take on any particular focus stakeholders desire; the *Kites* team will work with organizers on special programs. The video *Up the Ridge* is available in 56-, 45-, 36-, or 15-minute, and 30-second versions. On DVD, it can easily be screened at house parties, sent to legislators, and shared with audiences such as college students in a classroom. The theatre piece *Thousand Kites* provides a community-building, face-to-face process of story-gathering. The script, adaptable to different situations, can be down-loaded free from the web and rewritten with or without Roadside's help. Internet components include a dedicated website with access to the above tools, which can also be embedded on any other organization's website. Using viral marketing, the internet provides a low-cost communication network that spreads the message.

Note that usefulness to the cause is valued more here than keeping a piece of art intact. Some artists who work in both the mainstream art world and community contexts have identified criteria that fit both, creating work that is at once useful and aesthetically satisfying. One criterion is the element of surprise, even astonishment, that choreographer Liz Lerman holds dear. An example from her work is seeing a 75-year-old woman leap into the arms of a 20-year-old man. The *Kites* team, too, surprises. Hearing and watching the mix of humanity at the play readings make their way through the text has been, for me, a moving experience of witnessing someone discover the pleasure of saying what they believe publicly; or, conversely, of having to speak a contradictory opinion and hence consider it.

Theorizing culture as political strategy

A classic question that arises in artistic projects allied to politics is – is it art or activism? It's time to get over the bias that art must be one or another. We have interdisciplinary specialists in everything from bio-ethics to social psychology. *Thousand Kites* is at once art and organizing. Much organizing in the 1970s and 1980s involved centralization – people already part of institutions such as unions, or living in the neighborhood with the problem. Activist Rinku Sen describes more recent organizing around "communities of interest," which "requires addressing issues that are ... rooted in the identities and subsequent attacks faced by the marginal – immigrants, youth, women of color, and the very poor" (Sen 2003). To that list one could add those affected by the criminal justice system. Because communities of interest may be more dispersed than those sharing an institutional or geographical home, organizing methods must be able to gather people. Viewing or performing art work become such occasions.

Political scientist Diana C. Mutz theorizes a role for cultural projects such as *Kites* in political activism, or in her terms, how "communicative interaction benefits democracy" (Mutz 2006: 5). First, she notes the benefits of exposure to oppositional viewpoints through deliberative, reasoned discourse. According to Jürgen Habermas, known for his seminal writings on the public sphere, contact with diverse views encourages greater reflection. Such exposure transcends the parochial nature of personal experience (Calhoun 1988). As noted in the epigram to this chapter, John Stuart Mill pithily describes the absence of such deliberation thus: "If the[ir] opinion is right, they are deprived of the opportunity of exchanging error for truth; if wrong, they lose what is almost as great a benefit, the clearer perception and livelier impression of truth produced by its collision with error"

(Mill 1859; 1956: 21). A film or play that communicates different perspectives in compelling ways is politically useful not by championing a particular position, but when it catalyzes conversations that bring these points of view into dialogue with those of the participants. We see this with *Thousand Kites*.

Mutz examines the conditions under which such exchanges take place. She defines a *network* as those with whom one has face-to-face communication, and *context* as the environment in which that takes place. Mutz finds that the contexts in which most people move not infrequently contain diversity, but their networks rarely do: she contends that like-minded people mostly talk to each other. Thus diversity for Mutz refers to "the extent that a given person is exposed to those of oppositional views versus those of like mind" (Mutz 2006: 13). Even less frequently do people from different social networks share ideas in depth. By setting up exchanges that engage the diverse group of people touched in any way by the prison industry, *Thousand Kites* overcomes such ubiquitous segregation.

For example, the first public performance of the play *Thousand Kites*, at which several of the communication strategies were employed together, was in Jackson, Mississippi. Carlton and Maurice Turner, activist artists (and brothers) who organized the event, approached not only prison activists in the area, but also several departments at Jackson State, a historically black college. They started with the English Department, approaching

Figure 4.3 Thousand Kites audience feedback. (Photo by *Thousand Kites*.)

a literary society which was interested in the script. The literary society students took on the staged reading, rehearsing in the afternoon and then performing that evening, scripts in hand. The Turners also reached out to the Law and Political Science departments, who saw the project's relevance to their studies about the criminal justice system.

The Turner brothers didn't know if their efforts with other departments had borne fruit until moments before the event began, when teachers arrived with their classes, bringing the audience to about 250 people. In addition to the reading, Szuberla and Kirby screened a 25-minute version of *Up the Ridge*. And then the audience spoke up, clearly grateful to be in a space where they could look for ways to improve the criminal justice system, with people coming at the problem from different positions. For example, Ellen Reddy, who works with "juvenile offenders," provided insight about systematic abuses she encounters. *Kites* organizers believe the event helped people see that even if they do not have a loved one behind the wall, they have stakes in a more just system.

Mutz's findings about networks and context differ from those of sociologist Robert Putnam on related themes. Putnam uses the term "bridging" social capital for the creation of ties among heterogenous groups, and endorses membership in voluntary organizations that do not require shared ideology or identity, like sports and the arts, as places in which bridging occurs. "Bonding" social capital arises from occasions for homogenous groups to build something of collective value together. Mutz finds that deeply intertwined and reciprocal networks are seldom characterized by a great deal of multi-perspective political discourse. The sites Putnam identifies as conducive to bridging social capital are not places characterized by in-depth political discussion. Voluntary organizations tend to be homogenous, promoting relationships among similar people. That's where capacity of the arts to gather diverse publics can make a significant contribution to activism and democratic deliberation generally.

But is there, asks Mutz, convincing evidence that hearing other opinions tangibly improves individuals or society? Variables in the research make it hard to measure. In one study, materials presenting different views were sent out in advance of face-to-face deliberations. So was it the materials or the face-to-faceness that made an impact on people? Or the presence of experts when people actually met? Or is it that people of different views actually talked together? (Mutz 2006: 59). Is more sustained contact among people with different points of view required for effective deliberative democracy? While these questions remain unanswered, Mutz found increased tolerance for difference through exposure to different views.

Mutz identifies a range of possible outcomes of linking deliberative democracy to social justice. On the beneficial end is "an awareness of oppositional perspectives, a deeper understanding of reasons behind one's own views, and support for the civil liberties of groups whose politics one dislikes" (Mutz 2006: 63). She cites a survey finding that people understood their own views better when they had to defend them in the face of opposing views. Their impact, when discussions reached sufficient levels of depth, was educational, providing new information. Mutz warns, however, that bringing together people of different opinions can have negative outcomes as well, such as bitter fights or more intransigent views:

> So although exposure to differing points of view holds the *potential* for tremendous benefits, to realize these benefits, exposure must occur in a context where the collective project of getting along with one another in society is primary, and the elucidation of differences secondary.
>
> (Mutz 2006: 62)

Mutz concludes that an extremely activist political culture is unlikely to be heavily deliberative:

> Although diverse political networks foster a better understanding of multiple perspectives on issues and encourage political tolerance, they *discourage* political participation, partly among those who are adverse to conflict. Those with diverse networks refrain from participation in part because of the social awkwardness that accompanies publicly taking a stand that friends or associates may oppose.
>
> (Mutz 2006: 3)

This speaks to the necessity to create contexts that balance the goals of deliberation and action.

That's where I take heart from Dudley Cocke's appreciation of conflict in democratic projects. The challenge to one's point of view, and to the possibility that the *status quo* might change, has got to threaten somebody, or nothing substantial is happening. The better question is, how do we work through the conflict, which is often a sign that the *status quo* is genuinely being questioned.

As if taking up where Mutz leaves off, social movement scholar Sidney Tarrow points out that "Although it is individuals who decide whether or not to take up collective action, it is in their face-to-face groups, their social networks, and the connective structures between them, that it is most often activated and sustained" (Tarrow 1998: 22). As applied to *Kites*, it's having something to do together, feeding the social network via screening the film, making the play, and holding events, that gets people activated because there's an event to gather them and provide a context for ongoing exchange. Indeed, Mutz cites studies that emphasize affect over cognition – the strength of *personal experience* in becoming tolerant of people different from oneself. The quality of personal relationships one develops improves with the number of deliberative discussions (Mutz 2006: 68).

I'd go a step farther. Participating in a dialogue with people one seldom encounters otherwise is one thing; but making a play together, as in Roadside's work with people from diverse positions within the prison system, creates a deeper experience together. If the Jackson State students follow through with Ellen Reddy and do, say, a literature workshop at a juvenile facility, that more sustained contact could lead to greater impact among people with different stakes and points of view. Such interpersonal contact is, according to Debra Friedman and Doug McAdam, "the key source of new recruits into social movements, far more ... than ... ideology or individual predispositions as the motivation" (Friedman and McAdam 1992: 99). Art's capacity to gather publics is thereby confirmed for its significant role in social justice movements.

Thousand Kites is a model of art providing a context for democratic deliberations conducive both to hearing various perspectives on an issue and to facilitating action. Whereas much art is considered complete once the artists finish making it, engaged art requires an ongoing sequence of call and response, and is not complete without waves of interaction with audiences. This interactivity is what positions *Kites* as a site for deliberative democracy. Cocke describes the *Kites* model as a feedback loop: based on the participation of the people most affected, artists create a formal articulation of criminal justice issues, an audience engages with it, responds, and that response feeds into the next iteration. The personal connection many of us have to people "inside", or to people who have people inside, keeps the deliberations from stopping at the necessary but insufficient step of hearing other views.

Art balances intimacy and distance. When preparing for readings of the *Kites* play, both informal conversations at rehearsals and formal performed readings allow people to connect to the issues through the screen of the characters' experiences. On the one hand, embodying ideas in characters and knowing that their words come from interviews involves a degree of intimacy, bringing people close to the real experience and humanizing the situation. Since the reader is not the original speaker, audience members can reflect and respond freely, at a remove from the source of suffering and violence.

Another condition for deliberative democracy to be useful is that such conversations not be purely theoretical, but tied to groups already engaged in action.

For example, Miss K was already employing *Kites* tools, calling in to the radio and arranging video screenings. She then organized a second *Kites* reading in Richmond, Virginia, as a follow-up to the screening of *Up the Ridge*. There was no rehearsal; people volunteered to read the various roles on the spot, which worked just fine. Some months later Miss K sponsored an awareness day, featuring another reading of the play, this time in a local park. It attracted a larger audience and was the centerpiece for a range of activities, including feeding the hungry people who congregate there. A third reading, in Lebanon, Virginia, organized by a prison support group, Virginia CURE, took on a particular poignancy when a man who'd been pardoned the day before came and joined the discussion. The reading was dedicated to him and celebrated his release. An officer from the sheriff's office also came, usefully expressing a different relationship to the system.

Part of the theatre piece's contribution to organizing is its flexibility concerning where, by whom, and when to perform it.[4] Roadside staff provide a theatrical structure that can be adapted as desired. More people's stories can be added; others can be removed. It is more personalized than a completely finished piece of dramatic literature, but more open-ended than Boal's tools, which tend to polarize people into oppressors or oppressed.

Integrating artists and activists

Eager to be as responsive as possible to the criminal justice movement, the *Thousand Kites* team of artists hired Working Films, an organization that strategizes ways to connect non-fiction films to activist contexts. For Szuberla and his colleagues recognized that organizing, like art, is a full-time occupation. Before co-founding Working Films, Robert West was a media programmer, producing independent film series and festivals. The experience of screening *It's Elementary*, spotlighting a program in California elementary schools about kids encountering gay and lesbian material, led West to further the organizing potential of political films. In Charlotte, North Carolina, where the film was being shown, school personnel were required to refer young people raising questions about their sexuality to their religious leaders.

In the question-and-answer session following the film, a young man in his 20s stood up and identified himself as a gay teacher who could be fired the next day for saying so. He condemned school policy around sexual questioning as counter to the reasons he became a teacher, including wanting to protect children and make schools safe. The silence around gay and lesbian sexuality, he proclaimed, was counter to making school safe. The room got quiet. This experience led the school board president, who had been invited and was, in fact, attending the screening, into a series of meetings that resulted in more openness about gay and lesbian sexuality in the schools. At enough of a remove to generate discussion, but close enough to real issues to be relevant, the film became a catalyst and the screening a context, for the teacher to move a political issue forward and diverse players to be brought together.

Although ultimately a success story, the film's role in affecting school policy was, West recognized, too accidental. An infrastructure was needed, a way for film-makers with political goals to show their films to people thinking through action strategies addressing the same issues. That is, West believed that in addition to the festival circuit, film-makers who hope their film will contribute to social change need to develop relationships with political activists on a separate and parallel track. Reaching organizers early enough for them to imbed a film in their work is an opportunity not to be missed.

Here's an example. In October 2001, Working Films co-founder Judith Helfant was completing a film called *Blue Vinyl*. She approached organizers of anti-toxin campaigns, for whom polyvinyl chloride (PVC), America's most popular plastic and the subject of her film, was the next target. Activists wanted consumers to take responsibility for the entire life cycle of this substance, known as a "bad" plastic, even though it is not harmful in the short term. How, she asked, can this film be of service? Greenpeace was getting ready to launch a campaign to persuade companies such as Bath and Body Works and Victoria's Secret, that market themselves as vaguely green, to stop using plastics in their packaging. So Working Films prepared 1,500 postcards asking CEOs of such companies to stop using PVCs, and launched the postcard campaign at Sundance, where the film was being screened. Since bad plastics such as PVCs figured in only 50% of their packaging, it was possible to stop. Offices called back to set up meetings with Working Films, committed themselves to becoming PVC-free in their packaging by 2005, and did so.

Working Films does an internet search to find organizers whose focus fits a given film. West calls them, and they generally love the idea of using media in their campaigns, but don't necessarily know how. West explains the high-profile release coming up that prompted his call, asks them to look at a DVD of it, and meets to suggest how they could include it in their organizing activities. West reports that a lot of non-profits and activists get called at the last minute to *help a film*, rather than being asked how the film serves *their* interests. He believes that every documentary film-maker needs community partners to vouch for their work; the authenticity of that relationship is crucial.

Appalshop envisions the role of culture in politics, as Szuberla explained to me, as helping facilitate a dialogue that isn't occurring, believing that solutions surface from the community: "The *Kites* staff members are not going to become criminal justice experts. Our area of expertise is not driving specific political goals and strategies but rather the skills to make art that generate dialogue and the trust that good things come out of dialogue." Szuberla states flatly that following up with grassroots activists is at the bottom of his "to do" list; he simply does not have the time.

This is where we see a conceptual shift from the model of one general campaign around an issue to numerous sharply focused campaigns. *Calls from Home*, for example, was one focused campaign. The StopMax (opposition to supermax prisons) work was another. In both cases, *Thousand Kites* produced content (a web page, a postcard) to support their projects. In fall 2008, the team began working with a group from the Virgin Islands whose men are being shipped to Virginia prisons, creating web pages, artistic productions, email blasts, and viral marketing to help them engage a broader audience and take action against this long-distance incarceration.

In October 2007, Working Films helped organize a meeting in Philadelphia between the *Kites* artists and prison justice activists. The goal was to develop strategies to use the multi-media resources to leverage the project's strengths, shed light on key issues, and implement reform on criminal justice issues. West's pitch to the activists was that art is meant to be a window into *another world*, to connect to people, invite them somewhere that perhaps they have never been, engage and empower them. In this case the *other world* is the criminal justice system. Working Films wanted to come out of the meeting with a sense of how to build an infrastructure so communities can use the art tools better to serve their cause.

The Philadelphia meeting generated numerous ideas about how to use *Kites* art for organizing. Most felt the need for a hook: prison artist Grady Hillman made the point, "The art work is great but it speaks to so many issues: family, human values, and how privatization and the profit base is destroying families and their connections to communities. For political organizing, we need to choose a focus." Someone hoped the theme of incarcerated children would be developed. Other themes included what happens to people we love as they go from arrest possibly all the way to being tortured; and, in light of a case in the news at that moment in Jena, Louisiana of institutional racism against several black teens, trying to map incidents of racial injustice. Several thought such a focus might segue into healing and restorative justice, directly responding to and improving the lot of the victims.

While all the artists were amenable, at issue was the capacity to develop the material. The theatrical component could accommodate such expansion of material most easily. Using the simple tool of the Story Circle, activists could be trained to gather stories specifically on that subject and insert them into the structure of the play. Dudley Cocke remarked that not only could the original material be reworked, but also they had already responded to a request for a Spanish-language version of the play and had made the translation. The activists shared examples of how the *Kites* tools had already proved expedient. A man from Richmond described a particular legislator who first said his constituency wasn't interested in prison reform, and later was turned around partly by seeing the film. West recognized the value of a full-time political strategist who could point to vulnerable districts and insert *Kites* in areas where the negative effects of the prison system were already felt. Someone else was interested in getting college students involved. Another activist emphasized marketing, not so much political strategy. He saw the value of producing images of youth who look like the kid next door, then seeing them change into a prison jumpsuit.

Not just *Kites'* content, but the caring message that its very existence sends to people ensconced in the criminal justice system, contributes to its value. It counters how the prison system takes advantage of the shame stirred up around a family member going to prison. The radio show *Holler to the Hood* (H2H) lifts that shame by supporting a caring community of inmates and their families. Miss K asserted that *H2H* gave her a way to call out, without her face, and now she can speak on it because for her, now, it's not just her son, it's everyone's sons, of many different races and religions in prison. Another activist recognized the negative impact of shame silencing people, and went public immediately when her son went to prison. It freed up a lot of people who'd been saying their children were away at college or the military. Because many people are talking about it now, she feels the prison reform movement can advance.

Arlene Goldbard applies Howard Gardner's theory of multiple ways of learning to different ways of persuading diverse audiences about the problems with the criminal justice system. Emphases include compassion, economics (your tax dollars wasted on these new prisons), the spiritual, human rights, civil rights, community development, and public safety. She proposes a button on the *Thousand Kites* website with these several different arguments. Others felt they could not focus on different ways of communicating with different audience sectors until they decided on one thematic focus for a political campaign. Keith DeBlasio noted that his organization's work to pass the Prison Rape Elimination Act – the high incidence of some prisoners raping others as the administration turns a blind eye – brought together people from the conservative Jerry Falwell to the progressive American Civil Liberties Union, because they all agreed that prison rape was wrong. The number of juveniles in the adult prison system made the issue all the more sympathetic. Having that common theme worked across many audiences. Yet others wanted to avoid specific goals, believing it's most important to get the material out there and discover in the process how it can be used.

The group identified multiple uses of the *Kites* materials geared to a range of audiences, and various ways of getting it into their hands:

- for policy-makers and other community leaders, make *Thousand Kites* toolkits, including cultural media to use in meetings
- for legislators whose constituency is represented in prison issues, provide places that are safe to come to and respond; perhaps insert a part for a legislator into the play

- for former prisoners, families, and support groups, forge connections as they re-enter society
- for StopMax conference attendees, prepare specific materials and workshops
- for people who aren't active and involved, but are affiliated with potentially sympathetic institutions like religious ones, announce *Kites* events in church bulletins; find a member of the faith community to approach churches
- for young African American males, articulate the link between the education system and the prison system whereby African American males in particular are pipelined from one to the other
- for engaged artists and arts teachers, post material on the online Community Arts Network
- for kids with incarcerated family members, create ways for them to network using the arts
- for high school students, integrate *Thousand Kites* material into the curriculum so as to present a more human and complex picture of incarceration.

Hearing the stories of celebrity ex-offenders is effective for some audiences. For example, the actor Charles Dutton was in prison, stabbed someone, and grabbed a book to bring to the hole. He accidentally took a collection of short plays. He came out 30 days later wanting to start a theatre company in that prison. When he got out, he went to community college and then to Yale.

The Philadelphia meeting ended with consideration of how to measure the success of *Thousand Kites* as an organizing tool. The level of opposition to *Thousand Kites* is likely to be an indicator that the strategy is, in fact, effective. Gathering statistics is also useful, such as noting the number of times the *Kites* DVD is shown, the play adapted, and how many new radio programs there are whose origins can be traced to *Kites*. It's important to evaluate how any given activist organization grows through integrating these tools. One can track the amount of media attention these events garner for the prison rights movement, as well as identifying actual policy changes after contact with *Kites*. The project is valuable as training for people who've never organized through the media before. Other indicators of success include celebrity buy-in: the film star Morgan Freeman, for example, has a foundation for juvenile justice. Growth in funding for cultural organizing, slowing the expansion of supermax prisons, and increasing reluctance to move prisoners across state lines are all signs of accomplishments.

Thousand Kites demonstrates the value of community cultural centers in political organizing. Appalshop facilitates multiple ways of telling a story, bringing artists from various media into collaboration because of their proximity, working together at Appalshop. At the same time, *Thousand Kites* teaches us the significance of story in political organizing. *Thousand Kites* asks: How do we uncover a story? How do individual stories of resistance hearten, and those of injustice enrage, energizing us to avoid paralysis and take action? What are the appealing ways in which stories create public awareness? Such art does not have to sacrifice aesthetics and complexity to accompany and support a social movement. Think about the beautiful aesthetics and power of songs in the civil rights movement, which both supported those already in the struggle and found their way to people as yet uncommitted. A movement, as activist singer and songwriter Berenice Reagan told Cocke, is about gaining territory. And so it is with *Thousand Kites*: using the feelings, ideas, multiple perspectives, and stories of people in a range of situations to generate an ever-expanding discussion questioning incarceration.

Workbook

The creation of scripts from stories and interviews

Ideally, these exercises would be done not just with students, but also with community participants. The more diversity and difference among participants, the richer the learning experience.

If you have not yet selected a theme

Pick a theme likely to be of interest to the participants for the Story Circle. For example, invite personal stories related to the criminal justice system. (As with *Thousand Kites*, the premise is that the prison system is so pervasive that any of us is only a couple steps away from it.) Do story rounds. Then take those stories and, in groups, compose scenes. Use assets the participants have; for example, if you have a lot of dancers, let the enactment be movement-driven. Set up some parameters, such as determining how many of the stories you heard you have the time to work with. Then lay out some compositional elements, such as allowing each dancer only four lines of text, staying close to the language of the original teller, and communicate the rest of the story through movement. Or require at least one moment when they speak directly to the audience, and another moment when they speak as a chorus. After each group has composed a scene, show them to each other.

If you have already chosen a theme and conducted at least one Story Circle

Reconvene several people from the Story Circle with whom you would like to continue to work and ask: Who do we want a play based on these stories to reach, and with what effect? What's the story we're trying to tell, and whose story is it? Create a research plan identifying a combination of sources according to the subject matter, which might include such elements as interviews, Story Circles, historical documents, and personal letters. A next step would be to bring together actors and work as their editor, collaborating on decisions about the play. Set up early public readings that include the people from whom the stories came. Follow the readings with Story Circles to inform future iterations of the script.

Either way

Bring together as many opposing points of view as possible. So the story here could be about a correction officer, a victim of crime, someone who is incarcerated, some impact on your community, or a friend with a family member incarcerated. You want conflict. Donna Porterfield of Roadside Theater has found that people are more open to hearing different points of view that come from the experience and first-person stories of those telling them. Such stories work better than argument in actually getting different people to hear each other. Therefore one of the principles in Roadside Story Circles is no cross-talk. According to Cocke, "Theatre, in a way, is based on political incorrectness. Disagreement and difference are good things."

Feel free to adapt and invent, based on the situation you are in and the assets of the participants. The principle in using these techniques is to tap into each person's creativity, including yours, sitting reading this text. Don't use these techniques as cookie-cutters.

Note that Roadside begins projects by articulating with its partners the values that will guide it. For an example of the form such partnership groundings take, see the Appendix.

5

GATHERING ASSETS

The art of local resources

A *theatre of local resources* builds on people and traditions present and able to respond to social calls. The whole becomes greater than the sum of the parts, as what one person adds summons a contribution from someone else. The need to act locally in New Orleans was catalyzed by Hurricane Katrina, which pushed already fragile neighborhoods into crisis. Hurricane Katrina struck New Orleans (and the Gulf Coast) on August 29, 2005, leaving 80% of the city under water by August 31. The cause of most of the flooding was not the storm itself, but rather the storm surge, responsible for breaches in over 50 drainage and navigational canal levees and precipitating the worst engineering disaster in US history (American Society of Civil Engineers 2007). The level of infrastructural neglect beforehand that accounted for Katrina's damage was equaled by the level of unresponsiveness on the part of local, state, and national government after it occurred.

Sociologists Robert Putnam and Lewis Feldstein identify the arts as "perhaps the most promising, if neglected, means of building social capital" (Putnam and Feldstein 2003: 4). My case study, HOME, *New Orleans?* (HNO), was one of numerous responses using local culture as a means of rebuilding communities post-Hurricane Katrina.

The choice: top-down or bottom-up

HNO was a neighborhood-based, arts-focused partnership among local organizations, universities, artists, and other residents, which began as a result of a meeting in June 2006, ten months after Hurricane Katrina. Ron Bechet, then Art Department Chair of Xavier University in New Orleans, convened some 15 higher education faculty from around the country who regularly do community arts with their students, to think together about campus–community arts collaborations in response to a crisis affecting an entire city (and region). I was among that group. Bechet brought us to a town meeting with about 100 local artists and a few interested parties from other fields discussing a role for art in rebuilding New Orleans.

111

Ron also took us on a "disastour" of the devastated city. The view on the ground was heart-rending: neighborhoods emptied of inhabitants, whose collapsed homes and crater-like pot holes bespoke how utterly at the mercy of the storm and levee breaks they were, and how little government aid had been forthcoming. Trailers parked alongside a smattering of homes on dark streets indicated as few as one per 30 households back in some areas. A dearth of re-opened hospitals, public transportation, grocery stores, working utilities, and businesses made returning wildly challenging, even for those with intact dwellings. Seemingly sturdy housing projects remained closed, their low-income, mostly black renters kept out of the city possibly forever. Was New Orleans going to rebuild itself as a different city, without the 70% African American population that included some of the most entrenched poverty but also many of the carriers of the city's celebrated culture?

Coincidently, a few days after I got home I heard from Richard Schechner, a noted theatre writer and director and a former professor of mine who, 40 years previously, had gone to graduate school and then taught in New Orleans and been part of the Free Southern Theater, a cultural wing of the civil rights movement there in the 1960s. He had also recently visited New Orleans at the invitation of local visual artist Jan Gilbert, and now imagined a project he called HOME, New Orleans? consisting of installations and theatre snippets in front of and inside ruined houses, briefly bringing back to life a range of memories before the houses were bulldozed or repaired, turned into condos, or otherwise irrevocably changed. He saw the project on a very large scale, necessitating many artists and students, generating artistic "home history" performances and installations from neighborhood to neighborhood, finally culminating in a giant parade to the Superdome[1] to exorcize the bad spirits from many people's ordeal there before being evacuated in the immediate aftermath of the storm. He wanted Gilbert to coordinate an artist component, and me to facilitate a university component.

Though I wasn't sure that people in a devastated city would want to create art about life before the storm, I was sure that I wanted to do something in New Orleans. I had never witnessed my government less responsive to a domestic disaster, and while not a substitute for official intervention, I felt that anyone who could contribute should do so. While many of the needs existed pre-Katrina, the storm was the catalyst to generate support as challenges got worse. I hoped that, given the level of need, people with various kinds of professional expertise would look to interact, so that together the components would achieve impact through building inter-sectoral momentum. I could do something in the modest realm of community-based art. Theatre by itself could not concretely change anything; but in conjunction with, say, the Neighborhood Housing Services (NHS) in the 7th Ward, might the presence of free arts programs for local children contribute to parents' sense of belonging in the neighbor-hood? Would they be more likely to work with the NHS to strive for home ownership and the neighborhood stability that comes with it? Was Katrina an opportunity for synergy among various neighborhood resources, further activated by at least some influx of money in response to the storm?

I also wondered if a role for art in rebuilding New Orleans would bring attention to art's social potential. Art as a reflection, as a creation, at a distance from everyday life, is the conventional norm. Would Katrina challenge those limits, and make a compelling statement about art that responds to very palpable and immediate social calls? Would it catalyze a crisis of meaning among artists, as I had witnessed in the immediate after-math of 9/11? At New York University (NYU) Tisch School of the Arts, where I was teaching at the time, my political theatre classes overflowed as young artists interrogated the uses of their métier in such an uncertain world. My office and those of my colleagues were sites of continuous, heartfelt conversations with each other and students alike about what kind of art mattered, if any, in a world seemingly bent on fratricide, if not self-extermination. In the wake of disasters like 9/11 and Katrina, how could one not question one's priorities?

I was grateful to Schechner for thinking that big; it had not occurred to me previously that I could just go to New Orleans and do something. As an outsider, I did not presume to head up HNO, but I emailed Schechner's proposal to Bechet and asked if he would take the lead in the university component. He asked if I'd come down and work with him, and I said yes. Bechet and I committed ourselves to the project, while letting Schechner know that it might change significantly in response to what people wanted in the various neighborhoods. And so we embarked upon HNO.

And change it did. The particulars of a community-based art approach became crystal clear a few months later, when Schechner brought Trinida-dian carnival master Peter Minshall, and I brought community-based artist Dudley Cocke, for a meeting to discuss the shape of the project with local artists in New Orleans. Here is how Ron Bechet and Amy Koritz, both partners in HNO, describe the difference between the two models presented on that occasion:

> Schechner['s] ... idea focused on the role of art and performance to memorialize, cleanse and celebrate so that the city could move on ... [reflecting] a tradition of aesthetic autonomy and creative expression powered by the unique vision of a gifted individual artist ... The tradition of community-based art, driven by a reci-procal relationship between artists and community, was repre-sented by Cocke and Cohen-Cruz. By the end of this meeting it was clear that these two orientations were incompatible, and that, while

the advocates of a more purely art-centered approach were not going to cede ground, neither were they going to commit the time and effort to make their vision a reality. The community-oriented artists, meanwhile, were not interested in expending their energy in the service of work that they did not feel would be responsive to community needs or provide long-term benefit to the people of New Orleans.

(Bechet and Koritz 2008: 1)

Note that both Schechner's model of top-down "aesthetic autonomy" and ours of grassroots community-based art intended to draw on local resources in creating HNO. But whereas Schechner's vision included a pre-selected director, Peter Minshall, and an already determined format, Bechet and I saw those as decisions to make with local participants.

Minshall's outsiderness was not the issue; it might have been wonderful to bring his formidable spectacle skills, having worked in numerous international settings,[2] into dialogue with local festival-makers, of which New Orleans has plenty. Projects grounded in the local are often enhanced by the presence of one or more outsiders. This was certainly true post-Katrina, where a level of trauma had affected those who went through it, only increased by the inadequate response to the crisis nationally, regionally, and locally. Even in more stable situations, it often takes an outside artist to bring attention to local life that is taken for granted. Rather, it was as yet unknown if community participants wanted to make a spectacle at all. Whereas Schechner never veered from his vision, Bechet, Koritz, and I identified neighborhood partners who collaborated in decision-making. People's need to lead their own recovery was of paramount importance on the cultural as well as the social plane.

And so the project proceeded with those of us on the ground. HNO leadership included visual artist Jan Gilbert; a faculty member from each of two historically black universities in New Orleans, Ron Bechet from Xavier and John Barnes of Dillard; and faculty members from each of two predominantly white institutions, Amy Koritz from Tulane, also in New Orleans, and me from NYU. Our focus was "home" in its many manifestations: individual dwellings, neighborhoods, and the city itself. Our process emphasized sustainable ways to use art to contribute to reinvigorating neighborhood life damaged by the storm, responding to local priorities through arts workshops, memorials, youth theatre, performance, and installation art.

Our work was twofold: to engage neighborhood residents in arts-based projects that modestly contributed to their communities; and, in the process, to train students in mixed teams from the four universities in how to engage and make art, with people, that integrated social purposes into the aesthetic. In response to what emerged through dialogue, we shaped four neighborhood projects. In the largely poor, black 7th Ward, our partners from the Porch Cultural Organization were most concerned about the kids becoming better readers and the neighbors coming together to create a sense of community. They saw dwelling on any aspect of Katrina, even life before it, as depressing.

Two communities wanted to make permanent memorials. In the 9th ward, our partners wanted their kids, who were going to school temporarily in an entirely different neighborhood, to have the pleasure of art-making in their lives. They began designing and making ceramic mosaics for a wall of the new school being built to replace the one damaged by the storm. They rejected the idea of the home histories project, wanting to rebuild as quickly as possible, not retain the shell of their damaged houses until we could mount the performances and installations. In Central City, there was a certain amount of chaos and instability, so the team's energy was focused on simply talking with people as they encountered them and gathering found objects for an eventual memorial. The seniors at the heart of that project met in a center, not necessarily near their homes at all, and lacked the mobility and interest to do something involving their homes. They preferred more activities at the center itself.

Only in the white, middle-class neighborhood of Lakeview, flooded by Lake Pontchartrain, was Schechner's idea of HNO pursued – the creation of installations and performances based on pre-Katrina home histories. The core Lakeview constituency was a group of artists, including Gilbert, from that neighborhood, for whom the plan to create performances and installations resonant of pre-Katrina life was meaningful. It provided a space for their own creative response to the storm which, in turn, was an occasion to bring residents who'd fled the city back together with those who'd remained, for them an important goal of the project.

The four of us leading HNO teams on the ground constituted the decision-making steering committee along with the facilitator of a fifth group, connecting the others by looking for opportunities for interaction among them. Each team included one faculty member or lead artist, students from at least two different universities, associate artists, and other local residents. Our grounding was a university course combining all the students and team leaders, and committed to reflecting on the work each team was doing by both specific problem-solving and discussion of general principles, practices, and theories of socially-engaged art.

Social capital and asset-based community organizing

I draw on two sets of ideas to explain the potential of community-based cultural recovery initiatives. One is social scientist Robert Putnam's "social capital" with its two variations, bonding and bridging. According to Putnam, the well-being of a place reflects its people's social capital, their ability to interact constructively around mutual interests. Social capital encompasses the networks of associations, norms, and trust that connect people beyond the confines of their homes. Bonding social capital centers on what groups have in common in order to advance their collective well-being. Bridging social capital extends reciprocity and trust to people who do not share identity based on markers such as shared neighborhood, age, gender, race, class, political orientation, and ethnicity (Putnam 2003: 22–24). The four neighborhood projects, building on the skills of local people, are examples of bonding; a later phase of HNO is intended to bridge people across the four neighborhoods.

The second idea illuminating HNO is John McKnight and John Kretzmann's "asset-based community organizing." As explained in their book *Building Communities from the Inside Out* (McKnight and Kretzmann 1993), asset-based community development means beginning by building on what a neighborhood has, instead of focusing on what it lacks. McKnight and Kretzmann argue for the need to shift the self-perception of people recovering from crisis from victims, reliant on and awaiting help from outside, to proactive self-starters, taking what steps are possible themselves. The danger of this approach is the elimination of government responsibility for aid. Therefore it must always accompany ongoing pressure for the much vaster level of resources from the city, state, and nation. In the meantime, an asset-based approach maximizes what people can do when they pool their strengths.

The notion of a theatre built on local assets most assuredly includes the artists involved themselves. Director John Malpede of Los Angeles Poverty Department, for example, looks for what the mostly homeless people in his company do best. Many are uncomfortable with social interaction, so Malpede frequently constructs the company's plays as a series of monologues. Malpede collaborator Elia Arce explains, "the style came from taking the limits of the circumstances and making them positive" (Arce and Malpede 2002). Los Angeles Poverty Department has done several long projects articulating the history of Skid Row as a means of expressing the meaningfulness of the lives of the people who live there.

Community cultural consultant Tom Borrup sees a connection between activists and artists who prioritize asset-based community building: "They are not simply making do with what they've got. They're using creativity to see what you've got and using it to leverage more – building on strengths to overcome weaknesses" (Borrup 2005). He emphasizes, however, first focusing on values. For example, a real estate developer might look at all the empty lots in the 7th Ward and see a huge profit for himself, whereas a community organizer might see these same lots as sites for current residents building and owning their first homes, and creating community gardens and a local library (Borrup 2006: 35).

Though *HNO* unfolded in four neighborhoods, in what follows I focus on the project I co-facilitated in the 7th Ward to illustrate the centrality of local resources in cultural projects helping to rebuild community. Our partner there, the Porch Cultural Organization, is a volunteer association whose mission statement asserts its intention:

> to promote and sustain the cultures of the neighborhood, city, and region and to foster exchange between cultural groups. The Porch is a place where all can come and do, to share their culture, and to take care of each other and our communities.
>
> (http://ny2no.net/theporch/the-organization)

Balancing local culture with that coming from outside, the organization's name refers to the quintessential space between the private and the public. According to Michael Dolan, the Porch came to America from Africa through Brazil and the Caribbean (citing Dietsch 2002: H01), so the name also bespeaks the neighborhood's roots.

Porch members say the 7th Ward is rich in culture but poor in economic resources. They want the assets they *have* to be more visible, even as they try to get more of the resources they lack. So when university architecture departments from around the country offered to help with rebuilding post-Katrina, the Porch requested they construct an outdoor theatre in their backyard. A team from the University of Kansas did just that. The outdoor stage became a way to celebrate neighborhood strengths, building on New Orleans's rich cultural tradition of outdoor parades and other public performances, with particular forms specific to black communities, as I shall describe.

The Porch is governed by a council whose members live within a few blocks of each other. The original five council members themselves demonstrate an asset-based approach to local leadership. Ed Buckner grew up in a housing project, lived on the streets at one point, became a machinist and lost four fingers in an accident. He is now a baker of pies, which he delivers from his truck, and is married with three kids. Through many years' work as a football coach, he knows most of the neighborhood families. Willie Birch is a well-known visual artist whose work reflects contemporary black life. While he lives and works in the 7th Ward, Birch brings funders and other interested people to the neighborhood through his extensive connections beyond. Hubert Dixon is a local retiree, particularly interested in developing health and exercise opportunities, such as a neighborhood walk/run event, for the full age range of people in the neighborhood. Carrie Burks, a retired teacher, has lived in the neighborhood many years and gained the respect of generations of neighbors. Helen Regis is a cultural anthropologist specializing in New Orleans second-line culture and public space. She partnered with Rachel Breunlin

117

(co-director of the Neighborhood Story Project) to create Seventh Ward Speaks, a public anthropology and oral history project, to highlight cultural creativity and activism in the neighborhood. The diverse skills and backgrounds the Porch membership brings to community development reflect the neighborhood's draw to a diverse range of people, due partly to its rich cultural history and central location. I observed admirable efforts to collaborate across race and class, though serious disagreements do arise.[3]

In spring 2007, I asked Regis about general neighborhood support for the Porch. She said that when they began, in January 2006, they got good local turnout at meetings, maybe 50 people, but over time those numbers have dwindled. She thinks that people don't see enough getting accomplished, especially the fact that the Porch's community center building was not ready to be occupied until a year after its founding. Regis explained, too, that a lot of people have left the neighborhood, not because of their homes being directly hit by Katrina, but because rents have gone up with landlords' expenses for repairing properties they own in this and other parts of town. This secondary layer of consequences from the storm is forcing more poor people, mostly black, to leave this city. Some people resent middle-class white people moving into the neighborhood. I heard about a teenager who said to one, albeit engaged, white newcomer, "One day we gonna buy our house back."

Regis says the overtness of institutional racism since Katrina is also deeply dispiriting. For example, the Porch neighborhood was getting no trash pick-up in spring 2007 while the adjacent area, the Marigny, especially its white middle-class section, was getting pick-up twice a week. Regis called the responsible city agency often, being sure there was someone who could fix it, in the way middle-class whites expect systems in place that function for us. Regis would walk the neighborhood with her cell phone and make calls – "Come to the corner of Pauger and Urquhart and pick up a big pile of trash." Neighbors would call out, "Good, girl, you tell 'em," but did not think their calling would have the same success and, so far as Regis knows, did not make additional calls themselves.

Regis is active in the 7th Ward and has good relations with most of her neighbors. How she feels as a middle-class white person there, she says, much like most of her neighbors, depends on the day. They don't like the gun shots or the drug dealers cutting through the back yards or police harassment of the teenagers. Regis gave this example: "A teenager cut through my back yard one day, gave me a big hug, and kept running, climbing the next fence. He smiled apologetically, as he hovered there before leaping over into the next yard, saying 'You unnerstand'."

Nonetheless, the active second-line parade and Mardi Gras Indian traditions, as well as the close-knit families on the block, drew Regis to the area and keep her there for now. However, the post-Katrina crisis means these traditions are now at risk city-wide, and rising housing prices in the 7th Ward will only make things worse. Regis says Porch founders were aware of this tension, and worried that the Porch's focus on arts and culture might enhance the neighborhood's cachet and unwittingly contribute to the acceleration of displacement for long-term renters in the neighborhood as well as homeowners (who could also get priced out by escalating insurance costs and rising property taxes). For this reason, the Porch partnered with an affordable housing organization, Neighborhood Housing Services, to develop a plan to stabilize and extend affordable housing in this section of the 7th Ward.

While New Orleans evidences Richard Florida's contention that an active and participatory cultural scene attracts people to a city or neighborhood, it does not necessarily lead to economic strength for all. Tourists have long been attracted to the creativity and free-wheeling atmosphere of New Orleans. But most jobs supporting the tourism industry pay poorly, such as minimum-wage hotel and restaurant workers. Critic Amy Koritz further points out,

> Florida has argued that strong social capital has a negative correlation with economic development. This was reflected in an early Urban Institute brief Maria Jackson wrote on culture in New Orleans after Katrina. She wonders to what extent the cultural traditions of the neighborhoods depend on their poverty and relative isolation for survival – and who wants to preserve poverty as a way of preserving culture! Ron [Bechet] and I saw some of this in the middle-class black students who had grown up in New Orleans with little knowledge of, and no connection to, the Mardi Gras Indians or second-line traditions.
>
> (Amy Koritz, "New Orleans chapter," email, August 12, 2009)

Grassroots culture-bearers, so plentiful in New Orleans, are seldom recompensed, but rather many poor and working-class people *pay* to participate in Mardi Gras krewes, second-line parades, and other locally-rooted culture. If projects like the 7th Ward theatre troupe are to create cross-neighborhood events, ways of funding project participants are necessary to make New Orleans cultural life sustainable in the face of post-Katrina challenges.

There's some concern, too, that outside interest may lead to gentrification, and the Porch leadership is concerned that the largely poor renters who have long lived there will be displaced. Near to the French Quarter, and on higher land than many poor neighborhoods, the 7th Ward was not as badly hit by Katrina as some places, although it still assumed substantial damage. Even before the storm, the neighborhood enjoyed no parks, no green places, "not even a basketball hoop," until neighborhood residents, including local environmentalist and active Porch member Dan Etheridge, created its first community garden.

Gentrification is inevitably a fear when a neighborhood's desirability raises housing prices such that outsiders are more able to afford them than long-term residents. One hopeful trend is that many 7th Warders welcome diverse new residents who contribute to its development. A Chicano man from Houston, a good cook and a good electrician, came to NOLA post-Katrina and made a good living as an electrician. He decided it was morally wrong to take that money out of NOLA, so he moved there and opened a Mexican restaurant in the 7th Ward. A lot of Mexican-Americans have been moving into town because of the labor opportunities, and they need to eat. Etheridge says the owner is very friendly and his small business is good for the 7th. And the food is good, which people around there care about.

In contrast, at a cultural meeting I heard a white man who lived briefly in the 7th Ward accuse some of the Porch leaders of reverse racism because they did not embrace his participation; after a few months he moved out. Someone else at the meeting suggested that the ill feelings he experienced may have been the result of incompatible personalities rather than racism. Certainly my experience was deep appreciation for co-founding the youth theatre troupe, and no ill will for being white and middle class.

The youth theatre workshop: adapting method to context

In the context of *HNO*, Porch council member Willie Birch, a close friend of Bechet, asked me to create a political street theatre company incorporating Boal, with teenagers that would perform on the Porch's outdoor stage. The prospect of working in an under-resourced New Orleans neighborhood whose cultural leadership saw an outdoor theatre as a rebuilding priority thrilled me. When I was 21, I was part of a street theatre troupe and retain great memories of the accessibility and joy of performing on the back of a flat-bed truck on inner-city streets, in Native American reservations, and at public parks across the country. So there was an appropriate fit as concerned me as a facilitator.

The youth troupe was conceived not only for the kids themselves, but for neighborhood bonding and New Orleans-wide bridging. The idea was, first, to involve teenagers as performers; second, to bring out local people as spectators, following the shows with barbecues where informal conversation could lead to more neighbor involvement; and third, to draw in people from around the city to experience a richer portrait of the neighborhood than that represented by the media.

I arrived in New Orleans with two NYU drama majors, Jack Judson and Jenny Soo. Reliance on local assets was basic to our approach.

Jenny and Jack made a workshop recruitment flier that Porch council member Ed Buckner distributed when he delivered his pies. As a former football coach at the local school, Buckner's endorsement of the workshop was the key to neighborhood trust and hence participation. Further support came from the local NHS office, whose staff saw involving kids as a way to involve parents, leading to relationship-building and efforts to teach them how to move from being renters to owners. Two local artists working for NHS, Stephanie McKee and Chris Williams, did some of their AmeriCorps hours with our workshop, as well as additional hours on our payroll.

Our efforts on behalf of the youth theatre brought us inside the community. One day, for example, when Jack, Jenny, and I were delivering fliers about the workshop, Willie Birch invited us into his home and studio. Birch takes photos of black New Orleans life and then recreates the images as large paintings in various shades of gray, often attaching several of them together – one was actually six conjoined, two each of post-Katrina houses caved in, fierce national guards, and protesting people. He also showed us the ironwork on his porch which, he explained, draws from the African, Yoruban, spiritual imagery of the crossroads. Even the porch itself as a structure, he says, comes from Africa. Then he took us to his backyard, his playground, where he had hung bottles and mirrors from the tree and on the fence, in the tradition of bright, shiny protection.[4] He is knowledgeable of all his plants and trees. He shared his interest in the browning edge of an elephant leaf, showing life go through its process into death.

Because the Porch's own building was in the midst of renovation, we needed a space to hold the workshop. With the help of Troi Bechet of NHS (and Ron's wife), and through the generosity of Father Terry, we got use of nearby St Anna's Church. Father Terry wants the church, whose post-Katrina congregation is even smaller than it was before the storm, to be a neighborhood cultural center into which our troupe fit nicely, alongside a musical ministry, a medical clinic one evening a week, and free classes in English as a second language.

But where were the teenagers who the Porch wanted us to involve in the workshop? Hanging on the corner, working after school jobs, dealing drugs. The first to join our workshop was a silent six-year-old with a very determined mother looking for something for him to do after school. Stephanie McKee and I looked at each other in dismay – we realized we might not find teenagers, but what could we do with six-year-old children? On the other hand, as Ed put it, they'll be teenagers someday – and so Brandon joined the workshop, underscoring a key principle of community-based work: to make it with whoever is in the room.

As we succeeded in workshop recruitment of 6–14-year-olds, it became clear to me that we would not be basing the work in Boal. Why not?

Working with children made an approach based in critical analysis less viable. What's more, it was unclear how focusing on the problems was going to help solve them, when nobody has a quick solution to the ravages of Katrina. Nor was there one general problem that bubbled to the top, that everyone wanted to address, which Boal articulates as a condition for successful Theatre of the Oppressed work, especially forum theatre. In the aftermath of Katrina, the list of concerns was legion: people needed homes, repairs, jobs, schools, roads, health care facilities, cultural organizations, and relief from post-traumatic stress. We trusted that other techniques would prove engaging, educational, and useful, and began trying a range of exercises to see which ones engendered the most enthusiasm. We did incorporate a variation of Boal's image theatre, not focused on oppression, but as a way to find vivid physical expression of whatever subject matter we were exploring.

We began by getting the kids comfortable playing theatre games together, setting a standard for behavior that excluded hitting and mocking, and building on what they found most engaging. We used the workshop to address needs that existed pre-Katrina, such as the low level of literacy and the paucity of positive activities for young people. Each child got a journal, and we often paused between exercises to write individual reflections or to gather thoughts for a new character or scene.

Why did we not turn to another community-based art stronghold, a primarily story-based approach? The stories the kids told initially were either violent or recyclings of television shows. We tried a Story Circle inviting the kids' stories of escape, knowing that retelling an experience can help reposition the subject from victim to survivor. But it largely brought back the terrible abandonment, fear, and chaos of Katrina. As James Thompson writes in _Digging Up Stories_, "giving dramatic structure to painful experiences can deny as much as it reveals. It can enhance the hurt as much as it heals the grief; it can stoke blame and the desire for vengeance as much as it delivers understanding and forgiveness" (Thompson 2005: 25). There was not enough distance to revisit escape fruitfully as families struggled to stay in New Orleans despite damaged homes, loss of jobs, and a disorganized school system.

If we wanted the kids to tell a different kind of story, we had to provide them with different kinds of experiences. It was a few weeks into the workshop that Willie Birch and fellow artist/activist and _HNO_ co-instigator Ron Bechet told me about a postering project they were planning about local heroes for upcoming black history month. First, Ron and Willie chose ten black New Orlineans who contributed in a variety of ways to local life. Then Ron and his Xavier University print-making class created multiple prints of each of their images. Then, early one morning, they hung the prints throughout the neighborhood, on street posts where they could be seen, turning the street into a gallery. The next step was to educate the community about the people portrayed. We realized that was a job for our youth troupe. So we created our first play, which identified and brought the ten people to life, teaching the kids about them along the way.

The kids thoroughly enjoyed playing the range of characters associated with the ten heroes, and learning some history along the way. Shifting gears into a simple performance was a welcome change of pace; playing with modest costumes and props and, most of all, using mikes from the outdoor stage, brought a level of significance to the work that the kids embraced. In a few weeks we'd developed a very short play, perhaps 15 minutes long, which we publicized with flyers and a parade through the neighborhood the evening before.

Performing in the Porch's backyard welcomed audiences not in the habit of frequenting more formal theatre buildings. The audience consisted of about 50 people, perhaps half community residents, most of whom knew the kids and registered real respect for the previously unrecognized skill they exhibited in performance. But not all the kids had acquaintances and family members there. And one of the kids, with whom we'd had a bit of a breakthrough when he got to play a drum, wasn't there himself because his father had appeared from out of town and taken him to lunch. About eight years old, he appeared to be mentally limited though not retarded. He had a 12-year-old brother who sold crack, and a 15-year-old sister who often watched the kids during the mother's frequent absences. His 11-year-old sister, who was also in our group, said to me softly as the audience was gathering, "I don't know anyone here." I asked if she'd like to meet people and she said yes, so I took her with one hand, and another participant, who said she wanted to meet people, too, by the other, and we went around introducing ourselves, shaking hands.

Another child who had participated enthusiastically in the workshop had suddenly stopped coming a week or two earlier. Buckner said he disappeared, which I thought he meant figuratively – that he had simply stopped attending. In fact, he meant it literally; there had been a custody battle and no-one in the neighborhood had seen the child since. There were two shy brothers who lived with their grandma and whose attendance had become spotty. The workshop had become less fun when we began rehearsing for the show. We later tried to split the workshop so one day could be open for theatre games and the other two days could focus more on building something towards performance.

We began the show with a warm-up circle of audience and actors, sharing the vocal, physical, and ensemble exercises we had been doing all along, in which the kids were now experts. University student assistants led the different exercises, as did McKee and Williams. Ranging in age from five to 75, diverse in race and class, people happily connected with each other. Then we did the show. All the kids rose to the occasion, with several of the youth absolutely shining, ad-libbing like never before. It was significant for all the kids to play local heroes, and for everyone to see them as such.

The show was followed by eating together. Just as people enjoyed each other's company, in what could be described as both the bonding of neighbors and bridging with people from different neighborhoods who attended, the kids themselves played together more peaceably than ever before. The name-calling and hitting that used to break out at any moment were absent. They seemed to understand that their success was collective, and to appreciate each other for making it possible. Even the rain passed us by after threatening all morning.

The next project was also the result of building relationships in the neighborhood. Local environmentalist Dan Etheridge, particularly supportive of our first thespian effort, asked me if I thought the kids would like to take a trip to a nearby bayou to see what the 7th Ward looked like 100 years ago. I was pretty sure they would. Etheridge said the bayou was also where enslaved people years ago would have escaped to, taken in by Native Americans and often intermarrying. In addition to the opportunity to get out of the city into nature, we hoped that seeing the bayou would lead to a conversation about how much a place can change. That could

Figure 5.1 Home, New Orleans? youth troupe performance at the Porch Cultural Organization in 2007. (Photo by Rachel Steele.)

then lead to a conversation about what they'd like the neighborhood to look like in the future.

About ten days later, we piled into four cars and spent a glorious day seeing what for most of them was not only their first alligator, but also their first frog. Less than an hour out of the city, we were enveloped in tall trees and balmy breezes. The bayou was preserved as a state park, with wooden walkways suspended just a little above the swampy terrain, and with a plethora of plants, trees, birds, and other wildlife. We wandered down the paths in small groups, stopping to look more closely, sketch unusual bugs in our journals, and finally sit silently and just listen. We picnicked on a lovely deck, with friendly rangers explaining more about what we'd seen. At our next workshop, we invented a creation myth of the 7th Ward based on the bayou. It featured helicopter and cypress seeds that grew into trees that developed magical roots called elephant knees, that held the earth in place and created the land we now call the 7th Ward. And from the water interspersed with that land came alligators, snakes, frogs, lizards, turtles, and egrets. It became the jumping-off point for our second show.

Both local heroes as an educational experience, and the bayou as an affective experience, led to stories and scenes profoundly different from those the kids had made before. If we are the sum total of our experiences, we made ourselves as we made our plays. We built on the available assets, particularly who was in the neighborhood, facilitated by the efforts of the Porch 7th Ward Cultural Organization. But the most significant test of the workshop will be its sustainability. When Jack, Jenny, and I left four months later, we were able to pass the leadership of the workshop to McKee, Buckner, and a young local theatre director and former NYU student of mine, Andrew Larimer. We had modest funds to tide them over until more could be raised.

While McKee was already a trained choreographer and dancer, and Larimer was well-steeped in theatre, particularly as a director, recognition of Buckner's leadership role with the troupe is very much linked to an asset-based perspective. Buckner knows about performance as part of a second-line tradition. He knows about the neighborhood issues, since he lives in the midst of them. He was quick to absorb the methods that Andrew, Stephanie, and I used in the workshops, even asking me for a list of exercises before I left town. Whereas in some contexts his capacity to use the skills he has and develop more might not have been recognized, he has been seminal in keeping the company together in the two years since it was formed.

The university connection brought with it numerous resources, the greatest of which was the participation of five students from Xavier, NYU, and Tulane, at least three of whom were present at every session. The kids had rarely had so much adult attention, by and large attending overcrowded schools, and mostly living in single-parent homes. They were fascinated with Jenny's hair, Rachel's camera, and Jack's gentle nature and athleticism. Given the lack of outside responsiveness during the storm, the children absolutely ate up the individual care and attention our team of students lavished on them. The university students also stood as a beacon of possibility: they were a racially mixed group who had made it to college and university, making higher education feel more attainable to the Porch youth. Our props and modest set-pieces were produced at Xavier by students and art professor Ron Bechet. Students made weekly pick-ups at Whole Foods for tasty and nutritious donated snacks, featuring bananas and carrots, apples and peanut butter, which were also a big hit.

Incorporating some of the good initiatives and proactive people in the neighborhood, rather than focusing on Katrina-induced problems that nobody had experience of solving, was a concrete way to begin and to offer the kids something of meaning with potential continuity. At the same time, our approach was iterative: it evolved as a kind of call and response, with artist/facilitators responding to the will of the participants, as it gradually revealed itself. A vision generated solely by an individual artist, as Schechner had proposed, would not have been as good a fit in this situation. The artist has to be on the ground, in a relationship with the other participants, allowing the project to take form as a result of the actual engagement.

The art of cultural resources

Consideration of local assets in situating art as a response to social calls would be incomplete without some discussion of a community's culture. Cultural capital constitutes a set of resources: the particular music, performance, poetry, folk wisdom, customs, food, and dress that are frequently sources of collective strength and pride and a way to bring people together. Theatre of local resources looks to local culture as a way to express and enhance social capital – to use meaningful, well-rooted cultural expression to bring social networks together.

Dudley Cocke describes the evolution of Roadside Theater's culturally specific approach:

> We first developed our community engagement methodology at home in the mountains and then exported it, always calling attention to the imperative of local translation. Our methodology's use of story is a case in point: Appalachian culture (like many cultures that have some history of being marginalized) has a strong oral tradition, so naturally we tap it. Another culture using our methods may have a strong visual arts tradition, so our process would emphasize tapping it. When working at home in Appalachia,

Roadside doesn't ignore or otherwise avoid its region's recent history of oppression; rather, it uses its performance traditions, especially music and storytelling, to analyze community problems and wage change, all the while celebrating local life.

(Dudley Cocke, "Roadside's cultural organizing," email, October 4, 2009)

I wonder if the 7th Ward youth theatre troupe could investigate its roots in social aid and pleasure clubs, a long-standing, African American, New Orlinean socio-political tradition of mutual assistance, and the related aesthetic tradition of second lines – street celebrations often braided with the expression of loss. This is the strength of Buckner, the troupe's leader; and is a performance vocabulary meaningful to local audiences? Second lines, according to anthropologist Helen Regis,

> are thought to have originated in 18th century Congo Square on the margins of colonial New Orleans where enslaved Africans, free people of color and Native Americans gathered, along with a few curious onlookers, to engage in commerce, music, dance, and religious ceremonies. Born of suffering but also of longing for freedom, second-line parades today continue to speak to the contemporary struggles of the city's majority black and working class population. Parades invite an embodied knowledge of the city experienced at ground level by club members, brass band musicians, and a heterogeneous cohort of marchers, dancers and second-liners often numbering in the thousands. The parades are interactive, participatory, and often break down the barriers between audience and performers through call-and-response chanting as well as dancing.
>
> (Regis 2010: 9)

The New Orleans second lines, like our youth workshop, represent alternative images of blackness from those routinely broadcast by the mainstream media.[5]

Creating performance through culturally-specific performance traditions draws people in because of the collective meaningfulness of the form as much as the content, thus explaining why it is one of the strongest, most time-tested approaches to art in social context. As Dwight Conquergood writes about Thai people in Laotian refugee camps, "suspended between past and future, they fall back on the performance of their traditions as an empowering way of securing continuity and some semblance of stability" (Conquergood 2006: 221).

There is resonance of New Orleans' African American cultural legacy in a three-part web series some of the members of the youth troupe

127

made in the summer of 2009. Most poignant is the use of performance to mourn the dead – the video is a lightly fictionalized account of the shooting death of Buckner's oldest son, in a case of mistaken identity. The project was initiated by Andrew Larimer, the young local director who has been a facilitator of the group since the beginning. Larimer explains:

> Ed and I had been talking for awhile about trying to get some mixed media into our theatrical performances, specifically around the violence in the community, and I'm pretty sure we were talking about that even before his son was murdered … The idea started with Ed wanting to film every street corner where someone had been murdered, either with a kid lying there to "reenact" the death or just the empty corners. Then it evolved into an idea for a play about all these street corners disappearing as the violence overtook the neighborhood, and then we moved it into the web series that it became … Commemorating the dead is definitely a big part of things down here.
>
> (Andrew Larimer, "The Web Series," email, December 7, 2009)

Creating a series of scenes which they then videoed, Larimer provided a context for the group to reflect on black-on-black violence and mourn the death of one of their own.

One of the most important elements of tradition is its capacity for innovation. The web series is connected to second lines in its purposeful marking of a local death, but is very different in the form used and also in its tone, as Larimer explains:

> Right now, we're on such a future-oriented, positive, go get 'em kick, I don't think we are focusing on the dead in quite the same way as we used to. Maybe less celebratory acceptance of the entropy of it all and more active desire to fix the problems. And the passion is so palpable, and the understanding of what people love about this town is so strong that I think we finally believe/understand that we can preserve what makes us such an amazing city without the corruption and the crime and lack of education, jobs and opportunities.
>
> (Larimer, email, 2009, *op. cit.*)

If response to senseless shootings and unequal opportunities can take the form of political efficacy, will that change the cultural landscape?

May the occasions to celebrate local life be more numerous than the occasions to mourn it, and may performance in the 7th Ward as elsewhere continue to be a source of strength to help people through.

Workbook

Facilitating theatre workshops

The workshop is the process component of theatre, whether or not one ever makes a play. Ideally, at least two people facilitate any given workshop, whether they be equally experienced, or one more seasoned than the other. Facilitators not only direct the sessions but also act as models, and dual leadership expands the possibilities for participants seeing themselves in an active role. I've co-facilitated with partners different from me in terms of personality (soft-spoken and a bit introverted in contrast to my stage voice and outgoingness), gender, race, age, ethnicity, experience level, and disciplinary expertise. Two facilitators are also invaluable because of the many occasions when one participant needs attention, allowing the other facilitator to keep the workshop moving for the rest of the group. And it's helpful to have someone with whom to plan and reflect.

It may seem odd, in a chapter on the specificity of the local, to focus the exercises on a generic workshop structure. But the point is to incorporate specific local formats within it. Having an overall sense of what you hope to accomplish helps set a course for individual sessions. A typical workshop consists of three parts: warm-up, main event, and closing. This cycle characterizes the entire sequence of sessions as well as each individual workshop. As concerns the entire sequence, the introductory phase is about getting to know each other, creating a sense of ensemble and the ability to work well together, and finding out the content and forms to which participants gravitate. The main activity involves going into depth about something mutually engaging. Closure is how the sequence of sessions ends, usually with some kind of performance, even for a modest audience, and a party to celebrate the group's accomplishments. In individual sessions, the warm-up consists of games and short exercises that focus the participants on each other and themselves in the present. I advocate bringing a plan of activities to every workshop, even if one ends up dropping one thing or expanding another, depending on who shows up and how things go over.

One way to use this workbook section is to put participants into groups of twos or threes and have them create templates for workshops they would like to facilitate, organized around the populations with whom they imagine working – for example, the elderly, prisoners, female teens, elementary school-age students, etc. If participants are already facilitating workshops, they could use this section to help plan and then take turns practicing facilitation in class throughout the semester. Note that community-based projects often begin with a discussion leading to a written document articulating its values and mission, and to which the group can return when conflict arises. See the Appendix for an example. What follows here are examples of exercises/activities that I have found fruitful for each workshop phase.

Warm-ups

Think about how the warm-up helps prepare participants for the main activity. In the 7th Ward, some of the most popular were as follows.

Zip zap zop: Everyone stands in a circle. Someone begins by saying "zip" as they direct their hands, palms together, arms extended, towards another player. The receiving player repeats the action to a third person saying "Zap," who then points their hands to yet another person, shooting energy as they say "Zop." Repeat, picking up speed.

Moving through different kinds of space: Ask everyone to walk around the room, taking a moment to notice their breathing, relax, and just take in the environment. Then have them move as if they were walking through honey. Give them a range of different environments to move through: space without gravity, surfaces that bounce, underwater, etc.

Machine: A good ensemble-building exercise that I first encountered through Viola Spolin's "bible" for workshop facilitators, *Improvisation for the Theater* (Spolin 1999). One person goes to the center of the space and makes a repetitive sound and movement, reminiscent of a part of a machine. A second person links themselves to that machine part with an interlocking, repetitive sound and movement, and so forth, till everyone is up and participating. Augusto Boal adds a variation to this exercise by giving machines themes of, say, an emotion, inviting the group to make a machine of fear or surprise; or a particular place, such as a machine of the neighborhood or city in which you are working.

Body leads: At the end of a warm-up, participants spread themselves throughout the space. The facilitator instructs them to walk around the room freely. After everyone is moving, ask the participants to "lead" – to initiate a movement – with a specific part of the body, such as their fingers, chest, hips, the top of the head. The body part leading keeps changing as the exercise moves along, giving them a few moments to experience each. Ask the participants to think about where their weight is placed as they lead with each body part. How does this compare with the way they move in daily life? Alternate between normal walking and leading with a specific part to juxtapose these differences.

Main exercises

These often begin in a training mode and at some point shift into creation and rehearsal.

Developing character through the body: Ask the participants to choose one body lead that they especially enjoyed doing. Everyone working at the same time, have them develop a character around this movement center. Perhaps they first find one repeatable gesture coming from this same lead. Then they find a repeatable phrase to accompany that gesture. Have them encounter each other, moving with that lead exaggerated, introduce themselves, say their sentence/do their gesture, and then find a way to say goodbye and move on. Have them also try to originate their speech from that body center. Perform these encounters in pairs for the whole group.

Musical chairs poetry: This exercise was developed by Dana Edell and the ViBe Theater Experience (Dana Edell, "ViBe Exercises", email, March 1, 2008). The goals are to create group poems, collaborate and build the ensemble, and overcome shyness and fear of writing. This is a great game for groups where individuals might be hesitant to share or create original, uncensored poetry.

Gather the materials needed: paper, pens, music, and movable chairs. Make a circle of chairs, with a piece of paper on each of which is written a first line for a poem. These first lines can be generated by the group, created by the facilitator, or pulled from published poems. Music plays while the participants, each with a pen in hand, dance around the circle. Music stops. Everyone finds a chair, picks up the paper, reads the first line and adds to it, continuing the poem. After a few minutes, the facilitator plays the music again and the participants immediately stop writing, leave the paper on the chair, and dance around the circle again. Music stops again and participants sit on the chair closest to them. They read the poem on the chair and add to it. Instruct them to follow the theme, content, and style that the first writer set up. The goal is for each poem to flow as an individual piece without broadcasting that more than one writer contributed to it. The music continues to start and stop. When ready, the facilitator starts to remove chairs. Each time the music stops, the participant left without a chair must sit on the chair that was just removed and finish that poem. The game continues until all the chairs have been removed from the circle, and each participant has written the final lines of an individual poem. Then the poems should be read aloud so everyone can hear how their words and lines have blended together.

Small group work: When developing work for performance, we often break into sub-groups, for several reasons: not all participants come to every session so small groups allow progress towards creating a performance to continue; the student assistants develop leadership skills by facilitating the small groups; in the case of youth workshops, some kids are best separated from each other; and participants are often hungry for the greater involvement and attention that small groups make possible.

Participatory choreography: Stephanie McKee brought this exercise to our 7th Ward workshop. Choose a theme grounded in nouns, for example, the four elements (water, air, fire, earth). Break into groups, asking each to

131

write down four to six action words describing their element. Water may evoke "runs, flows, drips, boils, and evaporates." Then ask one person in each group to create a movement that embodies one of the action words, and teach it to the others in the group. Compose a dance that incorporates all the movements. Each group shows their dance to the others.

Field trips: These were foundational in the New Orleans workshop, whose participants rarely left their neighborhood and most of whom had never left the city except when they evacuated from Hurricane Katrina. Whether to stimulate ideas for a production (a trip to a bayou to get them thinking about how much neighborhoods change), experience live performance (a terrific high-school production of *Dream Girls*), or just a fun break in the routine (a trip to the local aquarium), field trips are opportunities to stretch participants' experiences and build commonality.

Note: At some point during the main activity, a break for snacks is both an energy infusion and a way to informally get to know each other better. Participants often love helping prepare the snacks and cleaning up afterwards, thus also instilling good habits.

Closure

Closure refers to the formal ending of a session, the transition from the special time of the workshop to regular life. Some of the ways to end include the following:

Sharing small-group work: Sharing with each other is a typical way to close a workshop. This habituates everyone to performing in front of an audience.

Pebbles: Everyone sits in a circle and "throws" one or two words into the center about anything they saw, experienced, or remember from the day. In addition to encouraging each person to reflect on their own experience, this teaches them what other people found valuable that they may not have noticed.

Singing together: Singing is another pleasurable way to end a session. Some groups prefer always ending with the same song, while others like to sing different songs each session, led by a facilitator or any workshop participant.

Miscellaneous

Getting attention: With kids younger than 12, this game-like way of getting everyone to be quiet and listen proves very successful. The facilitator simply says, without raising her voice, "If you hear my voice clap once" (some do). Then, in a somewhat quieter room, she says, "If you hear my voice clap twice" (most do). Then, in an even quieter room, she says, "If you hear my voice clap three times" (ideally all do).

Exercise sources: Whatever facilitators have done themselves becomes a workshop source. Good catalogues of exercises and theatre games include: *Improvisation for the Theatre* (Spolin 1999); *Games for Actors and Non-Actors* (Boal 1992); *Theatre for Community, Conflict & Dialogue* (Rohd 1998); *Impro* (Johnstone 1979); *Playwriting: A Practical Guide* (Greig 2005); and the website Tisch Community Connections (www.community.tisch.nyu.edu).

Underpinnings that set the tone

Key positive experience: Susan Ingalls articulated this idea after 30 years directing arts programs for kids, and it is equally applicable to adults. Key positive experiences are highly charged experiences that come in tandem with major challenges, unlocking the door to reaching one's full potential. Sometimes through meeting physical challenges such as Outward Bound, sometimes through the social and aesthetic stretching of performance, people discover vast reservoirs of determination and persistence, resulting in successfully accomplishing the endeavor and enhancing their sense of their own potential thereafter, whatever the challenge.

Workshops balance various continuums: developing actors and whole persons, instilling discipline and fun, propagating process and product.

6

PARTICULARIZING PLACE
Revitalizing cities and neighborhoods

> What is specific about a place, its identity, is always formed by
> the juxtaposition and co-presence there of particular sets of
> social interrelations, and by the effects which that juxtaposition
> and co-presence produce.
>
> (Doreen Massey 1994: 168–69)

It's a well-known story: manufacturing jobs leaving US cities since the
1950s, CEOs moving their plants elsewhere to lower costs. Working-class
neighborhoods suffer the neglect that comes from high unemployment;
gradually, run-down and boarded-up houses become part of the familiar
landscape. The economies of said cities sputter and stall as people are
forced to rent instead of buy, the tax base drops, and necessities of everyday life, including schools, roads, and social services, are undermined by
insufficient funds. Once-busy shopping streets are empty except for a few
discount stores, resulting in less foot traffic and an increased perception of
danger and crime. As a result of urban renewal across the USA in the
1960s, multi-lane interstate highways dissect and isolate selected neighborhoods. Increasingly, people with the means to do so move to the suburbs.
Automobiles provide easy access to malls with vast parking lots, familiar
chain stores, and private security. Customers never have to leave well-lit
shops to get from one to another, nor brave the rain or snow.

Over a decade ago, geographer Doreen Massey described the movement
of capital, and with it jobs and people, globally, also paying attention
to places whose populations have grown as a result. She asked, "How, in
the face of all this movement and intermixing, can we retain any sense of a
local place and its particularity?" (Massey 1994: 146). In what follows,
I consider artistic experiments, under way in Syracuse, New York, which
respond to Massey's question. Syracuse struggles with an economic
trajectory as described above, despite formidable assets. I examine how art
contributes to a sense of the particularity of a place, and why that is
important. Echoing Massey, I interrogate how one builds on the "particular
constellation of social relations, meeting and weaving together at a particular locus" (Massey 1994: 154). I look at how artists provide experiences

of the particularity of place through interaction with actual residents, specific places, and meaning-making activities. Art thus becomes a component of the inter-sectoral effort to reverse a city's downward spiral, like each professional arena – job development, education, government, transportation, to name just a few – contributing what it is best suited to do.

The city is the quintessential context for call and response. Its sectors are totally bound up with one another. A university cannot thrive if there's nothing off campus for students to do, and no way to make their parents comfortable about a four-year stay. Companies won't want to move to a place where the schools are so bad, and the quality of life so anemic, that only the wealthiest, who can afford private school for their children and frequent traveling for themselves, sidestep that dilemma. A city with a compromised tax base and concomitant service curtailment can most effectively become better for some if it is better for all.

Art can also address the emotional and psychological effects of decline, which cities do not suffer equally. While New Orleans, too, has long struggled with sub-standard schools, housing, jobs, transportation, and other public goods, its vibrant cultural life continues to attract people there to visit and to live. As I described in chapter five, New Orleans is teeming with music, neighborhood- and city-wide culture, and a heady mix of traditional and experimental performance. Developing cultural projects for specific neighborhoods there is not to introduce art into the city's identity, but to suture the richness of its art to other sectors. The examples I gave in chapter five were how a youth theatre might also improve literacy, and a cultural center with a strong sense of neighborhood ownership contributes to people wanting to move from renters to owners in an effort to stabilize a neighborhood and avoid gentrification.

While New Orleans's cultural identity as a jazz center, as the "big easy," a place for dancing and drinking in the streets, greatly oversimplifies that city and erases the everyday struggles of the majority of its inhabitants, music and street performance do permeate nearly every neighborhood. Syracuse, by contrast, does not have a reputation as a place to visit and live for its cultural vitality. But a considerable number of artists nevertheless reside in Syracuse, many of whom enthusiastically contribute to a renewed and more vital cultural image and reality. In this chapter, I investigate recent artistic experiments to communicate Syracuse's particularity, focusing on two neighborhoods: the downtown business area and the Near West Side (NWS), the ninth poorest census tract in the country. I consider how such a project interfaces with efforts from other sectors to improve local life equitably. I look at both successes and failures, each instructive in their own way. I explore the tension over where projects come from – organically from residents, bubbling up from communities, or out of resources and ideas from external sources. I contend that there are limitations to what can be accomplished without integrating meaningful, grassroots processes.

Revitalizing downtowns

As William H. Whyte, sociologist of public spaces, said, what people want from cities is other people.

(Kaufman 1999)

Why revitalize downtowns? One of the great appeals of cities is density – the energy of diverse people going about their lives. Many people take pleasure in rubbing shoulders with each other, and in being exposed to the range of expressions and products people make. Others, as Doreen Massey reminds us, hold on to "an (idealized) notion of an era when places were (supposedly) inhabited by coherent and homogenous communities" which "is set against the current fragmentation and disruption" (Massey 1994). I dare to hope that those holding on to a nostalgic vision of homogenous community may be surprised by the pleasure of difference, an experience art-making and art-viewing can provide. While supporting commercial enterprise, such art responds to a fundamentally social impulse. Downtowns are where people gather and mix in the traditional North American, industrial city. While residential neighborhoods tend to reflect the same class, and often ethnicity or race as well, downtowns are our best chance to experience heterogeneity. The presence of an energetic downtown is one of the reasons people choose to settle one place rather than another, ultimately increasing the tax base and improving civic amenities like public education and transportation.

There's broad consensus that cities need people not only to frequent, but also to *live* downtown, providing a steady human presence, clientele for newspaper and coffee shops, boutiques and bakeries, the slow build to a place teeming with life. There is a trend in mid-sized US cities for empty-nesters, who moved out of cities to raise their families, to move back when the kids leave home, attracted to a walkable lifestyle, low residential upkeep, and the cultural pleasures that city living offers. City living has always had an appeal for young professionals. Some of both these demographics are slowly moving into downtown Syracuse. The formerly grand Hotel Syracuse is converting some of its units into condominiums, among the 1,000 new living spaces under construction as I write this in 2009. But, for now, Syracuse streets are sparsely populated, particularly after dark, although there are parked cars aplenty, especially near restaurants and bars. With no substantial grocery markets downtown, people can't live there without an easily-accessible car. With few people living downtown, Syracuse is not a 24/7 city, with a steady flow of people in the streets and the concomitant feeling of energy and safety.

136

The idea animating revitalization in downtown Syracuse is connecting and enhancing its existing assets. This concept, the Connective Corridor, is an L-shaped strip that originates on University Hill, home of the "eds and meds" (a cluster of universities and hospitals), extends down the hill several blocks, and cuts west for another mile. The activities to which most people connect at one end of the Corridor are inter-collegiate football and basketball games at the Carrier Dome, the Syracuse University (SU) stadium. From the campus, the Corridor extends north a few blocks and turns at Syracuse Stage, the premier regional theatre of central New York. Within a few blocks of the subsequent mile-long strip, traversing the main arteries of downtown, are the Syracuse Symphony, the Syracuse Opera, the interdisciplinary Redhouse, the Everson Museum (which includes in its holdings one of the great ceramics collections in the north-east), and another two dozen arts and cultural institutions, interspersed with office buildings. Restaurants, bars, and a smattering of shops are largely concentrated in the several-block area of downtown called Armory Square.

Richard Florida has theorized that art contributes to revitalization of cities by helping to create a buzz and sense of unique identity, "branding" them as desirable places to live, drawing people and economic development (Florida 2002). The Erie Canal contributed to Syracuse's ascendency in the 19th century, facilitating the movement of goods, ideas, and people across central and upstate New York; the Connective Corridor is intended to generate similar energy now, throughout the city and the region. Both the Canal and the Corridor build on natural and cultural assets particular to the region, with the intention of generating commercial activity and making Syracuse a *somewhere* people will want to come. Syracuse is receiving some $20 million from the state and $10 million from the federal government and the central New York electric and gas company, National Grid, to develop the downtown, $20 million of which will pay for new Corridor design amenities. The goal is to create a vibrant city center, with people riding bicycles and walking down a tree-lined path along a stream (largely concreted over), enjoying urban cultural amenities as well.

The challenges are formidable. Even before the economic downturn of 2008, cultural venues were struggling to draw consistently robust audiences. In the city itself, population has fallen from 250,000 in the 1950s to 147,000 in 2009; the suburbs bring the population close to half a million. Recognizing that only together will local cultural institutions constitute an artistically lively Syracuse, there have been steps to increase audiences through collaborating. All of the museums and galleries stay open late on the third Thursday of each month (www.th3syracuse.com). When the Everson hosted a blockbuster Impressionist show in fall 2009, Syracuse Stage presented an original solo performance there, *Woman in the Blue Dress (La Parisienne)*, based on a famous Renoir painting that was on display. Whereas paucity of audience can increase competition among a city's cultural venues, recognition that a patron who enjoys the Everson might also enjoy Syracuse Stage is necessary for developing a reputation as a city with a critical mass of cultural energy.

Another major stakeholder in the city's revitalization is SU, the largest employer in the city. Universities have always been closely tied to local economies; as goes the city, so goes the university. Chancellor and president since 2004 Nancy Cantor has aligned the university's role as regards its local economy with a vision of the purpose of education to develop individuals' potential not just to serve themselves, but also to contribute to civic life:

> Cantor is helping forge a new understanding of the role of universities in society as SU pursues its vision, Scholarship in Action [SiA]. This entails a view of the university not as a traditional "ivory tower" but as a public good, an anchor institution that collaborates with partners from all sectors of the economy to more effectively serve the needs of society.
>
> (www.syr.edu/chancellor/about)

SiA posits that education comes alive when students experience its effect in the world. Reciprocity is core: students learn from, and contribute to, communities of experts that include both academics and people engaged in various issues on the ground, even as the initiatives thus undertaken are enhanced through university expertise. Philosophically grounded in SiA, Cantor has dedicated substantial resources towards Syracuse's revitalization, believing that applied learning provides at once a concrete public good and a training ground for future leaders.

Within a year of her arrival, Cantor called for the renovation of a boarded-up former furniture warehouse on the western edge of downtown. The School of Architecture moved in while its building on campus was being renovated, increasing activity in the neighborhood. Although the School of Architecture has since returned to campus, the former warehouse has been permanently repurposed for SU design programs. About the same time, under Cantor's leadership, SU initiated a planning process and a Corridor design competition with a series of public meetings facilitated by policy expert Eric Persons. In fall 2008, to concentrate SU's downtown efforts, Cantor hired Marilyn Higgins, who was vice-president for economic development in the central New York offices of National Grid, to head up SU's new Office of Community Engagement and Economic Development.

Nevertheless, Corridor progress has been slow, leading to accusations of too much talk, endless meetings, and nothing physical demonstrating progress. Lesson: don't roll out an idea in the press without an associated action. Executing ideas has stalled because of the protocols for acquiring public funds; for example, federal highway money, explains Higgins, "is extraordinarily restricted and has to go through a very long complicated vetting process."[1] Detailed studies such as traffic counts and manhole cover examinations must take place before any designing can begin.

To the additional charge that the university is making unilateral decisions, Persons (now part of Higgins's staff) reminds critics that many of the design objectives SU is pursuing came out of the community meetings he facilitated, and were also articulated in other studies and recommendations[2] – better lighting, bike paths, and better signage, to name a few. While understanding the mistrust some people feel about "the 900 pound gorilla, the University," Persons is frustrated by accusations that the university is "just doing what it wants, ignoring that it's what the grass roots and community-based organizations have also been saying for years" (Eric Persons, "SU and community development", email, July 23, 2009). Harkening back to Massey, this resistance may also be an unwillingness to change at all, preferring a nostalgic picture of a homogenous Syracuse to a city that embraces those who live there today.

Many people forget, never understood, or are not acquainted with the community-informed vision. Some reporters for the local newspaper, the *Post-Standard*, are skeptical about the Corridor and the $20 million then-Governor Eliot Spitzer announced that the state of New York would contribute. In a 2007 column, reporter Dick Case criticized Spitzer for promising money the legislature had yet to pass. Fair enough. But Case didn't stop there. He described the Corridor as merely "new street lights, bus stops, sculpture, and trees," with the only thing to show for itself "a bus line, carrying students from SU and townies to the campus." And what expert does Case cite in his critique? "A student" who he quoted as follows: "I think it's a good idea in theory but I don't think it will add much of a difference" (Case 2007: B1). The Corridor to which Case writes he would connect includes "a crew to sweep the sidewalks, repair the busted pavers, wash a few windows, [and] reopen the stores and restaurants that have closed, or are about to." I want those things, too; they and the Corridor are not mutually exclusive. But it is futile to sweep streets that remain virtually empty, other than a few businessmen and unemployed passing through. That use of money has no possibility of generating more.

The importance of promoting interaction in public space for revitalizing cities has been well-documented. Sociologist William H. Whyte wrote that crowded, pedestrian-friendly, active spaces are safer, more economically productive, and more conducive to healthy civic communities (Whyte 2001). More pedestrians eventually generate an increase in jobs, from café servers to clothing-shop clerks, and more collaboration between artists and business-owners to create more activity as enough people are there to participate. As downtowns become the nexus of activity, more people want to live there. No-one is suggesting that benches, street lights, trees, and art single-handedly turn cities around, but nobody has come up with any single ticket item that will reanimate downtown districts. So in 2008–09, Corridor advocates hastened the process forward anywhere possible – and that included art.

The Urban Video Project

The Urban Video Project (UVP) began in 2007 with a couple of SU students projecting footage on the side of a downtown building. As it has expanded, the UVP has become a fascinating site to explore the relationship between the specifically artistic and more broadly cultural, as well as the question of who instigates public art projects, and particularly the notion of "the university" as an outside instigator even though its employees may also be insiders (such as long-time Syracuse residents). Both how the project as a whole is conceived, and who controls its imagery, relate to the larger question of ownership of publicly-displayed art work.

Seeing the UVP as a way to make Syracuse unique culturally, the university acquired funding to install permanent projections onto walls at three sites along the Corridor. Students and faculty from SU's College of Visual and Performing Arts, and Educated Guess Work, an interactive design firm from Philadelphia that designed and installed the system, created the short videos and still images that launched the project. The UVP website (http://urbanvideoproject.org) noted that it would hold workshops for local artists, art educators, children, and teachers interested in providing artwork in the future.

A year into the process, the UVP's identity is vacillating between broadly cultural and specifically artistic. For example, can the UVP feature images of the ultra-popular college basketball and football games? These images are cultural in displaying locally meaningful activities, but they are not art in the sense of being crafted to reflect an individual creator's point of view. Emphasizing the cultural over the artistic, UVP co-ordinator Denise Heckman, from SU's Industrial Design faculty, hopes that UVP will function as a mirror on the city, affecting people's experience of Syracuse, in tune with the Connective Corridor's purpose:

> I love the fact that people in the city can submit images and we can show them publicly. We can take a 4th grade class and have them all draw fish. An SU design student can make an underwater scene using the children's fish imagery and the children can come see it. I want families watching this, so in some ways it's about interactive design. That fits in with the city because one of the ways you revitalize an area is to get people to interact with it and have ownership.
>
> (Denise Heckman, "UVP," email, October 10, 2008)

Community participation in the image-*making* is likely to lead to community participation in the image-*viewing* – people will have a direct relationship to the works' makers. An emphasis on process is in keeping with the project's cultural aspirations. But how to generate enough interest in the UVP and create a viable infrastructure for such interaction to happen?

The UVP, like most cultural initiatives in Syracuse, is struggling with building an audience. UVP projections currently appear on the very broad wall adjacent to a parking lot used for the symphony, the opera, a restaurant, and the court system; and around the corner, on a long, narrow strip of the outside wall of the Onondaga Historical Association, across from a YMCA whose programs include the most extensive writers center in the county and a men's shelter. (A third projection site, on Syracuse Stage's façade, has not as of this writing been programmed beyond colored lights.) Other than coming and going from their cars, if they are attending an event or eating at one of the handful of restaurants in the immediate area, very few people frequent these streets at night. In response, Heckman proposes developing UVP's educational component:

> We need to have a presence on the web, too, because when you walk or drive by the UVP, it goes away very quickly. You should be able to go home, sit down, and read the artist statement, watch it again, look at other work by the artist, link to it, talk about it with your friends, and leave a message. We're looking to leverage that kind of technology, and we're looking for where, around town, we can put a card every month about the featured artist, reminding you to go.
>
> (Heckman, email, 2008, *op. cit.*)

These locations were chosen precisely to expand foot traffic. But until there's more of a reason to be on these blocks at night, the UVP lacks a context to draw the unintentional audience on which public art depends. Armory Square is the one downtown stretch with enough restaurants and bars to generate people in the street. If the UVP succeeded in generating regular pedestrian audiences by projecting images there, where they would be encountered, the pleasure might motivate people to visit projections in less-frequented areas.

Another challenge to the UVP is its instigation by the university, which some view with apprehension. Some skepticism is evident at the municipal Public Art Commission (PAC), an 11-member body initiated, like the UVP, in 2007, and another engine to make Syracuse an artistically more interesting city. According to the city ordinance creating it, PAC's purpose is "to facilitate and encourage public art in the City of Syracuse by creating a streamlined application and review process" (www.syracuse.ny.us/Pdfs/Public%20Arts/PublicArtsOrdinance.pdf). This includes reviewing and

vetting UVP content. As a member of PAC, I have been involved in discussions regarding the project. The most extreme position is that our
volunteer body is merely going through the motions of deciding about
university proposals, given its boundless capacity to move initiatives
forward. Nevertheless, most members recognize that PAC's and the university's goals for an artistically vibrant city are complementary.

Some PAC members are concerned not with equity in dealing with
the university, but rather with a definition of public art sometimes at odds
with the UVP. One issue is intentionality: PAC encourages artists to create
work specifically for large-scale contexts, not work that becomes public
because it is projected onto a large wall. Then, too, as the UVP has clarified
its goal to generate excitement downtown, it has expanded its means.
Persons (who has helped move the UVP forward as part of his Office
of Community Engagement and Economic Development position) and
Heckman describe the UVP as a format for sharing "who we are and
what we care about," for celebrating current events relevant to the community, and for showing interesting work by local students and residents
(conversation with Eric Persons and Denise Heckman, June 2009).
Meanwhile, the PAC has been moving the opposite direction in its self-
defining process: while initially open to nearly every proposal in order to
get expressive work out into the city, commission members now want
to set a higher bar artistically.

At issue here is PAC's embrace of art over culture more broadly
construed, and UVP's exploration of both. Tracing the meaning of the
two words, Raymond Williams observed that, since the mid-19th century,
art had increasingly come to refer to "a special domain of creativity, spontaneity, and purity, a realm of refined sensibility and expressive 'genius'"
(cited in Clifford 1988: 233), not least in resistance to growing industrializa-
tion. At the same time, culture had come to foreground "those elements
that seem to give continuity and depth to collective existence" (cited in
Clifford 1988: 232). Whereas UVP projections of local events conform
more closely to the above definition of culture than to that of art, the
majority of PAC members are simply interested in displaying good public
art. My own position is that there is room for both.

Another point of contention has been the use of aesthetically-pleasing
images with commercial ramifications to promote local arts and culture.
For example, Syracuse Stage wants to display dress-rehearsal photographs
of current productions on the UVP screen on its façade. Their photo-
grapher is known for both artistic and commercial projects. In this case, the
art is at once a form of advertising, a way to generate enthusiasm for art
and culture in Syracuse, and an aesthetic form compliant with PAC guidelines.[3] Indeed, commercial images are a well-established component of the
art world continuum in general. But the intention of public art in Syracuse,
according to PAC, is not commercial.

For all its challenges, the UVP is a promising fit for Syracuse, viewable by a large public at multiple venues most evenings from dusk to 11 pm, from cars or on foot. The long winters are less a deterrent than the absence of a viewership habit. The project can accommodate ever more image-makers and content; indeed it must, to fulfill its goal of enticing people downtown to see it. The UVP needs the freedom to experiment, and PAC ought not to be asked to perform a task for which it was not established, namely to make decisions about those components of the UVP that make no claim to being public art. Indeed, the ambiguous boundary between art and other visual meaning-making is part of the UVP's potential richness. The biggest challenge for the UVP is how to fulfill its role as a culturally meaningful expression, entailing a plan for community involvement. Unlike art *per se*, which may survive with only a modest audience, meaningful cultural activity is call and response: it is not complete without a robust audience who are, in fact, a next rung of participants.

Towards a participatory performance spectacle

I used to love to get into the thick of crowds ... The tussling beefiness of everybody poured into me like broth; I felt exuberant, enhanced by the soul-mix.

(Edward Hoagland 1979: 77)

In 2008–09, Higgins and the Community Engagement and Economic Development office formed committees to further design, visual art, and performance on the Corridor. I participated in the performance group. In contrast to situating the UVP where people do not congregate, our consensus was to create a public performance at the site of greatest activity. Informed by that committee, I am producing a project with Geoff Navias, artistic director of the local, multi-size puppet-and-mask-based Open Hand Theater, and Lauren Unbekampt, education director for Syracuse Stage and SU Drama Department instructor, with a particular strength in physically large expression. Both Navias's and Unbekampt's aesthetics are larger than life, so they are a good fit for a performance scaled for downtown. People from the four quadrants of the city will explore in workshops what is particular about themselves, and then share that in a downtown performance event.

Animating the project is the desire to create a yearly performance experience particular to Syracuse, building on local enthusiasm for annually-recurring festivals. Nearly every weekend between May and September, the city features an outdoor event, most often with the food and music of a different ethnic group rooted in the local population, including Greek, Puerto Rican, Polish, and others. While perhaps they once reflected the particularity of these cultures, now the main difference is

Figure 6.1 Open Hand Theatre performing outdoors for incoming Syracuse University students, Syracuse, New York. (Photo by Syracuse University Photo & Imaging Center.)

the music played and a couple of food items for sale, though some also provide culturally-specific dance performance, much of it folkloric rather than contemporary. Indeed, they rarely reflect the life of that culture now. Somewhat more successful are events that build around proficiencies people are actively involved with now, with annual jazz and craft festivals being well-attended and popular. This new event will be focused on how art-*making*, as well as *viewing* a final event, brings people together. Workshops will be offered in diverse neighborhoods to facilitate modest but broad participation.

The project, then, is an inquiry: what is particular about Syracuse, and how might it be shared through performance? With seed money from the university, the project integrates town and gown as participants and audience, providing local residents with pleasurable and unusual activities, and university students a meaningful experience off-campus that might engage them in the city's life. Workshops will take place over an eight-month period, punctuated by a number of small performances intended for neighborhood contexts. At the end of eight months, one large downtown performance will take place.

In sync with Massey, "constructed out of a particular constellation of social relations, meeting and weaving together at a particular locus," the event brings together a broad cross-section of Syracuseans: from the student population at SU, the children and families who already participate in

Open Hand events, Latinos largely from the NWS and African Americans from the Near West and South Sides, and others from the large immigrant and refugee population. Central New York State is one of six major portals for resettling refugees in the USA. Arts workshops provide not only a pleasurable way to practice English, but also a social network. Immigrant youth in Syracuse, as elsewhere, frequently experience a great deal of isolation, dispersed across a variety of classes and schools. Especially middle- and upper-school kids are mortified at sticking out, so language challenges are often a source of deep embarrassment and shame. By integrating these youth in the performance, we hope to provide a relaxed environment within which people from different nationalities can get to know each other. We also hope to bring in some of their rich puppet-and-mask performance traditions.

By focusing on the cultural contributions that refugees and immigrants, as well as other residents, can offer the entire populace, our project embraces an asset-based rather than deficit model, as elaborated in chapter five. That is, we are building on the community's strengths, not approaching the challenge strictly in terms of what is lacking. In this case, the goal is to move from a perception of refugees as nothing more than a drain on local finances, to recognition that they also contribute towards making Syracuse an international city.

Then there is the challenge of drawing people downtown at all, in our case through the energy of a large, annual, participatory performance event. Navias notes:

> One of the aims and inherent problems with the Connective Corridor is that it is connecting to a downtown that is a underpopulated. People reminisce about how it was. But no one goes downtown if they have a free afternoon. We go downtown for an event that happens to be down there, we may eat while there, or drink in Armory Square, but that's about it ... The Connective Corridor has been brilliant in opening the conversation, and, by example, SU has attempted to breathe some life back in, anchoring the Corridor with the Warehouse. We need to create a new public ritual that can happen within the great setting of downtown's historic buildings and vibrant past, but to make it kick, it has to weave a new story even with some of the old threads.
> (Geoff Navias, "Connective Corridor," email, October 6, 2009)

In tune with Massey, we are focusing on neighborhood imagry and expressions generally known only to the people who live there now.

Numerous urban areas use art to draw people to struggling downtowns. Some towns try "arts passports," entailing the purchase of a booklet that assures entry to multiple cultural venues over a set period. Other towns have had success with art/wine walks. Patrons buy a map of participating venues where, over a given weekend, they can see art and have a bit of wine and a snack at each, upon showing ID. Some festivals build upon a book that residents are reading together, often coordinated by public libraries. For example, the book *Don Quixote* celebrated its 400th birthday in 2005. Partly in recognition of the growing Latino population, the Bethlehem, PA school system and civic organizations encouraged mass readings, and the local Touchstone Theater created a site-specific performance based on it, moving audiences throughout the city. Scenes were devised for resonant sites in front of which they were performed. For example, the final scene, Quixote's death, took place at a cemetery on a high hill overlooking the town as the sun set.

Cultural festivals are particularly promising because they are capable of involving so many people of different skill level; are typically free to view; and tend to bring in various groups, in addition to the arts, in their planning and production (Jackson 2008: 99). The relationships built in the relatively conflict-free context of festival-building can be continued in other community efforts. As urban policy researcher Marie Rosario Jackson notes, one of the indicators of how meaningful such occasions are is how long people prepare for them. Years ago, when I worked on New York City's Greenwich Village Halloween Parade, I recall people who began building their next year's costume literally the day after the previous Halloween.

A compelling example of an aesthetic event building on the particularities of an under-inhabited urban space is WaterFire, conceived by Barnaby Evans. On select summer weekends in Providence, RI, this six-hour public ritual features 100 bonfires blazing just above the surface of three rivers that pass through the middle of downtown. Meanwhile, international music selections play through a sound system all along the route. People are drawn to walk along the river, spend time with friends, eat at local restaurants, and view (for free) a few carefully spaced performances that change each weekend, all along the fire-lit river. The overall purpose is to experience the elemental joy of the water, fire, sky, and each other, just passing the evening together.

Performances that celebrate place draw on a range of aesthetics of site specificity. Michael Rohd, artistic director of Sojourn Theater, has developed methods to tether such performances within three spatial frames. The broadest is place, which he defines, citing Bill Savage, as "space plus value." How does a given performance resonate within that city, town, or neighborhood? Concentrating in closer is the second frame, space, referring to the three-dimensional geography of the performance, where it actually happens. Tightening the focus, we arrive at the third frame, site, a point of meaning (Michael Rohd, unpublished comments to workshop participants, Imagination Stage, Bethesda, MD, June 28–30, 2009) – for us, the diversity of people we are bringing together to perform and, we hope, to spectate. (See exercises for exploring site specificity in the workbook section at the end of this chapter.) Our hope is that this will become an annual performance event, along the lines (but in its own unique way) of WaterFire.

Revitalizing urban neighborhoods

> Each place is the focus of a distinct mixture of wider and more local social relations ... [and] from the accumulated history of a place, with that history itself imagined as the product of layer upon layer of different sets of linkages, both local and to the wider world.
>
> (Massey 1994: 156)

Following Massey, I subscribe to a municipal identity that is neither static nor nostalgic – that is, not trying to resuscitate a homogeneity imagined to have existed at some earlier time, and thus demarcating a hostile line between us and them. Nor, as Massey writes, is a place's identity single and coherent – "If it is now recognized that people have multiple identities then the same point can be made in relation to places. Moreover such multiple identities can either be a source of richness, or conflict, or both" (Massey 1994: 153). How can the process and product of art provide an experience of the multiplicity of place as Massey describes, experiencing its specific character in the ways that our segregated lives do not typically encompass?

Syracuse's Near West Side (NWS), just beyond the western edge of downtown, is characterized by old houses, many boarded up, and abandoned warehouses. Of neighborhood households, 78% rent,[4] well beyond the percentage considered healthy to contribute to a city's tax base and to encourage a sense of ownership in the neighborhood at large. Many of the landlords are absentee, meaning that money earned leaves the city entirely. Developed in order to house workers whose labor fueled manufacturing during Syracuse's economic heyday, the NWS was abandoned when those jobs were outsourced, and no new industry was provided for neighborhood residents.

Nonetheless, cultural practices imbedded in everyday life exist and could be more fully supported, by recognizing that acts such as hair-braiding and deejaying, which take place on the NWS, are also forms of expression. Now a plan for school improvement, home rehabilitation, and business development includes incentives for encouraging artists to live and work in the NWS. For artists are often willing to move into marginal neighborhoods in search of sufficient, affordable space such as former warehouses abundantly offer. In turn, their presence can help shift neighborhoods from desolate to desirable. Ironically, they can also hasten a process of making neighborhoods unaffordable for both the original residents and themselves – to which I shall return.

Local leaders, coalescing as the Near West Side Initiative (NWSI), are collaborating on the effort. They include four major Syracuse institutions: Home Headquarters, a not-for-profit whose purpose is revitalizing and stabilizing neighborhoods; Gifford, a local family foundation; the Center of Excellence, "a federation of firms, organizations, and institutions that creates innovations to improve health, productivity, security, and sustainability in built and urban environments" (www.syracusecoe.org); and Syracuse University. Chaired by Higgins, the committee additionally includes private businesses and entrepreneurs; community economic development leaders; neighborhood institutions and residents; and neighborhood advocates and service providers (Marilyn Higgins, "Near West Side Initiative", email, July 27, 2009).

The NWSI hopes to develop a thriving neighborhood of small businesses with an emphasis on technology, artist housing, gallery and performance space, cafés and restaurants. I wonder if Syracuse has the population to support such activity, although it is linked to efforts to draw new residents by encouraging more companies to settle and bring new jobs. The renewed energy owes much to Say Yes to Education, a private foundation that, in 2008, made a commitment to the entire Syracuse city school district to enrich education through after-school and summer programs, and to guarantee every senior the financial support to attend any of a list of colleges and universities into which they are accepted.

Efforts to create an arts district

The role of the arts in the redevelopment plan is reflected in the name the NWSI has adopted for the Initiative: SALT – Syracuse Art, Life, and Technology Quarter, the acronym also a reference to the product that once brought the city great wealth. Indeed, Syracuse has sometimes been known as Salt City, as its salt springs provided the natural resource that the Erie Canal transported in the 19th century. Our team working on the performance project also considered "salt" as part of that event's name. We liked salt's additional connotation of something that adds flavor to daily life, and its association to the working class, "the salt of the earth." But we decided against it. Geoff Navias, who has lived in Syracuse for 30 years, has seen multiple unsuccessful organizational names featuring salt: the Salt City Miners (folk music), the Salt City Players (theatre), the Salt City Story. Navias posits that these names had "a media buzz that evoked 'unearthing the past' and not a lot of excitement about the future" (Navias, email, 2009, *op. cit.*).

Moreover, in the case of the NWS, SALT was chosen by a committee, not agreed upon by neighborhood residents. While an effort to evoke something positive and specific to the community, the name highlights not the majority of people who live there now, few of whom are artists or technology experts, but an idea of who the committee hopes to draw. So what of the current residents? And can art districts be planned, or do they have to evolve organically, as artists seeking abundant, inexpensive live/work space move into raw areas? Can this strategy work in a city like Syracuse, with so much low-priced housing and no artist areas to extend in the first place?

And how to avoid gentrification, which is often set in motion when artists resettle marginal neighborhoods and make them so desirable that rents and housing costs rise and new, more prosperous people move in, eventually displacing not just the artists but also the people who lived there before them? Sociologists H. Briavel Holcomb and Robert A. Beauregard define gentrification as an upwardly-mobile middle class's "search for safe and rapidly growing housing investments with employment ties to the city" inflating housing costs and displacing working-class and poor from viable neighborhoods with handsome and rehabitable housing stock (Holcomb and Beauregard 1981: 23). While not a concern anytime soon, since Syracuse is what planners call a "weak market" city, decisions made now will have an impact on the future. Some people say they'd love the problem of gentrification – they'd love an influx of people who want to be there, and who will demand improved conditions. But not the poor, who fear that such an influx will mean they'll lose what little they have. Responding to my concern, Higgins noted,

> Although this fear [of gentrification] was voiced early in the process – reflexive almost – engagement in the project actually reverses that fear. The neighbors I have spoken with – (which is now quite a number) – recognize pretty clearly that they will get better services and a higher return on THEIR investment after all these years when more homeowners locate in their neighborhood and really they WANT it to happen.
> (Marilyn Higgins, "Gentrification?," email, July 7, 2009)

Nonetheless, a successful NWSI will result in higher rents and taxes, and not necessarily more jobs. Government must make provisions to protect current dwellers if neighborhood values rise.[5] And while a neighborhood may become artist-friendly, the root cause of its initial deterioration, poverty, often just moves somewhere else.

Artists must be conscious of their effect on a neighborhood and look to contribute. One frequent benefit of artist-dense neighborhoods is the creation of artist centers, "dedicated spaces ... where membership and access to programming are open to all comers, and where workspace, residencies, grants, mentorships, and exhibition and performance space are available" (Markusen and Johnson 2006: 7). Nationally, artist centers have contributed to community development by helping communities use art to solve problems, connect residents with each other, express identity and pride ... [and enhance] commercial vitality ... by investing in historic or new buildings, bringing artists and audiences to the neighborhood day and night, encouraging restaurant and service start-ups ... serv[ing] artists and amateurs ... [and] balanc[ing] programming that is inclusive with that which is competitive and meritocratic.

(Markusen and Johnson 2006: 10)

It's easy to see that artist centers could just as well divide as unite neighborhoods; some form of access to all is essential. And local residents must have a hand in shaping such a center if it is to be *of* the neighborhood, not merely *in* it. Sometimes people most want gardening, or cooking, or board games available as a social activity, and are only marginally interested in the more conventional arts.

Originally, SU pursued an artist relocation program for the NWS, fashioned after the revitalization of Paducah, Kentucky, led by artist Mark Barone. Barone had studied city planning in college and then made his living as an artist, buying a house and settling in Paducah. He became increasingly angry as slum landlords neglecting their rental properties drove down the value of the houses in his neighborhood. Barone and a team of city planners got widespread city support to enforce housing inspections and take derelict property away from irresponsible landlords. They encouraged the city to sell such properties for almost nothing to artists and others with the will and the money to renovate them, with low-cost loans. A good number of homes were thus renovated and an influx of middle-class people in the arts and related fields moved to Paducah.

Given the inexpensive housing stock and abandoned factories in the NWS, Chancellor Cantor invited Barone to lead an effort to create a live–work art and cultural community there. Barone came to Syracuse, identifying four elements necessary to his model:

1   the city's will to enforce housing codes, do inspections, and dispossess slum landlords from properties that are not kept up
2   increased police presence in blighted areas
3   local banks willing to make non-traditional and interest-free loans to people responsible for renovating the houses they get from the city for a minimal cost
4   the creation of a national marketing campaign to attract artists from far as well as those who participate locally.

(Mark Barone, class presentation, Syracuse University, Syracuse, NY, February 7, 2008)

150

Barone was convinced that veering away from any of the four points would result in failure. For example, I asked him if he'd consider some rentals and some sales, since the need to build up sheer numbers of people in the neighborhood is so great. His answer was an unequivocal no, as the city is in such great need of a more robust tax base. Barone's model looked more and more like outright gentrification, dependent on people who could afford even subsidized home ownership, and just moving the problem of poverty somewhere else.

After two years, Barone did not feel he had garnered enough support from Syracuse local government for housing code enforcement and police presence. Nor were local banks able to make affordable loan terms as the economy worsened over the course of 2008. His four conditions were simply never able to be put in place. Banks nationwide were struggling in that period of failed mortgages, the near demise of Fannie Mae and Freddie Mac, and the most hostile investment climate on Wall Street since the Depression. It's unlikely that Paducah, Kentucky could have done in 2007–08 what it did in 2000.

But timing is not the only reason the Paducah model failed in Syracuse. One factor is size: as of the 2000 census, Paducah had a population of 26,307, less than a fifth the size of Syracuse; its county population was 65,514 to Onondaga County's 458,336. Higgins has analyzed other significant differences between the two projects' goals and contexts, as follows:

> The Paducah model was a purely residential, arts-based revitalization strategy. The NWS model, in addition to artist relocation, includes the creation of a green neighborhood, the attraction of green tech companies, and a requirement to foster new business development and jobs for area residents.
>
> Syracuse has many neighborhoods that require the attention of code-enforcement and police, whereas Paducah was able to concentrate on just one distressed neighborhood.
>
> The NWS project involves the acquisition, financing, and renovation of large commercial structures (former warehouses), making product development (what we have to sell to the artists) a much more complicated matter than Paducah's offer of residential properties.
>
> The NWSI aims at maintaining the existing social fabric of the neighborhood while attracting others to locate here. The Paducah model was admittedly aimed at gentrifying its Lowertown neighborhood.
>
> (Marilyn Higgins, "Revitalization Models,"
> unpublished document, 2008)

After careful consideration, the NWS collaborative concluded that, unlike Paducah, Syracuse needed a model through which to collaborate with local artists, draw upon the contacts of the plentiful local universities, secure the private investment needed to renovate the warehouses, take full advantage of the New York City market [five hours to the south-east], improve the safety and physical appearance of the neighborhood, and fully engage the local residents and cultural institutions in the effort.

(Higgins, unpublished, 2008, *op. cit.*)

Mark Barone provided a vision of the arts' contribution to neighborhood revitalization, but not particulars that fit the Syracuse context. Barone left Syracuse. While the vision articulated above makes space for local input in shaping the neighborhood in which people actually live, how it is carried out will be the test.

Art and community-building

Bringing artists from elsewhere is not the only way in which culture contributes to neighborhood revitalization. Enthusiasm for the role of a neighborhood's own imbedded arts and culture activity in community development is strong at the local Gifford Foundation, one of the major partners in the NWSI. The people who live in the neighborhood form the basis of Massey's emphasis on building with people who are actually there, to which newcomers of goodwill can be added. Kathy Goldfarb-Findling, Gifford's executive director, explains the Foundation's perspective:

It's not possible to engage people through typical economic development methods. If you really want to create revitalization within a neighborhood, which is where we work, you have to engage the residents. And the only thing we've come up with that is able to cross over all the boundaries that exist within neighborhoods and communities is the arts. So the first thing that we did both on the Southside and the Near West Side was to form neighborhood residents into arts' councils.

(Gifford Foundation staff, group interview with the author,
Syracuse, New York, December 8, 2008)

Unlike other components of community development, the arts cuts across ages and economic divisions; one can be proficient in and connected to an art form without substantial material resources. And, unlike a model dependent on resources that exist elsewhere, everyone has culture.

During initial brainstorming sessions for an earlier effort on Syracuse's Southside, also a low-income area, a former consultant for Gifford asked a group of neighborhood residents to list what was already going on in the arts in their community. Heidi Holtz, a Gifford Foundation program

152

director, explained what she learned that day: "I had this picture of what the arts are yet what they talked about was things I hadn't thought of as art – like hair braiding and hair styling." Gifford staffer Brian Moore described their success on the Southside integrating local musicians, summer Syracuse Symphony concerts, and city-wide audiences. In the first year of their Southside initiative, Gifford sponsored one Syracuse Symphony performance in the Southside. The second year, a community concert featuring local musicians preceded the Symphony performance. Moore explains that the Symphony brought people to the neighborhood to hear the music, which then enabled them to experience some of the positive aspects of the Southside, which was mostly known for its poverty. According to Holtz, "The perception of that neighborhood began to change."

But the challenge was moving the Initiative from enthusiasm and some initial projects to a way for neighborhood residents to sustain both the arts and community development. Holtz believes she took too strong an administrative lead for too long; rather, people willing to take on local leadership should have been identified sooner, and then trained to develop such skills. Goldfarb-Findling adds,

> We made a really significant error very early on in not providing the residents with more opportunities to understand the linkage between the arts and their social issues, neighborhood improvement, and economic development. They saw the arts as the icing on the cake, or a plug-in, and they were almost entirely devoted to things that they could do for their children. Our staff might have actually been hampered by the fact that we're all embedded in the arts in our own lives because we took it for granted that they would get that sense of the value.
>
> (Gifford Foundation staff, interview, 2008, *op. cit.*)

The Gifford Foundation demonstrates the value of community funders with long-term connections to the people they are supporting. They continue relationships with people beyond individual grants, can see what is and is not sustained, and proceed accordingly.

Holtz points out that Gifford also put too much reliance on the artists already in the community: "We asked local artists if they wanted to work with this community, and we didn't get a strong response. I should have aggressively sought out specific artists." In other words, the ability to create community arts projects is a specialty which not all artists share, emphasizing the capacity to be responsive to what the community itself values.

The Gifford staff also came to appreciate the need for a permanent location for cultural activity in a community. In early brainstorming sessions, Southside residents had expressed enthusiasm for etiquette lessons for girls, dance classes for kids, and generally a place to gather. Holtz explains that

153

they had access to a gorgeous old building, which had been used for a very successful dance and theatre program, and which they hoped to make into a community center. The building was owned by a church, which could not negotiate a price with the local Community Development Corporation, and instead closed it. Not rehabilitating that space, both Holtz and Moore attest, was a mistake. According to Holtz, "Once we lost that physical meeting space even before there were any classes in it, something shriveled up and died."

Community development through the arts entails casting off pervasive habits privileging art-making as a specialty only for formally trained individuals, and relegating the rest of the population to passive consumption of their products. Urban policy expert Maria Rosario Jackson points out the value of the process of making art, whether on the part of those formally trained, or amateurs who are informally trained or self-taught. She also resists the dichotomy between art for art's sake and art with a purpose, while recognizing that many people do not:

> [A]n artist may be involved in work that has both artistic and community development value. However, it is likely that in the arts world, the community development value of the work will be overlooked. Similarly, in the community development field, the artistic value of the work may not be fully appreciated. There are very few mechanisms that can validate the work across the spectrum.
>
> (Jackson 2008: 95)

Expressing the value of both art, with its allegiance to disciplinary norms, and culture, which emphasizes meaning for a particular group of people, is one way to bridge this gap.

Jackson emphasizes the role of neighborhood arts and culture in preserving a sense of the meaningfulness and particularity of specific places, recognizing that art is larger than conventional theatres, museum, and concert halls. It includes

> murals, altars, choirs, music bands, ethnic dance troupes, embroidery and quilting groups, drumming circles, theater troupes, parades and festivals [in] schools, churches, parks, community centers, social service organizations, social clubs and benevolent societies, and sometimes businesses and commercial retail establishments.
>
> (Jackson 2008: 92)

These are activities that already exist to some degree in the NWS, and could be enhanced. The art-makers who already live in the NWS must be recognized even as more artists are invited to further enliven the neighborhood.

154

The Gifford staff established a NWS resident's art council to be part of decision-making about art in the neighborhood. In exchange for a free live/work space, nationally-recognized artist Juan Cruz, who has long ties to Syracuse and had recently moved back permanently, will do workshops with local inhabitants, with many of whom he already has a good relationship. This choice is meaningful given the large Latino population in the neighborhood, and Cruz's status as an artist recognized beyond Syracuse but also appreciated for what he has done there. The agreement faltered temporarily due to too short a commitment on the NWSI's part: Cruz needed a promise of at least five years' free space for the move to be worth his while. Some NWSI members were concerned about Cruz making good on his part of the bargain, but the arrangement requires trust to go forward, and it has.

In conjunction with an effort by Home Headquarters, Higgins's office is attempting to recruit Syracuse area artists, not necessarily from the NWS, to purchase inexpensive homes there in need of rehabilitation. Complicating matters, since the recent great recession, access to credit for renovation has tightened up considerably, resulting in only those with some financial means being able to partake in the opportunity. A Syracuse entrepreneur and artist has purchased one of the houses, and a policeman with a steady income may be buying another. Scott Allyn, whose family runs the very successful central New York company, Welch Allyn, is putting a recording studio into yet another building on the neighborhood's border with downtown. Higgins's staff is approaching local artists with studios in the Delavan, a former factory also near the edge of the neighborhood, to consider living in the NWS, close enough to walk to their work spaces.

Two SU programs are out-and-out recipients of NWS houses for art and teaching projects. Visual artist Marion Wilson will be downstairs and writer Steve Parks upstairs in one property. The idea is that renovating abandoned houses can be art projects and concomitant teaching opportunities in themselves, in addition to what is created within them. Wilson looks at this work as "social sculpture," an idea of German artist Joseph Beuys (1921–86), which transforms the idea of sculpture from an art form to a social activity.

In approaching the house-as-art project, Wilson builds on her 2008 creation of the Mobile Literacy Arts Bus (MLAB). In collaboration with a class, she transformed a 1984 RV bus into a mobile arts studio for students in the Syracuse School District. MLAB houses vibrant courses in photography, poetry, and literacy created through partnerships with SU faculty in those disciplines, responding to the schools' perennial lack of space and resources. MLAB "serves as a mobile classroom, digital photo lab, gallery space, and community center. As a team, we did it all: demolition, design, and construction" (mobileliteracyartsbus.blogspot.com).

155

The vision for Wilson's new project, also to be carried out with a class of SU art students, is the community-based, collaborative, and interdisciplinary design and construction of a sustainable storefront and art/literacy community center. Students and faculty of nearby Fowler High School Business Academy will serve as clients, design partners, building collaborators, and eventual co-managers of the small business to be housed in the storefront. Wilson is also working with the Business Academy curriculum of Fowler High School, so participation in the project fulfills college or high school credit. This formal recognition of learning that takes place through higher education and community partnerships is an example of a concept called university-without-walls, discussed in chapter seven.

Artist and community activist Rick Lowe's organization Project Row Houses provides a useful precedent for Wilson:

> Project Row Houses (PRH) is a neighborhood-based nonprofit art and cultural organization in Houston's Northern Third Ward, one of the city's oldest African-American communities. PRH began in 1993 as a result of discussions among African-American artists who wanted to establish a positive, creative presence in their own community ... Lowe spearheaded the pursuit of this vision when he discovered the abandoned 1-block site of twenty-two shotgun-style houses in Houston's Third Ward. The shotgun houses became the perfect opportunity to pursue the creation of a new form of art. They had two key elements: 1) a beautiful form recognized by the renowned Houston artist Dr. John Biggers to be filled with architectural, spiritual, and social significance, and 2) a need for social action among the community to bring the project to life.
>
> (www.projectrowhouses.org)

Artist involvement in Project Row Houses in Houston and the NWS in Syracuse shares an emphasis on creating community through art. Dr John Biggers articulated a model of art integrated in everyday life, further necessitating the move off-campus, to more ongoing communities. The aesthetic value of art integrated in everyday life, which flourished in many traditional societies, reappears in an eclectic range of 20th-century philosophies, including those of John Cage, Allan Kaprow, and the third wave of feminists in the USA in the early 1970s. Another worthwhile model is the Puerto Rican Pregones Theater in the Bronx, which produces a range of performances and workshop opportunities for both area residents and audiences from all over New York City and beyond.

The importance of a living culture was a strong rationale for two Latino SU faculty to develop an off-campus component in the NWS.

156

Entitled "La Casita Project," the emerging program seeks to bring diverse Latinos and others interested in Latino culture together in

> a space of creativity, learning and collaborative cultural production and for sustainable dialogue ... [It] will create occasions for interaction among students, scholars, activists, and artists ... [and] promote and encourage research and discussion with local communities to enhance our understanding of phenomena such as migration, cultural hybridity, bilingualism, transnational cultures, transnational family relations or other areas of common interest.
> (Inmaculata Lara-Bonilla, "La Casita," email, February 22, 2008)

With its substantial Latino population, the NWS provides a living context for Latino cultural activities of real value to students and faculty who are of, or drawn to, Latino cultures, at the same time as contributing to the quality of life there.

Inmaculata Lara-Bonilla, the key instigator of La Casita, aspires to make university resources available in the NWS by way of "speakers, workshop leaders, readers, and performers, in addition to providing space for community organizations and groups to meet on a regular basis, offering classes, and granting access to a physical library as well as online resources" (Lara-Bonilla, email, 2008, *op. cit.*). An ambitious undertaking with much goodwill, La Casita's university activators must be careful not to overdetermine its shape before having a neighborhood presence and strong local partners. Although Lara-Bonilla meets regularly with university and community advisors, many of these ideas were part of her initial plan.

Lara-Bonilla and her project partner, former director of Latino/a Studies Silvio Torres-Saillant, have much to offer and also much to gain by situating themselves in the community. Questions abound. Do they want Latino students to have continuity as concerns a relationship to cultural celebrations, connection with Latino families, and the Spanish language itself? Have they mapped the neighborhood to make sure they are not inadvertently putting themselves into competition with more modest organizations carrying out some of the same goals? At one point, they were enthusiastic about creating a bilingual library. There already is a bilingual library in the NWS; why not add to their resources, rather than in effect creating competition by duplicating what good already exists, but with greater resources?

While it is appropriate and generous for a university to provide funds for its own faculty to develop projects in the neighborhood that at once educate students and serve the public good, some community members seek opportunities to develop projects of their own? There is a balance to achieve between university and locally driven efforts, or, despite the best intentions of reciprocity, university personnel will be relentlessly in the driver's seat. The *de facto* message to the community could become that they are not capable of turning their community around; only these experts are.

For example, a consultant for the Gifford Foundation and a staffer from Higgins's SU office worked together in the NWS to bring local people into arts revitalization efforts. They gained the trust of a local deejay who, in turn, brought 17 aspiring musicians and dancers in their late teens and twenties together to advocate for a community music studio in one of two large former factory buildings that the university has bought and is in the process of renovating. At 225,000 square feet, one of the two buildings is large enough to accommodate such an initiative, even though overall space usage plans were still unclear. The deejay, two staffers, and a group of supportive community members began spackling and painting a space in the factory with the vision of music, dance, and art studios and concomitant classroom spaces where the artists benefitting from the space would provide other community members with free classes.

But after several weeks of growing involvement, inevitable expenses became apparent. A pipe froze, another broke and caused a flood, and the idea to bring a local Latino youth theatre to rehearse there became problematic because of the vast, open space of the building and concerns the kids might wander off and get hurt. The local artists were then told that plans had changed and space would not in fact be available for them. How much was that decision due to growing awareness of costs, coupled with a change of plans to move the public television and radio studios there rather than building on an adjacent vacant lot Might it be in the communities interest to develop a space unaffiliated with the university, given the desire for autonomy? Certainly institutions of higher education are under institutions of higher education are under greater constants than are grassroots collectives.

And while the university cannot be expected to pay for everything, there are a few troubling aspects to this incident. Why did people allowed to move forward before the space was guaranteed? Were they hoping that their sweat equity would convince those in control to let them have the space? What other leverage did local people have to prove their commitment and try to gain a foothold in the space? Was there an internal argument going on between those who saw the local buy-in as worth the expense, and those who saw it as a potential problem? Did that reflect a lack of trust in local people, or a concern about the financial burden? Would not a music studio provide something better for young people, many unemployed or underemployed, to do, or were they perceived as too much of a risk? Is there a belief that, given options, people can and will make other choices? Which local people are being given the means to help shape their neighborhood? As Massey suggests, how can one improve a place if one does not include the agency of a spectrum of people who

158

actually live there? Or can the NWSI simply not give attention to every aspect of revitalization at the same time? Happily, as I write this, neighborhood planning for a community center with university support is being resumed.

The arts' contribution to urban development

Urban welfare and history professor Mark Stern has found that the influence of local cultural activity in revitalizing neighborhoods "is not primarily about tourists or jobs or even revenue. Nonetheless, clusters of small community programs can have a substantial impact on the economic fortunes of their respective neighborhoods" (Stockton Rush Bartol Foundation, undated). In Philadelphia, Stern saw cultural activities drawing new residents into communities, reducing poverty, and increasing population, without trying to bring in people of greater means. He notes that "Cultural participation and diverse communities are mutually reinforcing and tend to promote gradual growth rather than rapid gentrification," thus allaying that fear.

Stern's research further reflects that "culture creates a positive social environment resulting in greater civic participation, lower truancy rates and lower delinquency rates," echoing the Gifford Foundation's experience in the Southside of Syracuse. And Stern found that "cultural participation builds bridges across neighborhood, ethnic and class divides in ways that many other forms of civic engagement do not" (Stockton Rush Bartol Foundation, undated). One of Stern's conclusions is that community-based organizations should be assessed on the strengths of the networks they generate and the impact they have on their communities. Recognition that the arts are exclusively about neither aesthetic pleasure nor income generation further supports my thesis that art's maximum value at the community level involves the relationships it supports and develops.

What I've been describing here is essentially a new civic art. It depends both on participation (so, as with ritual, *being there* through recurring iterations of the same event is part of how one enacts shared identity), and on aesthetic excellence (so the event provides a more heightened experience that is different from everyday activities). Participation occurs in many ways and serves many purposes. Jackson adjures that "Through making art – amateur and professional, formal and informal – communities preserve, invent, and assert their identities; transmit heritage; and comment on their existence" (Jackson 2008: 92). A more general appreciation of the many ways in which people express themselves, from forms such as painting to making houses themselves into art, also goes a way towards knitting a community together and lifting up the whole. Jackson further measures the value of art in community settings through aesthetic development, the creation of social capital as people work together to create something, the increased "stewardship of place," and art's capacity to serve as a social glue, connecting various sectors together (Jackson 2008: 100). So while the establishment of artists' live-work spaces may contribute economically, it must be balanced with artists becoming part of the communities, offering free workshops, for example, in exchange for low-cost studios and homes.

Enhancing arts events downtown may contribute to people wanting to live nearby. The biggest challenge in that regard in Syracuse, says Eric Persons, is *marketing*:

> Suburbanites, especially those with families, don't generally see downtown as a place to spend quality time versus going to the mall or some other activity. People just don't know what there is to do – and there is a lot to do. I met a local guy who travels across the country to visit jazz clubs but didn't know where Syracuse's Jazz Central [an organization that sponsors jazz performances] was located. The big exceptions to that rule are the summer weekend festivals, when there seems to be the collective acceptance by the community to be downtown.
>
> (Persons, email, 2009, *op. cit.*)

Persons does, however, see the allure growing, especially among people whose children have left home, and young professionals. Indeed, a local group called 40 Below – a play on how cold it gets in central New York, but referring to people under the age of 40 – prioritizes increasing local arts events as an impetus for that age group to stay in Syracuse.

At what price choose shopping centers over a robust downtown? Malls are generic, all the stores local outposts of chains. Nothing reflects this place or the people who manage them. Suburban culture keeps people in their old enclaves, not providing the experience of local diversity. The downtown is still the seat of municipal government, many business offices, arts and cultural venues, restaurants, and individualized retail shops. While malls are here to stay, the downtown, offering other pleasures, can experience a comeback.

Nonetheless, it's important to keep in mind what the arts *can't* do. Artists are put in a tricky position when they are expected to serve commercial and aesthetic interests, which is sometimes the only way they get support. As critic Elizabeth Strom points out, "Whereas once the arts were considered a luxury, supported by philanthropy and enjoyed by an elite group of connoisseurs, today's cultural institutions are constructed as an explicit part of a city's economic revitalization program" (Strom 2002: 5). Ironically, such a conception of art still keeps control in the hands of the rich and powerful, who choose which fund.

Cultural policy expert Ruth Ann Stewart warns against positioning the nonprofit arts as economic engines. One, they do not tend to employ large staffs, nor are salaries so high. Volunteers are a significant component of their operations. Two, many of the people and events that arts organizations present are only visiting, in touring shows and exhibitions, so the money paid leaves with them. Three, the nonprofit arts are always dependent themselves on raising money. Four, their status exempts them from the city property taxes, which fund necessary city services including police, parks, and education (Stewart 2008: 113). Nor do the arts address the underlying problem of low or no economic productivity.

Stewart does, nevertheless, see a significant role for nonprofits as part of a multi-sector revitalization effort: "Relieved of weighty economic expectations and appropriately embedded in a larger strategic vision, the arts can play a central role in a city's revitalization plan ... generat[ing] social capital and public goods" and sending a message to residents and outsiders alike about renewed energy in formerly "distressed and abandoned urban centers" (Stewart 2008: 115). It's finally art's non-materiality that most contributes to a community's well-being.

When I first moved to Syracuse, I had the sensation that I didn't know where it was; all I saw were generic shopping centers. The first time I felt I was *somewhere* was when a local artist brought me to a small, totally unique lingerie shop downtown. The second time was when I ate at Dinosaur Barbecue, also a home-grown and very popular spot downtown; and the third time was when I got a tour of north Syracuse, just off a main street, and suddenly saw shop signs in multiple languages and veiled women, and smelled tantalizing spices bespeaking a fabulous mix of cultures. Immigrants everywhere open modest restaurants and clothing shops, sell their crafts and music; why not in Syracuse?

The following exercises suggest some of the ways in which performance contributes to the experience of the particularity of place.

Workbook

Making site-specific performance

The goal of these exercises is to imagine a downtown event or festival that features performance, contributes to a specific and recognizable, surprising and multi-layered sense of identity in a particular city, and draws people downtown. They can be combined easily with exercises suggested elsewhere in this book, such as Story Circles and one-on-one interviews, to also bring forth the specificity of the people with whom one is working.

Begin by researching examples of site-specific initiatives in other towns – a downtown river, perhaps, or an established link to a particular cultural form such as Peducah's quilters. The online Community Arts Network is a good place to begin. Notice how, as community-based dance theatre artist Martha Bowers puts it, site-specific performance is a creative exploration of locational identity. Here's an adaptation of an exercise she gives her students.

Go to some point in your local downtown that you see as a potential public performance site. Explore the area within a three-block radius of that point. As you walk, record your thoughts and observations. Imagine it as the site of a large, repeatable public performance.

If you have a recording device or a camera on your cell phone, use them to capture images of particular locations. If not, simply take a journal and make notes and sketches. What is there to see, hear, smell, touch, and taste? What associations do you bring to these perceptions? Where are you looking ... eye level, up, down, inward? What are you looking at ... buildings, people, sidewalks, signs, animals, space, trash, items for sale? Is there any compelling natural or architectural feature in this area that anchors an event? Is there an open space with the potential to be filled in some compelling way? Who and what is and isn't there? What shops and cultural venues there offer potential partnership for a big event? What are you thinking and feeling? How are you responding physically? What are you hearing ... sounds, bits of conversation, horns, silence, a song in your head?

Also include the following elements in your report back to the class:

- Identify two local individuals or groups of performers who you could imagine participating in such an event, and describe what they might do. (This may take more time than a short-term assignment allows.)
- Note what time of year the event would happen, and how you would try to make it a recurring event.
- Make a timeline for producing such an event.
- Prepare a budget for it.
- Identify potential participants, audiences, and marketing ideas to inform and get them there.

Another approach is to create a performance initially viewable from one's car, accepting that sometimes more people drive than walk through downtowns lacking density. Bowers mused on such an art project for downtown Syracuse:

> How differently we experience a place when we drive through as opposed to walking through it. The kind of privacy of the car is perhaps replicated for walkers by insulating ourselves with audio devices. Then we experience our environment through a kind of sound track. What if instead of veiling the environment with sound, one created a narrator who guided you through a specific walk or drive – an audio tour that could be played in a car – and helped bring your attention in a more acute way to specific details,

while providing narrative and historical contexts. Though you wouldn't want to take the driver's attention off the road, maybe one could incorporate places to pull over and listen/look or get people out of their cars.

(Martha Bowers, "Site-specificity", email, February 28, 2009)

In considering a site-specific piece viewable from a car, one would have to determine if the limited opportunity for face-to-face contact was in keeping with the project's intentions.

Here's an exercise Michael Rohd does to begin to explore site specific art:

First warm up the group with a physical exercise. "The diamond" – a variation on flocking, which possibly originated in the dance world – is a good start. Make groups of four on some thematic basis. For our purposes, we might organize groups around particular architecturally-interesting spaces in Syracuse: the art museum; the university's downtown "Warehouse", which houses the design program; a restaurant in a 19th-century church that was part of the underground railroad; the old, baroque city hall; and the science museum located in the vast, former armory. Each group of four (or some groups of three, depending on numbers, in triangle formation) stands facing the same way, in the shape of a diamond. Whoever cannot see the others begins a movement, slowly enough that others can do it close to simultaneously. When the initiator sees someone else in the diamond, that person becomes the new initiator. The idea is to pass movement initiation from person to person, moving as much as possible in sync with each other.

Then each group sits down and talks about their building. The focus could be on any of the following categories, taking on the next each time the group does the exercise: the narrative/functional meaning of the building, e.g. what one literally does there; the historical/associative meanings of the building, the former of which will require additional research; the physical/landscape of the building, e.g. its purely spatial, architectural qualities; and the political/interactional rules of action governing how people actually behave there (Rohd, unpublished comments to workshop participants, 2009, op. cit.). This might, in the case of the Syracuse public performance project, also be done in relationship to particular buildings with which particular participants have a special relationship.

Focusing, for example, on the first category, the functional meaning of the building, create an activity together that people typically do in that space. Show it to the others. Team up groups so one group then suggests to another two ways to heighten the event from ordinary to extraordinary. Do that. Then the group making suggestions decides which of the heightened actions to keep and which to let go of, so there's more of a balance between ordinary and extraordinary.

A next step, drawing on another of Rohd's exercises, is to devise a way for the audience to experience the piece more fully. Maybe their physical location induces more connection, or perhaps they are addressed in a way that makes them part of the scene, though not compelled to do anything in particular. Don't forget the contract with the audience, which Rohd describes as their feeling that they are in good hands.

7

TRAINING

An engaged artist prepares

Training – Ah, there it is – the eternal argument for and against dramatic schools and the necessary apprenticeship for our profession which can never, unfortunately, be sealed by a diploma.

(John Gielgud 1936)

There's a moment in the 1936 film *Modern Times* when Charlie Chaplin, as the "little tramp," escapes from a policeman by hopping on the back of a passing truck. It is carrying explosives and thus also sports a red danger flag. When the truck hits a bump, Chaplin and the red flag are thrown off. Chaplin runs after the truck to return the flag, waving it to get the driver's attention. At just that moment, a large group of people, in the midst of a protest march, cross his path and, taking him for the leader and the red flag for a beacon, fall in line behind him.

While people do occasionally head up marches without having been part of the process that led to them, artists who would create engaged work would do well to immerse themselves socially as well as aesthetically, to be positioned to hear a call, and sufficiently skilled and informed to fashion a fitting response, before leading the charge. Such art requires deliberate, not accidental relationships with the people whose experience is the basis of the engaged performance process. Retrieving a flag is a single act of kindness, but does not reflect an understanding of the larger context in which brandishing that flag takes on deeper meaning and has an effect in the world.

In this chapter, I lay out an educational template that prepares artists to make well-informed, socially-engaged art. I focus on programs that are situated in US colleges and universities, with some attention to educational opportunities provided by individual artists and companies. The interviews and survey responses that inform this chapter were gathered through The Curriculum Project,[1] a research project I co-facilitated with cultural consultant Arlene Goldbard and Appalachia-based theater director Dudley Cocke. We framed the study as education for community cultural development (CCD), defined by Goldbard as encompassing "a range of initiatives undertaken by artists in collaboration with other community members to express identity, concerns, and aspirations through the arts and communications media, while building the capacity for social action and contributing to social change" (http://curriculumproject.net/glossary.html). The components of training that follow are relevant not only to CCD, but equally to the closely related fields of applied theatre and engaged art.

The dynamic triangle of a socially-engaged arts curriculum

How do artists, whose education typically focuses on the accumulation of craft skills, the cultivation of an intuitive formal sensitivity, or knowledge of conventional art history and theory prepare for the complex ethical questions that are raised by projects that take them into unfamiliar spaces and contexts?

(Kester 2004: 140)

The Curriculum Project began with a hypothesis with which most interviewees and survey respondents agreed: that a good engaged arts education contains three components of training – craft (the skills of art-making, including elements specific to such work including facilitation); scholarship (including reading, writing, reflecting, and researching underlying ideas, history, theory, and issues); and hands-on community-based experience – each of which must be well-developed. In The Curriculum Project report, Goldbard referred to this configuration as a dynamic triangle, whose three parts adhere through underlying democratic values and principles. In this spirit, one interviewee described the multi-faceted scholar–practitioner his applied theatre program in higher education hopes to produce:

Somebody who understands theory, even if not immersed in all aspects, and is aware of the historical antecedents and pedagogical, philosophical underpinnings of so much of what we do ... and what the perennial questions are to wrestle with and where to look to answer a range of other questions that will come up. They should be versed in research methodology and be as widely read as we can expect them to be over a period of a 36-credit program. At the same time they develop very concrete practical skills, particularly around facilitation, group-building, community development, and the practice of many different forms of theater and theatrical interventions, both in the studio and in community-based projects.[2]

Underdevelopment of any one component in the trinity, and the absence of democratic values, weaken the whole, which is greater than the sum of the parts.

But while engaged art requires a multi-dimensional education, many programs tend to be either strictly skills-based or too theoretical. As one interviewee said, "You get armchair scholars, who want to critique everything. They don't really know what the community is. You get people who just provide skills, conservatory training, and not the other components this field needs people to know." Sometimes this imbalance is the result of financial limitations. The administrator of a program that is strong in community engagement but weak in theory said, "We cannot afford to admit anyone who does not come without a certain level of social competence, awareness of economics, race, class, and gender, because there's nothing in our program yet that really prepares them for that."

I turn now to each of these three components.

Craft training

Engaged art does not require less craft than mainstream professional art; arguably it requires more. Trained artists are responsible for shaping collective expression when the participants lack not commitment and connection, but artistic means of expression. Such work depends upon two streams of training. One is a command of general community-based arts skills, such as group facilitation, story-gathering, and direction of collaborative work. The other is discipline-specific craft, which for theatre includes such areas as warm-up games and improvisation, also applicable to engaged art. People with both sets of theatre skills, whatever their credentials in academia or in mainstream art, need to be among those providing engaged art training in the studio as well as in the hands-on context.

Because learning a craft takes a great deal of time, there are some advantages to situating engaged programs within art schools (in the UK known as conservatoires) where students are already spending long hours in studio classes. A theatre major, for example, will have already begun developing a broad vocal and physical range, clear approaches to character development, and an understanding of how to shape monologues and dialogues. Young artists can apply these skills to community contexts and are frequently strengthened by the opportunity to share them in meaningful projects. New York University (NYU) acting teacher Rosemary Quinn, for example, focused a Theatre Skills and Ensemble Building class around community internship problem-solving. One student was preparing a clown contingent critiquing fast foods, which was to be part of a demonstration. Quinn had this student practice in class the facilitation skills that she would need in developing the piece. Students making theatre with children at an elementary school brought situations that had challenged them to Quinn's class to problem-solve. Their classmates suggested exercises to try, and ways to get the children to be more proactive, despite the school atmosphere rewarding acquiescence.

Another advantage of craft-based theatre programs is the positive atmosphere that they provide about the arts themselves, as a teacher in such a program noted:

> We don't have the disadvantage that most academic institutions have, of devaluing the arts. And unlike the conservatories, we don't put the arts in their own kind of ivory tower. We don't remove artists from the real world. We say, in effect, that art is a way to comprehend the world and make meaning in it.

The additional value of an engaged art education within a conservatory is stretching the parameters of theatre itself.

A downside of the art school context, however, is its tendency to separate technique from content. In the context of engaged art, technique is taught not for its own sake, but to facilitate expression of communally-meaningful content. And whereas culturally-specific traditions are important components for students coming from, or working with, non-mainstream communities, art schools may offer resistance to such practices when they fall out of mainstream notions of arts training. The non-Anglo director of a community-informed theatre company who we interviewed was glad that her daughter's conservatory program expected all their students to perform scenes from the European and white American canon. But she believed that her daughter and her daughter's non-Anglo classmates – and they concurred – also needed to do work coming from their own cultural roots. Artists who use culturally-specific methodologies in community settings, such as members of Roadside Theater, who assist people in identifying a culturally-grounded form to express their own communal stories, may be better trained in community-based art than graduates of many conservatory programs.

The notion of aesthetics also arises when folding engaged art training into conventional art schools. Aesthetics generally refers to a way of judging the qualities of an art experience, traditionally in such terms as beauty and good taste. Engaged artists do not seek to lower aesthetic standards, but rather to attain qualities of art appropriate to its goals. The underlying democratic values frequently find expression by shining a spotlight on people whose intelligence (for example, the refugees in *home land security* in chapter 3), and places whose beauty (such as particular spots in Syracuse, New York's neighborhoods discussed in chapter 6), are not instantly apparent. In contrast, some art-making systems call for the art object to be devoid of content, and focus rather on a general idea of beauty. Such criteria would be unproductive measures of an art form focused on local meaning and identity. Then, too, aesthetics may not be the highest priority of those who are motivated by a democratic impulse to expand whose expression is valued. If an inexperienced performer stumbles through her lines, but connects with the audience and brings attention to a compelling local issue, the fact of her giving voice to community needs tends to be valued above the way she communicates it.

Singularity about aesthetics is another drawback of some mainstream arts training. One of our interviewees, whose community-informed program is in a conventional arts training context, critiques such a stance while seeking more rigor in engaged art:

> We all know those "good theatre" kinds of statements. It devils me when it is simply used to crush the intention and to put up obstacles and road blocks. At the same time, the question of aesthetics is something that is dreadfully overlooked when it comes to community-based art making. As a field we need to be much more articulate and pro-active in getting the question of aesthetics on the table, so that we have an ability to stand up to the wind of conventional aesthetics.

Recognition of the need for its own aesthetic richness is a theme with many applied theatre commentators. In *Performance Affects*, James Thompson puts what anarchist Emma Goldman called "beautiful, radiant things" – such as affect, joy, and emotion – at the heart of applied theatre, and pulls away from a strictly utilitarian – effect-focused – emphasis (J. Thompson 2009: 1).

Increasingly, community-based artists seek a balance between exciting aesthetics and meaningful content with a high level of local participation. One arts practitioner told us,

> Aesthetics are really important in work that engages with communities. Not just to be replicating at a poorer level training that people don't have access to, but finding an artistic catalyst behind *their* creative work. There's a wide range of diverse cultural practices, such as Chuck Mike, whose work developed in Nigeria, and Augusto Boal in Brazil. But artistic possibilities are limited if we don't engage with contemporary indigenous practitioners on a first voice level.

In other words, one can uphold rich aesthetic standards that come from the cultures with which community groups are in tune.

Scholarship in an engaged art education

Engaged art challenges a deeply-entrenched myth about artists: that thinking gets in the way of creating. On the contrary, because engaged art goes beyond individual self-expression, other considerations arise. Given the interactive nature of engaged art, one needs sharp critical thinking skills so as to decide what technique to use in what situation. One must develop cultural sensitivity when community participants and artists are of different race, class, or circumstances. Sensitivity to the relationship with a particular audience or community calls upon skills that a conventional craft teacher may never have developed.

While there's little consensus about a set of intellectual components essential for all training, the following subjects are frequently taught as community-based arts scholarship: Freire- and Boal-inspired courses;[3] history and theory of community arts; principles and ethics of practice; race, class, and sexuality studies; feminist studies; community organizing history and theory; cultural policy; and community development history and theory.[4] Students learn about the history of art's potential, the development of related art forms and practices, ideas that drive the work, methods of research to collaborate with people around their identities and aspirations, the socio-economics of a given community, the issues under examination, and larger social, political, and ethical questions. They read, write, and reflect critically upon both theoretical and practical aspects of the work, studying why culture is arranged the way it is, and how policy regarding it can be changed.

Setting a standard curriculum may not be desirable, given the different points of focus of engaged art. A community organizer affiliated with higher education believes that engaged artists must pursue different scholarly paths accordingly:

> It's about rigor, it's understanding what it means to be a community organizer if you're saying you're one or, if you're saying you're anti-gentrification it's really understanding what gentrification means in its complexities. There's a scholarship component about what it is you're trying to change in the world if it's about social change and the history of those social movements gives you an analysis. It's learning how to develop an analysis and understanding enough content to be able to do that so you're not just dropping yourself into campaigns for something, but you have a theory of social change and you know how to act within it.

This is a good example of the hyphenated nature of engaged art, its positioning with one foot firmly grounded in each of several fields.

Whether combining art with organizing, therapy, education, or another discipline, the breadth of knowledge most engaged artists are expected to draw upon, like interdisciplinary programs in other areas, is not easy to master, given how much time it takes to stay current and produce work in one field. A touchstone for interdisciplinarity in the academy, where expertise in one's discipline is the gold standard, is that one must

170

nevertheless be grounded in deep knowledge about *something*.[5] Some programs integrate learning about theatre with one other body of knowledge. Buzz Alexander's much-respected program at the University of Michigan focuses on theatre and prison. Another practitioner who teaches in higher education imagines creating a master's program with one track in the arts, the other in community development. Those admitted need to have already mastered one or the other. They would take courses in the one they know least, as well as courses all together integrating the two.

Most people in the field agree that research needs to be part of such a curriculum. A director of color who directs a community arts organization noted that the art forms of *her* community were reflected in neither her university art courses nor the curriculum she was meant to teach to kids in public school. She thus began researching her family's cultural practices, and has since expanded that research to forms relevant to the diverse young people with whom she works. She brings that knowledge to her classrooms.

Critical thinking is also a necessary habit of the mind to cultivate in our work. The director of a program with a very balanced curriculum emphasizes the value of questioning, a classic tool of critical inquiry:

> It's important that our students also have a grasp of the questions that arise in the field. What does it mean to work in a community? What are the debates around your positioning of yourself? Are you a member of that community? How do you negotiate differences? What are the ethics of working with people and their stories and their experiences? We look at dimensions of cultural studies, some performance theory, the history of this work and antecedents both here and in other places such as the Latin American popular theater movement, for example. What is it that we stand on the shoulders of?

His words are sensitive to the community that arises around engaged art itself.

An important piece of engaged art scholarship is getting beyond one's own assumptions about social hierarchy. One professor we interviewed assigns Linda Tuhiwai Smith's book *Decolonizing Methodologies* (Smith 1999) so students experience a feminist, Maori, "first-nation" critique of Eurocentrism, the disciplines, and the Western system:

> I immediately have students try to locate their own subject positions and then begin to understand so-called "master narratives" or "master archives." So students understand that it's not simply black or white or a dualistic or binary in which they have to side with the good guys to work against the bad guys. We're all

171

complicated creatures who are affected by the various ways in which these hierarchies intersect in our lives. A book like that immediately creates attention to the dominant ways in which things operate. Not just the obvious things, but everyday practices, like assumptions of classroom relationships. I want to immediately create a space in which people can begin reflecting and talking about what's going on.

Becoming more conscious of their own assumptions, students are able to recognize inbred biases as they work with people different from themselves.

Reflection is a core component of engaged art training typically associated with classroom learning in higher education, and a site of the integration of the three components of the triangle (craft, scholarship, and community experience). A director of a community organization expressed hope that the university component would bring with it "a space in which critical issues are thought through that normally are not dealt with because of the crush of everyday practical matters." The arts in community contexts are highly dynamic; we make decisions as we go, with flexibility a core value. Without thinking about choices both during and after the process, we may miss the opportunity to learn from the experience. Many of our interviewees expressed the belief that practice without reflection is not a productive learning experience.

My own experience at the age of 21, co-facilitating a theatre workshop at a men's maximum security prison through membership in the NYC Street Theatre Company, is a case in point. While it's the experience that set me on a community-based arts path, there was never enough time for reflection, shared readings, or formal group discussion to put what was for me an overwhelming experience into a graspable context. Having never been confronted with an experience in such contrast with this country's claims of "liberty and justice for all," facilitating a drama workshop in that context, characterized by violence among the inmates and at the hands of the guards, turned my world on its head. That deeply informed how I set up internships for my students years later, with classroom time to reflect on their community-based practice.

Community engagement as a component of learning

The community engagement component of an applied art education is often strongest when directed by longtime practitioners of community-based art. Given the exigencies of academia, people who've taken the academic route will be hard-pressed to have had as much hands-on experience themselves. Numerous interviewees attested that they learned more about engaged art from mentors in the field than from formal education. Many engaged artists began as conventional practitioners, and gradually integrated their passion around certain issues into their art, or sought out a theoretical education to understand in more depth what they were encountering. Others began in related fields – community organizing, social work, education – and increasingly used art as a means towards achieving their goals.

Some practitioners advocate an immersion model of training, mirroring how they learned through hands-on experience, such as the program this interviewee set up:

> It's a month-long intensive where students come and live with the company in a community. The company members are both teachers and practitioners and the students are both students and practitioners and there are classes with the theatre's faculty and also guest faculty. At the same time the students and the teachers are together putting on a community-based play with the community that we're living in ... I was trying to recapture some of the intensity of the rural years of our company, living as well as working with the community ... Learning historical context, philosophical underpinnings, and all the aesthetic and political issues that are raised by community-engaged work are absolutely important, but I don't think that it can substitute for the experience of doing it.

But only some colleges and universities are flexible enough to accommodate artistic immersion experiences, given other courses the students need to take at the same time.

Nevertheless, there's general consensus that hands-on experience is an invaluable component of training. It sets up an iterative model of learning, where teachers respond to what students need as it comes up, as one practitioner/teacher describes:

> Students engaged in their own projects show us the letter they wrote to try to get a community partner on board or they tell us about the problems they are having. We dissect them together and point out the gaps and the abuses of privilege that are going on, or the assumptions being made. I'm so passionate about the practical being the essential component because it's where you start uncovering the real, not only the deep joys of this work, but the incredibly potent challenges.

Because challenges present themselves in very distinct ways, learning how to deal with them is best accomplished on the ground. Such work relies on skilled mentors, and a set of values on the basis of which solutions are selected, and which may be best articulated in a reflective context to the side of the work itself.

Learning by doing is not just a way to encounter the real problems, but also a way to de-romanticize the field. In one higher education program, students complete a five-semester community-based internship so, as an administrator of that program describes, they can "fall in and then out of love" with their site, and thus understand the whole cycle of work at such an organization. Five semesters, 10 to 20 hours a week, is also long enough for the students to become of real value to the organization, so the principle of reciprocity is strong.

Imbedded in community contexts, such programs are also well-situated to extend professional development opportunities to community partners, thus embodying the core value of reciprocity. Staff can be asked to make the time to participate in workshops when students are dedicating significant hours to them. One college offers regular day-and-a-half-long sessions:

> We find a room, buy food, pay for a guest presenter, ask the community organizations that we work with to bring a senior member of their staff, the graduate student intern, and a youth participant and come as a team and then work all together – doing creative work, thinking work, sharing and talking and networking.

The willingness of that administrator's institution to provide training for students and community members together is rare. In my experience, institutions fear that students will question why they are paying for their education when the community partners are not. But, given that those partners are providing their lived experience as part of the students' education, the situation is really more akin to barter.

Another value of the hands-on, community component of the training for community members and students alike is the relationship-making between people from different backgrounds. I have often been the first Jewish person that people in certain neighborhoods have met. As a 15-year-old, I was the first white person a group of kids on Chicago's Southside had ever seen in person. (One of the first questions I was asked was how I got "those spots" on my face, which were in fact freckles.) At the same time that people regard each other's differences, they also have a chance to discover commonalities. Cultural mapping, a favorite exercise in community-based arts circles, is a fascinating way to recognize similarities and differences that don't necessarily meet the eye.[6]

But students must be armed with enough real skills and sensitivity to go into communities. Some teachers prepare students for at least a semester before placing them in neighborhood contexts. An engaged artist who does residencies in higher education spends the first semester giving students the tools that she's spent 30 years developing. Then, in the second semester, she has the students apply them to something that they're already involved with on campus. "And then," she says, "maybe I'll trust them in community."

174

Values and principles underlying training

Engaged art is not value-free; more than a collection of artistic, cultural, and organizing skills, courses, and experiences, its education must be grounded in a perspective and purpose that includes and goes beyond the creation of art. Some practitioners see social justice as a useful way to identify the over-arching drive of this field – using one's art to support groups of people in their quest to participate fully in society. Others prefer the terminology of cultural democracy, also emphasizing the basic right to have a voice in determining their life's direction, regardless of cultural identity, race, gender, physical capacity, or class.[7]

By whatever language, engaged art is characterized by a high level of par-ticipation, whether in early phases of researching and building the art work, in the presentation phase, or in activities following, and often in all three. For people frequently get more out of making art than seeing the fruits of other people's creativity. That is, the process is often the phase of greatest insight, even more so than the product. Principles underlying the way the process unfolds include flexibility, respect, and good listening. Inclusion is another value. People are welcome whether or not they have artistic train-ing and no matter what their economic status, educational level, or racial/ ethnic identity. Reciprocity – a mutually nourishing relationship between artists and other participants – is also fundamental. The quality of partici-pation and the efficacy of the project for community partners must be equal to what the artists gain for themselves.

The scholarly component can bring to the fore values manifested in community experiences. A long-time professor of community-based arts suggested how:

> I don't think people are poorly motivated when they go out to a hospital where kids are dying, I think they feel that. But they may not be thinking about which hospital is accessible to them and which kids don't have hospitals. So how do you take the experience further and get into the economic analysis and look at agency on both sides? And begin to think about structures? Wonderful people do won-derful helpful work; I have no critique of that at all. What happens to those kids in that hospital when students come in and make them laugh and give them spirit is fabulous. But how will the students come to think about the kids who aren't there in that hospital?

Making the connection from the personal experience of those kids in that hospital to larger questions about access and health care is the kind of think-ing that educators committed to social justice values are likely to nurture.

Foregrounding the values underlying this work helps students discover what drives their passion, and thus helps them find their path in the world.

I've had many students recognize *how* they wanted to work when they encountered Freireian dialogical learning in practice, with its sharp contrast to an expert-driven "banking method" in which participants are objects receiving, not subjects co-enunciating a direction. Approached as an educational experience with concomitant analysis and reflection, the practice refers back to values in the interconnected loop of engaged scholarship.

Leaders of community art who came of age in the 1960s/early 1970s influenced values underlying the contemporary engaged art landscape. As one such educator put it:

> Social justice was respectable then and now it's not. There's this language about compassion exhaustion. Before the yuppie revolution, before it was hip to be rich, I grew up anti-commodity. I thought that it was good to shop in secondhand stores. And if you were a bourgeois person who dropped out you wanted to be poor. It used to be that community work grew out of work in communities and now universities are turning it into something academic and theoretical rather than a lived practice.

This last speaker suggests that a crisis in values sometimes occurs through situating engaged work in higher education, distant from the inherently activist nature of engagement.

Relatedly, mainstream US higher education's emphasis on individualism and culturally specific (tribal, historically black, etc.) colleges' commitment to community-oriented curricula represents another values clash. A tribal college president distinguishes between the two:

> It's something educational systems have a very difficult time doing, because they want to deal with the individual ... but we have a different culture; we have a different language basis; we have some different viewpoints about art, and we don't segregate things. If you take an anthropological look, very few people ever refer to the ongoing change in dynamics among themselves as culture, but that's what it is. The artistic parts of that tie directly back to the concept of environment, economics, spirituality ... erasing this boundary line between the college age students and working with the whole family ... When you penetrate into the K-12 system or some other context the education is going to be a lot better.

This emphasis on individual achievement characterizes many colleges and universities, despite the "public good" rhetoric familiar on most of their websites. It begins when the degree of competition to being admitted is promoted as evidence of a school's excellence. Tribal colleges and histori- cally black colleges and universities (HBCUs) serve students with an understanding that they need to take what they learn back to better their communities. In such a system, the school tries to admit everyone who wanted to come. It is a less self-serving conception of education, valuing more serving society. The two goals are not necessarily mutually exclusive.

Higher education as the site of engaged art pedagogy

Colleges and universities are anchor institutions in their communities, not constructed to move from one place to another. For some, this leads to more than a geographical relationship with the rest of the community – also a social and pedagogical one, connecting locally through service projects (generally extracurricular and more about what the student does for an organization than a reciprocal relationship),[8] curricular initiatives, and faculty research in collaboration with people whose expertise lies beyond higher education's walls. At the same time as the institution contributes locally, students are enriched by experiencing their education's value in real-world situations and learning from people on the ground.

The presence of community engagement on US campuses reflects a number of histories. In some cases, public engagement bespeaks the maturation of the generation that sought a more relevant education for themselves as students in the 1960s and 1970s, and who now occupy the roles of professors and administrators. Land grant institutions were estab- lished on property provided to each state by the federal government in order to provide practical higher education to working-class people, in keeping with provisions of the Morrill Acts of 1862 and 1890. Still other institutions, such as faith-based schools, HBCUs, and tribal colleges, are steeped in values calling for a vigorous relationship with the community. Community-engaged scholarship is part of conversations about changing definitions of what it means to be educated. On the self-serving end of the spectrum, colleges need to raise money, and one strategy for interesting local funders is contributing to local life. Beyond the fact of campus– community connections, one must interrogate the underlying values in such relationships, asking how power, money, resources, and decision-making are shared. On the other end of the spectrum, educating students for the public good, contributing to public life is both a means and an end of higher education.

Advantages of learning engaged art in higher education

Situating engaged art pedagogy in higher education can be an opportunity for students to make an ethical analysis of a system they themselves are in. Some instructors thus begin with the school itself as the first community to

177

explore with students. Albeit temporary members, they are nevertheless part of their school community in ways they may not be of the neighborhood where they work on projects. In the Grassroots Performance Project, part of the housing forum in which some students participated was educating other students about the impact on long-time, lower-income residents of the rents students are willing to pay in NYU's immediate neighborhood.

Some visions of higher education fit squarely within engaged art's value system, and are furthered by respected and articulate academic leaders who have access to the national stage. Nancy Cantor, Chancellor and President of Syracuse University, for example, has written extensively about reframing the university as a public good, providing the institutional context in which engaged arts can flourish. (See "Chancellor's speeches" on the Syracuse University website, www.syr.edu/chancellor/speeches.) She has put the resources of that university into initiatives intended to serve campus and community alike. (See chapter six for a sense of Syracuse University's commitment to local revitalization efforts.) The role of such high-profile advocates cannot be overestimated.

The opportunity to study the disciplines into which students may want to insert engaged art is abundantly available through higher education. Especially in liberal arts programs, where young people are expected to get a rounded education, courses in the arts and others in, say, environmental studies, urban policy, or writing are immediately available. Oral history classes may include community-based story-gathering. Through immersion in these various courses, students draw on the expertise of other classmates as well as other teachers, and bring this depth of knowledge to community arts contexts.

Courses that accompany hands-on arts engagement can illuminate the students' experience and sensitize them to people's lives. For example, some HOME, New Orleans? (HNO) students (see chapter five) were taking a course in cultural policy at the same time as they worked in neighborhood projects. Rather than see the poverty they encountered as either inexplicable or a reflection of the people's lack of motivation, they had some means of understanding root causes of where resources were and weren't placed, what jobs were available to people at what levels of education, and who had access to such education. The community-based experiences also added value to a range of professions for which students were preparing. A pre-med student experienced the importance of relationships with people rather than a purely "service" approach to community engagement, which she said affected how she thought about the kind of doctor she wanted to be.

Students engaged in community-based projects, in both the arts and other disciplines, come into contact with possible application of their studies post-graduation. The NYU Grassroots Performance Project included a vocal training course taught by Jonathan Hart Makwaia, which explored people's individual voices as well as group singing and musical composition. One student wrote a song in three parts, "The Lower East Side Anthem," which opened housing forum sessions in that neighborhood, and combined short scenes of difficult housing challenges with concrete information to solve them. The group was invited to sing the anthem at the GOLES (Good Old Lower East Side) benefit, and it was also sung by the graduating class of a local elementary school where several of the other students were interns. These students thus learned about uses of their musical training that were broader than for strictly theatrical settings.

Cross-institutional projects provide an additional context for students to learn across racial divides as does community-based work generally. *HNO* brought students from two HBCUs, Dillard and Xavier, together with those from Tulane, a largely white "Research One" institution. As Ron Bechet and Amy Koritz, professors from Xavier and Tulane respectively, in leadership roles with *HNO*, have written,

> We discovered that the Tulane students felt that they were being stereotyped by the Xavier students as "rich, spoiled white kids." Meanwhile, they expressed the opinion that the Xavier and Dillard students were held to lower standards and didn't work as hard as they did. Issues of race and class were raised and discussed in ways that may not have been possible without the experiences of the course. One student noted that she felt very uncomfortable as an African-American woman in her [community] placement, and learned how important it was to continue to help others see how narrowly they see African-Americans.
>
> (Bechet and Koritz 2008)

Building relationships among students and faculty across institutions in New Orleans has proven as important as developing community in and across neighborhoods, and as significant a component of the students' education.

Engaged art education also offers opportunities for faculty development. While some faculty members are nomadic, others try to stay at the same institution for a good stretch of time, especially if they have children in local schools. This sets up an opportunity for them to build deep local relationships and cultivate partnering skills over time. A criticism voiced in Curriculum Project interviews was that inexperienced faculty members were assigned to teach community-based art courses. Such teachers have the chance to develop into decent facilitators when working on multi-year projects such as *HNO*. Not only different students, but also rotating faculty, facilitating and team teaching, on a long- or short-term basis, have participated each year. Experienced faculty from one institution mentored those newer to community arts from partnering institutions.

Various higher educational resources are made accessible to community partners as well. The Grassroots Performance Project I co-facilitated at NYU provides examples. Partnering with GOLES, a housing organization for low-income people, several students developed scenes about the housing rights of New York City renters, and prepared a brochure to hand out after performances. Among them, the team of students had excellent skills in design, layout, and writing, and knowledge about urban housing issues, effectively translating what they'd learned from GOLES itself into a useful takeaway. More generally, students in community-based internships help prepare information materials and write newsletters, publicity copy, and grants. They share their access to libraries, technological resources, and networks, and help find financial support. Especially given limited public and private funds, higher education as a partner should not be cast aside lightly. Higher education can also provide a steady stream of young people with the commitment, resources, and desire to learn and contribute.

For most full-time faculty, higher education offers opportunities for exchange through conferences, institutionally-supported leave, and sabbaticals. Increasingly, university-supported gatherings in the community arts field include community partners. Higher education legitimates what people know, and is often a prerequisite for achieving job security. Even the most modest college or university fellowship for partnering artists may open the door to new avenues of employment. Institutions of higher education have space for workshops, guest artist housing, and meetings that can be shared.

When designed as learning experiences, engaged arts projects set up through colleges and universities are less reliant on outside funding than those generated by community-based organizations, since student tuition and faculty employment cover some of the costs. In the workshop phase of partnerships, the exchange of student and faculty participation for community expertise and integration replaces the exchange of money. Faculty are expected to produce and, when recognized as knowledge-building opportunities, community-based projects may be beneficiaries of research grants. Additional funding that is harder to access, however, is often needed to sustain projects. Hence learning to fund-raise is also a significant component of an engaged art education.

Obstacles to situating engaged art training in higher education

US higher education is not generally perceived as community-friendly. Typically described as the ivory tower, much of what it offers is far too expensive for general consumption, and its discourse can be off-putting and out of touch with real-world needs. Higher education is seen by many as aloof from the people beyond its walls, its contract with society broken. In the USA, historically known as a place of opportunity for all, education is now less often seen as the door to a better future regardless of family or class background, and more often considered out of reach for people of modest means.

Universities and communities operate in different time zones. Community life is continuous, not shaped by the semester, while particular constituents are only available at particular times, say during the day (retirees) or after school (youth). Students in higher education organize time and commitments within 10- to 15-week-semester segments, and must work around other intense courses and work schedules even within those parameters. Such use of time supports a concentrated pedagogical model better than it does the organic development of community-based projects, in which learning is more diffuse. These differences are reflected in Bechet and Koritz's account of student responses to the first iteration of "Building Community through the Arts," the course that accompanied their work in the different New Orleans neighborhoods:

> In an anonymous course evaluation ... [students] consistently expressed respect for what we were trying to do and felt they had benefited from the class ... [One] student noted, "I think the course was theoretically a good idea, but in practice it was less organized and communication with teachers was sometimes difficult. That being said, the class was a great experience." Another student wrote that the class "has good, noble intentions, which is respectable." This student also commented, "My understanding of community definitely has changed. I realized how proud people are of their communities and how two neighboring communities can seem like different countries. Integration is also harder than it seems."
>
> (Bechet and Koritz 2008)

These students suggest both the challenge and value of participating in a course spread across neighborhoods and classrooms. Like *HNO* assessments, students' Curriculum Project survey responses from around the country frequently reflected the difficulty of being available enough to make their hands-on activities worth the time it took to set up and get going, and the challenge of fitting both theory and practice into one course.

Professors, too, are stretched thin by the amount of time required for community engagement, in this case when it is the subject of one's research, as this interviewee attests:

> It takes time to document the history of community in a way that is empowering to a wide range of people, especially the youth in and around the community. To jet in and jet out, to think that one has represented that place, I don't think is really possible. There is

a fundamental problem with the academic production of knowledge, especially when it deals with people and communities.

This scholar calls for research to serve its subject community as well as the scholar's individual academic agenda. He also suggests that academic production of knowledge does not easily accommodate how knowledge is generated in community collaborations.

The above scholar alludes to philosophical contradictions as well. As one seasoned university administrator states, "Universities are not structured to be permeable; they are metaphorically gated communities in terms of rules, structures, and ownership of intellectual property." Yet the value of reciprocity underlying engaged art must stretch to the formation and uses of knowledge as well.

Numerous interviewees criticized universities for behaving imperiously toward their communities. In my own experience, NYU was the source of much community rage and frustration as it purchased more and more land and buildings. Similarly, Columbia University's expansion uptown in New York City, and similar trends at urban universities all across the country, drive up real estate costs as they spread into adjacent areas. While not controlled by those teaching community arts, these realities create tension between modestly-scaled community-based courses and projects and the formidable impact of the institution. In response, some faculty try and make even a modest intervention in the institution's policy regarding the surrounding community.

The nature of teaching community-based arts contrasts with traditional higher education pedagogy. One professor described opening a space where students and community participants share the teaching role in both the community practice and the classroom. Integrating learning with teaching so that everyone does some of each is a principle of such work, and is necessary for sustainability. It's Freirean pedagogy, and comes from situations where everyone is needed to take on leadership. But it is anathema to a top-down view of education or a narrow conception of expertise, and means valuing the ability to facilitate co-learning as much as a professor's material knowledge-base. Another interviewee noted that the person who "delivers" education for community-based art veers from the traditional notion of teacher as disciplinary expert to someone who brings and organizes different experiences, which may range from putting students in contact with a local minister to a young rap artist. The purpose is to bring in people who come from aspects of the path that students need to understand in order to make good choices and decisions in diverse community settings.

Then, too, some of the qualities that make strong community-based artists in the field, such as affirmation of community assets, feel lax to students in rigorous conservatory programs, who want to be challenged to take their craft further, not complimented excessively for what they can already do. I once hired a very accomplished and much beloved community artist to facilitate a project with university students and neighborhood partners. His constant affirmation of the students' work, so important in community contexts, was a source of student annoyance, who felt he was not sufficiently rigorous with them. Teaching by affirmation is exacerbated by the economics of learning in higher education: the costs place pressure on students to make sure they are getting "their money's worth," leading to some treating teachers as service-providers. And defying the stereotype that those who can, do, while those who can't, teach, teaching community arts is very much a doing, and deserves to be valued as such. The point is, the very place where training happens reinforces values that may be in contradiction with the values of the program.

Higher education-instigated community work risks taking a colonization-like stance. An arts practitioner with a university appointment noted, "When they come into communities, it borders on exploitation at worst and at best it's sort of like the community becomes an educative moment." That is, the university team may objectify a community situation narrowly for what students can learn from it, rather than broadly for what both sides might gain from working together. The goal is to make an educative moment useful for all parties, so the community is not the students' guinea pig.

Then there are challenging, while potentially transformative, issues dealing with race and class. Sometimes students participating in engaged arts projects are middle- and upper-class and/or white, in contrast to many of the people in the communities with whom they collaborate. Such work requires sensitivity to diverse cultural strengths that may not have been nurtured at school. For example, is the oral tradition as valued as the written word? Then, too, the values of higher education are sometimes more normed to the dominant culture than to marginalized groups. Higher education prepares students to compete, which contradicts the field's commitment to encouraging inclusion. And as costs skyrocket, universities are less and less places to experience diversity.

Seeing themselves as a business, some institutions are wary of the term "social justice", fearing it will make their program appear too radical. Some stakeholders doubt if the university system is compatible with issues of social change at all, because as one higher education-based administrator remarks, "Higher education in our capitalist system has become itself consumer driven from both the institution and the students. That gets in the way of a lot of the things that we're trying to teach and the work we try to promote in the world." Moreover, given the emphasis on consensus and dialogue embedded in democratic values, a social justice thrust may appear to demonstrate a preconceived agenda. In an effort to be maximally inclusive, one arts practitioner noted that "more profound social change can happen when people come together across various lines, including class, than only preaching to the choir or engaging one segment of a community." The language one uses to describe one's program will be seen as an invitation or obstacle to participating.

Higher education does not always value the knowledge generated outside its walls. More than one interviewee referred to higher education's ivory tower stance – its constituents not knowing what the community needs, even as they presume to think they are experts with everything to give. Relatedly, the missions of higher education and community-based organizations tend to be different. Another practitioner based in higher education finds that

> in community organizations, consciousness is stronger than in the university-based projects ... That's their mission, they're in the community and they're arts organizations that are advocates for their community and they have that activist consciousness. It is about self-determination and power relations on their constituents' behalf. There's a danger when you get into the university that you're removed from that and you can tell that even if you used to be that, suddenly you find yourself a "service provider." And you know, that's really the work of transforming a university.

It's almost ironic that scholars who do the work most meaningful to them in community contexts often discover they must work equally in their higher education communities in order to generate the institutional changes that support the community work.

Some university-based scholars do not see the practical study of the arts as valid subjects of a serious education at all. James Thompson, a director of the Centre for Applied Theatre Research at the University of Manchester in England, observes that the applied version of any discipline, be it mathematics, anthropology, physics, or theatre, tends to be contrasted with, and deemed lower than, its theoretical counterpart: "they are not suitable subjects for the academies but the lesser, applied versions of the 'real'" (Thompson 2003: 17). Some artists who value conventional training also dislike utilitarian or applied uses of art, assuming that a work can not be aesthetically exciting at the same time.

Even when engaged arts programs are established, some never develop beyond an immediate impulse to recognize the relatedness among a set of courses already on the books. Consider the arrested development of a minor in applied theatre that I shepherded just so far but no farther. In the late 1980s, teaching "political theatre" classes at NYU, I was approached by a group of students making a plea: It's fine to learn about artists motivated by social as much as aesthetic reasons, but what about doing it ourselves? Thus I developed my first "Theatre in the Community" class, which was soon joined by a plethora of other courses in the same spirit. In the mid-1990s, Una Chaudhuri, a very broad-minded Drama Department chair, noticed a through line connecting the various courses I and a few others were teaching. These included Community-based Theatre, The Actor Teacher, Radical Street Performance, Theatre and Therapy, Global Perspectives on Applied Theatre, Boal and Beyond, and others. Why not, Chaudhuri asked, make a ring around these courses and call it a minor? I only too happily agreed. The department had over a thousand *majors*, over 90% studying acting, so introducing alternative options for a life in the theatre seemed an ethical imperative, as well as a specific way to harvest the specialties of several faculty members. We described the program as a minor in applied theatre, reflecting "the growing recognition among professionals in a range of fields that theatrical techniques and practices have wide and vital applications in fields outside the theatre as traditionally conceived, including education, medicine, therapy, political activism, community work, and social services" (http://drama.tisch.nyu.edu/object/dr_minor. html). That simple act of noting kinship among pre-existing courses signaled to students excited by one such course a set of related others.

However, while a good way to *begin* a minor, merely highlighting what exists is not a way to *establish* a coherent program. One needs to be intentional, but quite a few programs are not: typically such classes are added to pre-existing curricula with standing faculty, many of whom lack community-based arts expertise. As one administrator we interviewed put it, "The challenging thing about my program is that we started a community arts concentration in an already existing arts management program that has faculty with really no background in community cultural development." Moving such programs to the next step requires money and the will to hire additional specialized faculty.

Moreover, some programs established with a strong conservatory component seek to institute applied theatre programs as a way to cut out students a year or two into the program without losing their tuition money. In such cases, more students are accepted than can fruitfully be accommodated, and applied theatre is seen as a place to move those who don't make the cut. This is a damaging approach that sends the message that applied theatre is a lower form of art than mainstream models.

Also of concern in institutionalizing community-based art education in higher education is that academic credentials may become necessary to make a career in this work. That is worrying, both in terms of what a credential conveys – who is setting the bar? – and also because not everybody goes, or needs to go, to college in order to become proficient in engaged art. Indeed, the community context is often the crucible where people who identify with the issues addressed rise to leadership positions as resources to solve problems become available. What they know from a life of experience cannot be taught.

Finally, engaged art as part of higher education will thrive or falter according to whether or not such activities "count" toward faculty promotion and tenure. Traditionally, faculty applying for tenure prepare dossiers with three categories of accomplishments to assess, valued in decreasing order: scholarship, teaching, and service. Generally, faculty have been expected to represent community projects in which they participate as service, despite the fact that such experiences may have been the basis of their research and scholarship, and have enlivened their teaching. Junior faculty have traditionally been counseled to wait until they have tenure to spend time in community pursuits.

Numerous strategies have been developed to articulate a place for public scholarship and practice within promotion and tenure guidelines. One is articulating a more expansive definition of scholarship itself. Ernest Boyer's seminal text *Scholarship Reconsidered* (Boyer 1990) articulates an expanded notion of scholarship that includes some of the activities hitherto regarded as service, asking, "Can we define scholarship in ways that respond more adequately to the urgent new realities both within the academy *and beyond?*" (Boyer 1990: 3; italics mine). Another way to expand promotion and tenure is by using national organizations that support public scholarship and practice to leverage local decisions. Julie Ellison and Tim Eatman (2008) wrote a report addressing promotion and tenure for public scholarship in the cultural disciplines under the auspices of the organization I direct, Imagining America: Artists and Scholars in Public Life. The report describes the dilemma publicly-engaged artists and scholars in the academy face, and offers concrete recommendations as well as a jumping-off point for an action-oriented process.

Assessing engaged art education

Engaged art programs typically assess student learning, but benefits to community partners are seldom as deliberately measured. For engaged art training to thrive, the value of the experience for all stakeholders must be seriously considered. Did the project effectively communicate an issue that those involved are facing? Did it involve the people who were targeted? Was the process of making it valuable and, as Thompson might ask, as affective as it was effective? Was progress made on solving the problem? Did people expand their networks in useful ways through the process? Were people with informal knowledge valued for their contribution? Was the project carried out in such a way as to make its sustainability likely? All these questions are seminal to a project's success and might be looked at, as scholar Bruce Burgett has suggested, as engagement goals.[9]

Learning goals can be situated within engagement goals: Is the student's capacity to engage with a broad range of people enhanced through the program? Is their practice deepened through applying the techniques they've been learning? Have their leadership skills been enhanced through the experience of collaborating on issues as they arise organically? Can they talk and write about the experience in such a way as to contribute to the field, and to bring it more respect and legitimization, more support and recognition, and more legibility to people in related fields? Can they challenge their audiences and open eyes, pointing out problems that insiders need to consider at the same time as recognizing insider knowledge? Can they communicate to policy-makers? Dwight Conquergood, for example, used to speak on behalf of gang members to Chicago courts, explaining that the culture of gangs is an asset for a young person alone in certain neighborhoods, as well as a problem.

One artist/educator we interviewed described how the underlying values of an engaged art project infuse the whole, and shape assessment:

> The focus is always the same: project-based, learner-centered, driven by diversity and what the art work is to achieve – and it's measured by that ... It is going to be evaluated by its relationship to the public, its carrying out of the goals that students set for themselves, which might be lowering the carbon footprint in one neighborhood. If it means building radio towers, they'll build radio towers. If it means putting a concert pianist on the roof, they'll do that. But the measurement will be, Is this an effective way to approach this?

She is articulating engaged art as part of an ecological system, and as such reasserting the tradition of art tightly woven within the life of a community.

It's important to assess engaged art projects according to one's own hyphenated goals, at once art and something else. If the planning process was thorough, the goals of such projects for all concerned have been well-articulated and will be the basis for assessment. Sometimes activating a community is the top goal of a project. Whereas craft may be weak in the early stages of such a project, performance can still be worthwhile for participants speaking on their own behalf. The significance of creating art at all in what are often difficult circumstances may trump waiting to achieve a certain aesthetic level. Getting people to show up regularly, believe their contribution is important, and begin to imagine what more rigorous craft might produce, means that the longer people keep at it, the better the chance that the art will improve. Establishing this broad sense of value in the educational phase will mean richer work when students become practitioners.

Infusing such values into engaged art practice and assessment must be deliberate, given the dominance of commercial values in much of the art world. As one interviewee who teaches visual arts in a university noted, students generally learn that "a successful career would mean selling their work to major collectors, be they individuals, galleries or major museums. So, they're object makers." This is a less complex conception of the artist than typifies engaged art.

Continuing, she points out how a curriculum absorbed with ideas about formal qualities of art, and leaving out values, context, and community engagement, sets the goals of an education:

> The European bias that the fine arts departments have developed sets up a segmented model of teaching. We would teach line, form, color, rhythm and the sum of it all would in the end be a perfect competition. None of it taught people what to say or how to say it or what was important to say. The only thing we did well was self-expression. And so that became increasingly self-indulgent and being interested in my self-expression beyond anything else and the problem was that it bred these art for art's sake sort of notions. It still did not leave you with a winning ticket to a creative approach.

Evaluating what such students learn would be unlikely to include questions of meaning and engagement. She goes on to analyze the problem with such an approach:

> We segment things, we break it down and we don't teach the whole person. We don't look at what they bring to the table, what they have inherently in their history and their nature that could be incredibly powerful tools upon which to act, which is the spring of the creative life.

This last interviewee puts the emphasis on discovering what each person has to contribute, in the ecological sense of where she comes from culturally and socially. It is this creative tension between what the individual artist brings and how she is a vehicle for a socially necessary expression that characterizes engaged art.

Finally, assessment must address the contradiction that, while hands-on community engagement is the most valued component of such an education, those who provide the venues and mentorship outside the university are typically under-recognized and under-supported. Why not draw a wider circle encompassing everywhere necessary learning takes place, and find ways to credentialize the entire system? Why not institutionalize a model of student learning that scholar Randy Martin calls "university without walls", and describes as follows:

> Community arts activists, organizations, and movements bear tremendous knowledge of cultural traditions, aesthetic forms, leadership in crafting and sustaining an organization, mobilizing

constituencies, disseminating and documenting work. Some of this is formalized in business plans, position papers, and other documents, some of it remains tacit knowledge. Across the country (and internationally) many people in all manner of settings have a formidable understanding of how this work gets done. The idea of a national University without Walls is to partner universities and community and cultural workers to make this knowledge legible and available to the broadest committed publics.

(Randy Martin, "University Without Walls,"
email, February 14, 2009)

This model gives equal value to both university- and community-based components, and appropriately remunerates community organizations as pedagogical partners.

The engaged artists featured throughout this book epitomize the fruits of the dynamic triangle. They have a command of craft, a critical analysis, and experience interacting with people in whose name the work is created and who, in most cases, have participated in making it. They are committed to the values of cultural democracy. The art they make contains the dimensions of craft, scholarship, and community engagement. Who'd have thought one could integrate as many ideas into a play as popular as Tony Kushner's *Angels in America*? How would Brecht have crafted his dramaturgy without a theory of epic theatre, informed by ideas spanning Marx, Hegel, and various forms of popular entertainment? Boal built on Brecht; and Wangh, Schutzman, and Aviles built on Boal. We all stand on the shoulders of those who preceded us, transmitted through the body and craft, the mind and scholarship, and the interrelationships with people striving for a more perfect world.

The curriculum project interviewees

Our thanks to the following individuals who gave so generously of their time and insights:

Buzz Alexander, University of Michigan, Prison Creative Arts Project, Ann Arbor, MI

Arnold Aprill, Chicago Arts Partnerships in Education (CAPE), Chicago, IL

Andrea Assaf, New WORLD Theater, University of Massachusetts, Amherst, MA

Caron Atlas, independent consultant, Arts & Democracy Project, Center for Civic Participation, Brooklyn, NY

Judy Baca, University of California at Los Angeles and Social and Public Art Resource Center (SPARC), Venice, CA

Ron Bechet, Xavier University, New Orleans, LA

Nancy Cantor, Syracuse University, Syracuse, NY

Nicole Garneau, Columbia College Chicago, Arts in Youth and Community Development, Chicago, IL

Pam Heinz, Mary Ann Shaw Center for Public & Community Service, Syracuse University, Syracuse, NY

Nick Jaffe, *Teaching Artist Journal*, Chicago, IL

Erica Kohl, Institute of the Study of Social Change, University of California, Berkeley, CA

Bob Leonard, Virginia Tech, Blacksburg, VA

Liz Lerman, Liz Lerman Dance Exchange, Takoma Park, MD

Sonia BasSheva Mañjon, Wesleyan University, Middletown, CT

Randy Martin, New York University, New York, NY

Susan Perlstein, National Center for Creative Aging, Washington, DC and Brooklyn, NY

Bill Rauch, Oregon Shakespeare Festival, Ashland, OR

Nick Rabkin, Center for Arts Policy, Columbia College Chicago, Chicago, IL

Michael Rohd, Sojourn Theatre, Portland, OR and Northwestern University, Evanston, IL

Rosalba Rolón, Pregones Theater, Bronx, NY

Jim Shanley, Fort Peck Community College, Poplar, MT

Judith Tannenbaum, WritersCorps, El Cerrito, CA

Jack Tchen, New York University, New York, NY

Carlton Turner, Alternate ROOTS, M.U.G.A.B.E.E., Raymond, MS

Roberta Uno, Ford Foundation, New York, NY

Marta Moreno Vega, Franklin H. Williams Caribbean Cultural Center African Diaspora Institute, New York, NY

Chris Vine, Creative Arts Team, City University of New York, New York, NY

Billy Yalowitz, Temple University, Philadelphia, PA

Workbook

Beginning engaged art partnerships

Entering community partnerships for engaged art projects requires a great deal of initial planning. The following exercises are designed to practice the hands-on process of building a new project. The first two are role-play exercises in which participants enact partners in the planning stage of a collaboration. There are many ways to enact a role-play; by all means draw on the expertise in the room, applying the improvisational techniques familiar to the participants, or try one of the following.

1   Agree upon a possible project focus for the purpose of the exercise; say, developing community-based performances and follow-up discussions to address the need to clean up a local lake. Let's say that the people who've come together to discuss it include a local activist group, a few native Americans committed to the clean-up of their sacred places including this lake, an arts professor, and at least one student. Give everyone a role on a folded piece of paper, including at least one participating student and one faculty member from the university, at least one engaged and one skeptical community partner, at least one participating artist, and a keen observer who doesn't say anything but just analyzes the power dynamic and then reports back. Take a few minutes to fill out each of the roles.

Set a modest amount of time to perform a scene in which the players try to arrive at the shape of the collaboration. State the project's goals and an aesthetic structure that might support that. Discuss who the actors and audiences might be, and what will attract them to participate. Take an inventory of artistic methods that potential partners already know, and ascertain if any of them might serve this project. If not, determine who else you might bring in, or how you might otherwise expand your collective toolbox. Think through the intellectual needs of the research. What must one know about the ecology of the lake and the history of toxic dumping in order to address it competently? What courses could be generated as a structure for student participation and the furthering of research? Think about how you would assess success in the project, and what benchmarks along the way would indicate that you are on a good path.

Discuss some of the underlying values you agree to uphold in the course of the collaboration. Figure out who has the money, which already creates a power imbalance. Set up challenges such as: the university having all of the money; a faculty or staff member who doesn't want to get too involved; someone who hopes the project works out but doesn't want to be impli-cated in any problems that may arise. Perhaps enact a second scene in which the principals report back to the funder. In setting up the role-play, go for conflict and dramatic moments, bringing antagonists together just as characterizes drama generally.

One of the most important lessons to experience here is that you don't have to be afraid of confrontation and difference. That's what has to be negotiated. In order to tease out this and other insights, follow the role-play with reporting on what happened from the point of view of each different character. Focus on issues reflecting the project's principles and values, such as, are we creating a truly equitable partnership? Discuss dilemmas each actor experienced in the scene, and brainstorm how they might have worked through them.

191

2   Michael Rohd facilitates an exercise to practice engaging a potential but as-yet-unconvinced partner, which works as follows. Workshop participants make two circles, one inside the other, with the same number of people in each. People in the two circles face each other to make partnerships. Each describes to the other a community arts project in which they are engaged or which they are just beginning. Then each identifies one prospective, significant partner who has not yet bought in to the project. Then all the people in the inner circle rotate one person to the right so they are facing a new person in the outer circle. The people in the inner circle describe their character to the new partner in 30 seconds and then the new partner portrays them in a role-play in which the teller tries to get them to buy in. After a few minutes, the role-play ends and the people who played the characters give the tellers feedback on their efforts to bring them in. Then the other half of the people do the same exercise around their unconvinced potential partner. Again, the people playing the characters give the tellers feedback about their persuasive efforts.

3   Another way to think through partnerships, especially at a project's outset, is to articulate in writing the principles upon which the collaboration is based. As disagreements arise later, agree to go back to this statement of principles as the basis for finding solutions. Include the following, adapted from a form that Roadside Theater uses in its partnerships:

> partner's ongoing goals (big picture)
> goals and activities specific to this partnership
> your individual goals
> issues (not included above)
> notes
> evaluation.

See the Appendix for examples of values and mission statements in two actual community arts and higher education partnerships. The Appendix also includes resources recommended by respondents to The Curriculum Project survey.

AFTERWORD

The centrality of relationships in engaging performance

Cultural responses to social calls rely on a set of relationships: between the precipitating circumstances and a community; the community and an artist, including cultural expression meaningful to both; the artist's own artistic inclinations and principles; and other partners available to situate the work in a broadly social realm. Returning to the question of choosing theatrical methods that I was asked at the Pedagogy and Theatre of the Oppressed conference, where the idea for this book was planted, I see these relationships at the crux of that choice.

The relationship between the precipitating act and a community immediately sets up particular needs. In the wake of Hurricane Katrina, and in the absence of government response, New Orlineans had to rebuild using their own assets. So projects that were rooted in what was both available and sustainable there, aesthetic and otherwise, were of primary importance.

The artist's relationship with the people whose circumstances precipitate the process leads to particular aesthetic choices. Pottenger's decision to include not only refugees but also powerful officials, including the Portland mayor and police chief, to tell the story of the border raids together, provided an opportunity for people of very different status to get to know one another. In other circumstances, Pottenger has chosen to perform stories she has gathered herself, or to cast professional actors in those roles, when non-actors were unavailable to take on a performance schedule. But Pottenger recognized that part of the value of *home land security* was that the people involved could work together, and then speak publicly themselves. Moreover, Pottenger's relationship with the people directly affected was not eclipsed by the play itself. Even in the midst of the considerable effort of creating *home land security*, she tried to arrange, for example, for the homeless actor to move in with another cast member who was living alone and lonely, having lost his wife.

Mindfulness of people's own cultural forms also shapes aesthetic choices. Roadside Theater in Appalachia bases its local work in the culturally-syntonic forms of bluegrass music and the oral tradition. Brecht and Kushner shaped their artistic expression into plays, culturally in tune with audiences they wanted to reach. Performances grounded in local culture and drawing on traditional forms gather spectators; once convened, they may address the political issue at hand. The effort to make a spectacle in Syracuse in a celebratory key, outdoors, during the day, draws on the pleasure many people there take in such a cultural format.

Relatedly, engaged performance draws on the opportunities as well as the challenges of its frequent separateness from the mainstream. Cocke notes that he and his colleagues invented Roadside within a culture that had no precedent of professional theatre. That fact, along with the absence of art school training, made them artistically uninhibited. Cornerstone came of age in small towns all across the USA, where company members had to rely upon each other and local partners. Roadside and Cornerstone share a long-term commitment to the longevity, talent, and stability of the ensemble, enabling them to reflect on, and then incorporate, what they learn.

Underlying the array of artistic forms that engaged performance can take is the relationship between the theatrical method and a set of principles. This is demonstrated by how the artists referred to in this book intertwine approaches that might seem mutually exclusive. From Brecht, we see that one can be simultaneously didactic and endlessly generative of dramaturgical methods that catalyze thinking for oneself – because the emphasis is on an active spectator, what's key is seeing a situation and characters in their contradictions, not being told *what* to think, but being shaken up regarding *how* to think. From Kushner, we behold fantastically imaginative images in dialogue with heavy theory one wouldn't think fit within a piece of dramatic literature, especially one headed for Broadway. His plays reflect commitment to theatre that provides what he calls the three Ps – politics, poetry, and popcorn. Cornerstone founders Rauch and Carey offer ways to draw on the strengths of the dramatic canon as well as the self-expression of people from every walk of life. The relevance of those productions to their local audiences is primary.

I've learned most about the inextricable relationship between principles and techniques that embody them through Boal. Early on in our experience with the theatre of the oppressed, Mady Schutzman and I were jokering (Boal's term for facilitating) a scene about a Mexican family trying to drive across the border into the USA, introduced by the now-grown son of the man who had been driving. We were using the technique known as Rashomon – replaying the same scene from the point of view of the various characters involved – including in this case the border patroller, the father who was driving the car and accused of trying to cross illegally, and the man's son, who witnessed his father's humiliation. But rather than finding insight in the process, the now-grown son was becoming increasingly agitated with each replaying. Later, Schutzman and I asked Boal what we should have done, and he responded that we should have replaced the son, for example by having someone else play his part so he could watch. But replacing the protagonist wasn't part of the technique we were using, so we hadn't thought to do it. We realized then that by knowing the principles, one can bring together techniques from different exercises, adapting methodology to the circumstances. So we foregrounded studying Boal's theory and not just the "how to" of the techniques. Boal developed a remarkably systematized body of work, the principles of which are as well-developed as its techniques.

Looking at the engaged artists in this book supports my claim that one does not become less of an artist by making engaged work. All are endlessly inventive, all are meticulous in experimenting with what they have done and pushing it further. Brecht embraced various theatrical forms, from expressionism through adaptation of classical plays, in response to the situations in which he found himself. Cocke is committed to a face-to-face, story-based approach, but has been an avid partner in *Thousand Kites*, wholeheartedly embracing what the internet, radio, and video bring to the overall project. Pottenger continues to bring a playwright's sensibility to her work shaping interviews and personal stories into plays; nor has she left behind her community organizing skills in carrying out the work she pursues, but learns more about the combination the longer she's at it.

Artists may be in constant flux in relationship to aesthetic choices, yet recognizable over the course of their careers. In a way, Boal has been the most unfaithful disciple of his own techniques, constantly adding new ones as new circumstances arose. Living in a country under a military dictatorship, he came up with invisible theatre, in which theatrical messages were camouflaged as real life. Influenced by his wife when she became a psychotherapist, he stretched his understanding of oppression to include internalized forms. Becoming a city councilor in Rio de Janeiro, he adapted his techniques to have a direct impact on policy, as he was, amazingly, in the position to do so. Yet through all the changes, ideas such as metaxis and the active subject remain constant.

This critical analysis of the situation is central to engaged performance. The platform from which an artist creates is bigger than individual self-expression; it must neither leave the artist out – or why engage performance? – nor dwarf other elements that call for addressing and redressing. If being an artist is just part of one's identity, and one recognizes art's limitations in responding to concerns about the world, than engaged art-making is a way to bring art to a larger endeavor. For engaged art requires looking at the ecological system within which the seed for art-making is situated.

Looking ecologically becomes a tool of analysis and understanding. The relationship between precipitant and people affected, for example, can be so

195

charged that it's often a mistake to hold first-person stories to the level of fact. When the Holocaust survivor I mention in chapter three recounted four chimneys at a concentration camp going up in flames, while the documentation supports only one chimney exploding, psychologist Dori Laub does not say the informant was wrong; rather, that her words must be interpreted for the knowledge they carry, not the knowledge they don't carry. Other people can quantify the number of chimneys destroyed by camp inmates; this person is witness to the emotional meaning, despite the odds, of fighting back in an impossible situation and winning that one victory, which surely felt at least four times more amazing than the numbers reflect.

Artists who aspire to make a difference in a social situation must assess the relationship between their goals and the scale on which they are able to work. I've witnessed many inspiring performance processes that contributed materially as well as aesthetically to a specific situation, but have not been replicated and relevant in other situations. The model that The Curriculum Project articulates for engaged performance education *is* replicable, even while open to variation, which must nevertheless be rooted in a set of principles. And while engaged art programs already exist, they have considerable ground yet to gain concerning recognition for knowledge not produced exclusively within higher education's gates. Likewise, efforts to revitalize neighborhoods bring engaged art to greater scale by configuring it as part of the ecology of a whole city, rather than a specialized pleasure for some. Such a model makes the statement that art may be as important as good education and safe neighborhoods to the quality of life.

One of the insights this study has yielded is the loosened grip of place on much engaged performance. Whereas once relationship to place *was* relationship to a people, in its present life, shared past, and future aspirations, that's less frequently the case now. People move and places change at alarming rates; steadfastness to values must see us through the loss of the familiar. Indeed, sometimes the familiar is exactly what needs to be lost when it encompasses biases, prejudices, and unwillingness to accept changes that improve the lot of the many.

The engaged art of our time is, above all, characterized by relationships with people and activities from many sectors of society. Revitalizing democracy through broadening participation is a goal of much engaged art, be it through Freire's active subject, Boal's spect-actor, Pottenger's embrace of Archbishop Tutu's *ubuntu botho* – our interrelated humanity – or Cocke's Story Circles. Relatedly, the *Thousand Kites* team brings together people with diverse prison experiences and professional expertise.

In May 2004, the Community Arts Network hosted a gathering of some 35 stakeholders to assess the state of community arts in the USA. Arts consultant Bill Cleveland, noting who was missing, makes an important point regarding the necessity of inter-sectoral partners in engaged art:

> A significant number of the critical partners – this is all about partnerships – are not in this circle. I'm talking about community development corporations, educational institutions, housing authorities, boys and girls clubs, neighborhood associations, immigrant associations, all these folks who come and say, "This creative resource has incredible potential value for moving and advancing our issues and our agendas."
>
> (Bill Cleveland, quoted in an email from Linda Burnham, "Inter-sectorality," June 21, 2007)

For public, inclusive art to benefit our shared civic life, we need opportunities that create intersections between engaged artists and people from other disciplines and communities working toward the same goals.

What Cleveland calls for is, in fact, happening. Arts journalist Linda Burnham describes one of the most important trends in this field as artists looking "beyond their own communities and their accustomed colleagues for help, to plunge whole-heartedly into other fields and submerse themselves there. The implication is that the result is a new, hybrid kind of thinking, a synthesis of their experience in community arts and their deep investigation of other kinds of work" (Burnham et al. 2004). With this comes the need for expanded skill sets. Writing about artists who are conversant in another discipline as well as art, Caron Atlas and R. Lena Richardson note that the result is not just practical, but also creative (Atlas and Richardson 2008). Atlas finds that engaged artists must constantly create new networks as well as new art products.

A case in point is Susan Perlstein, who founded Elders Share the Arts in 1979, and now finds herself in the unfamiliar terrain of public policy. Tapped by several federal agencies to head the National Center for Creative Aging, Perlstein faced a steep learning curve:

> At present we are working with the National Endowment for the Arts, National Assembly of State Arts Agencies as well as National Council on Aging, Federal Administration on Aging and their Area Offices on Aging. And local groups in twenty states. We are trying to put into place systemic change that involves culture change – building a society for all people, especially including older folks ... There's this big shift going on where older people were looked at as a disease and a medical problem of the country, and now the shift is to look at older people as a resource and strength of our society ... I hear it, and I feel it, and I never

dreamed I would see that day, but it's here, so I need to learn how to step up.

(Atlas and Richardson 2008)

As Perlstein reports, sometimes one must leave one's arts base and immerse oneself in a related field. Rather than seeing engaged art as offering fewer aesthetic opportunities than the mainstream, this book bears testimony to the many artists for whom engaged art provides not only creative, but also social growth possibilities.

Engaged art is created in relationship to impossible visions, utopian callings, that the collaborators could not possibly have the means to carry out fully. In Syracuse, we want to generate a giant performance, bringing in people from all walks of local life, who do arts workshops together all year long and then perform downtown. We want the festival to become part of how people mark the end of summer and the beginning of the long winter, and how they make a connection to each other even as most of them would not in other circumstances meet. We want the streets to be as full of people as they were in the 1950s, with positive outcomes for other sectors as well, such as local restaurants selling lunch from outdoor stands set up for the purpose. We want immigrants and refugees to be seen for the cultural richness they bring central New York, not just for the economic needs such major life changes entail. We want teenagers to connect to elders, not be perceived as, respectively, threatening or dull.

Such art can help us recognize that there are various sides to the same situation and they are not mutually exclusive. A city with a large immigrant and refugee population is an international city even as its newcomers need substantial support. Teenagers and elders may enjoy different cultural forms and still enjoy each other. Yes, four chimneys were blown up at that concentration camp and yes, one chimney was destroyed in that act of resistance. And the same materials used for swords can make plowshares, and spears can make pruning hooks.

As James Baldwin is attributed with saying, "Life is more important than art; that's what makes art so important" (cited in Spinrad: 1991). Embedded in that statement is the importance of using art well to honor appropriately those people whose lives are most affected by the subject matter. Art keeps its makers in the picture; the *making* of the art is the joint task, the *object* of art is a piece of that whole. But the biggest picture is shaping one's own corner of the world, of which art-making is a small but vibrant element in a large, collectively-created mosaic.

APPENDIX

1 Selected Adaptations, Cornerstone Theater
2 Roadside Theater's Story Circle Methodology
3 Values and Mission Statement, Community Arts and Higher Education Partnership
4 Criteria, Syracuse Public Art Commission
5 Resources from The Curriculum Project Research

1 Selected Adaptations, Cornerstone Theater

This list is drawn from Kuftinec (2003: 195–99) and Cornerstone Theater staff (www.cornerstonetheater.org).

1986 *The Marmath Hamlet*. Adapted by the company and people of Marmath, North Dakota, from Shakespeare's *Hamlet*.

1988 *The House on Walker River*. Adapted by the company and people of the Walker River Paiute Tribe and Shurtz, Nevada, from *The Oresteia* of Aeschylus.

1989 *Three Sisters from West Virginia*, adapted by the company and people of Kanawha Valley, Montgomery, West Virginia, from *The Three Sisters* of Anton Chekhov.

1992 *The Toy Truck*, adapted by the company and Peter Sagal from *The Clay Cart* by King Sudraka as translated by J.A.B. Van Buitenen, and produced with residents of the Angelus Plaza Senior Center.

1997 *Candude, or The Optimistic Civil Servant*, adapted from Voltaire by Tracy Young. Produced with the Angeles Police Department, Metropolitan Transportation Authority, Los Angeles Public Library, and US Postal Service Employees.

1999 *A.K.A.: A Beverly Hills Musical Morality Play*. Adapted by Shem Bitterman from *The Marquis of Keith* by Frank Wedekind. Produced with residents of Beverly Hills.

2000 *Peter Pan*. Adapted by Alison Carey, produced with residents of Cleveland, Ohio.

2 Roadside Theater's Story Circle Methodology

Introduction

The stories we're able to tell ourselves and others, those we can understand and imagine, define not only what we believe to have already occurred, but what we believe to be possible in our individual and collective lives. Story Circles engender appreciation for the unique intellectual, emotional, and spiritual qualities of each participant, and develop oral expression and listening skills. Each one of our stories is a gift to those who are listening, with the quality of the listening a gift in return to the storyteller.

Roadside's ensemble members grew up without television, immersed in a world of local stories and oral histories. The oral tradition, often in ballad form, is the most prominent feature of our shared Scots–Irish heritage, and it has shaped the content and determined the form of our plays. If you have ever sat around with friends and kin singing, spinning tales, and recounting histories, you will quickly see where we're coming from: the play's lines suddenly doubling and overlapping within a general motif of call and response. In our Appalachian performance tradition, as well as in other performance traditions into which we have been invited to perform (the southern African American and Puerto Rican traditions come right to mind), *call and response* extends beyond the stage to include the audience. The grand result is the rich choral effect of harmony and counterpoint that is group storytelling, whether on a front porch or in an auditorium.

Not only can the oral tradition effectively generate content for building plays from scratch (Roadside has created 57 such plays), but, after performances of the staged play, Story Circles with audience and cast can provide a nuanced feedback loop for audience members to integrate the play's experience into their own lives, as well as for the play's artists to deepen their understanding of the performance. In effect, such circles continue the play's action into a new Act, providing a way for the community to talk to itself about the play's themes, and for the performance itself to mature. Based on this experience, sometimes community leaders will invite Roadside to help their community discover and publicly present its own songs, stories, and oral histories. A basic building block of these extended community cultural development residencies is the Story Circle.

In the course of sharing stories, difficulties in a community often rise to the surface, including issues from which its members are suffering. Roadside's Story Circle methodology supports a basic principle of such community change work: those who directly experience a problem must make up the generative base for devising and enacting the solution. In this work, Roadside first uses its Story Circle methodology to help individuals discover their own truth of the issue, and then to test and develop that truth in dialog with other community members. By periodically collecting and organizing the knowledge about the issue generated by the stories, communities have an informed basis for recommending change, abetted by an enhanced sense of mutual trust. To sustain the momentum for change, the process of individual and collective learning about the issue must continue to inspire and shape action.

What follows is a summary of the deceptively simple Story Circle methodology Roadside has developed for creating and developing original plays and for helping communities develop themselves. Because stories are so powerful, they can easily be used for purposes of domination and exploitation, rather than collective development. Consequently, Roadside is formal about its methodology, and we encourage those interested in the method to contact the company for training. The training includes how to become a Story Circle facilitator and how to use Story Circles to create plays, is a lot of fun, and can be accomplished in two days.

Story Circles

A Story Circle is a group of people sitting in a circle, telling personal stories, led by a Story Circle facilitator. Each Story Circle is different according to its purpose.

What is and is not a story?

- A story is a narrative of events drawn from the teller's personal experience.
- A story can be fashioned from a memory, a dream, a reflection, a moment in time, and more.
- A story typically has a beginning, middle, and end, as well as characters and atmosphere.
- A story is not a lecture, an argument, a debate, or an intellectualization, although these elements may be part of a story.

Story Circles should:

- Be preceded by an informal time to socialize (for example, a pot luck dinner).
- Take place in a quiet space with good acoustics where interruptions are unlikely to occur.
- Consist of from 5 to 15 people sitting in a circle without notepads, pocketbooks, etc., and in such a manner that each participant has a good view of every other participant.
- Have one trained facilitator who begins, oversees, and ends the Circle.
- Have a stated time period in which the Story Circle will take place.

- Have a purpose articulated by the leader and agreed to by the participants.
- Allow for silences between stories.
- Be as much about listening as about telling.

Story Circles should not:

- Primarily serve the agenda of any one participant.
- Give importance to one story, or one type of story, over another.

The facilitator's role:

- Be clear about the purpose of the particular circle. (Examples are reinforcement of cultural identity; examination of issues of race and class; identification of community concerns; introduction of a community storytelling project; and so on.)
- Know, or determine with the group, the theme for the particular circle. The theme must complement the Story Circle's purpose. For example, if the purpose is to explore cultural identity, a circle theme could be family holiday traditions. If the purpose is to better understand race and class, the theme of the circle might be a story about a moment when one realized that one was different.
- Introduce him or herself, describe the circle's purpose and theme, and state the time the Story Circle will end.
- Tell the rules of the Story Circle and answer participants' questions about them.
- Emphasize the idea that listening to the stories of others is as important as telling your own, noting that deep listening can engender a meditative quality in the circle.
- Discourage participants from thinking too much about what they will say when it is their turn, asking them to trust that their story will come from their listening to the stories of the others.
- Tell the group how long the circle will last, and ask participants to pace the length of their stories to the time available, taking into consideration the number of participants. For example, if there are 12 people in the Circle and 60 minutes for storytelling, each story should be approximately 5 minutes in length.
- Announce the manner in which the facilitator will politely indicate to a teller that he or she has passed the time limit and needs to wrap-up the story.
- Ask the participants to quickly name the typical elements of a story – narrative, plot, characters, atmosphere, etc.
- Begin the circle with a story that sets the tone for the purpose and theme of the circle, or state the theme and ask who in the circle would like to tell the first story.

- After the first story, go around the Circle clockwise or counter-clockwise, with each person telling or passing when it is their turn. The rotation continues until everyone has told a story.
- Reserve time after the telling for participants to reflect on what has just transpired by asking everyone for their observations and comments.
- When possible, end with a group song or poem (perhaps taught and led by a participant) that brings closure to the spirit of the particular Story Circle.
- End the Story Circle on time.
- Participants often want to talk personally to each other after the Circle breaks up, so the facilitator should ensure space is available for this purpose.

Story Circle rules:

- There is only one Story Circle facilitator.
- There are no observers – only participants.
- The Story Circle facilitator is also a participant, and must tell his or her story as well.
- Participants speak only when it is their turn.
- The order of telling is either clockwise or counterclockwise from the first teller.
- When it comes to one's turn, the person decides the timing of when to speak, and may decide to pass, knowing their turn will come around again.
- After everyone in the Circle has had the opportunity to speak or pass, the rotation begins again for those who have passed.
- Listening deeply is the most important part of the Story Circle experience.
- Participants should not distract themselves by thinking ahead about what story they will tell.
- Rather, participants should listen to the stories told, and, when it is their turn, tell a story brought to mind by the previous stories, or pass.
- Participants and the facilitator never argue with or debate another participant's story.
- Participants and the facilitator never comment upon another partici-pant's story other than to say, when it is their turn, "That story reminds me of … "
- There is no cross-talk in a Story Circle and all respondents to a parti-cular story wait their turn and are in story form.
- Story Circles are never tape recorded or videotaped without the parti-cipants' expressed permission.
- If the stories in a circle might be used to inform the development of a new play, all participants must understand this and give their permission.

When a Story Circle should be stopped by the facilitator:

It is not unusual for painful stories to emerge in a Story Circle. The facilitator must exercise judgment about when to continue a Story Circle and when to stop it. Story Circle facilitators should not try to serve as therapists, social workers, or doctors (even if these are their professional occupations), because participants did not come to the circle to receive these services. The facilitator can:

- Call for a break and talk individually with the distressed person; or
- Refer the distressed person to the proper professional; or
- Resume or reschedule the Story Circle.

The living word has a soul of which the written word is properly no more than an image.

Socrates

© Roadside Theater 1999
  Roadside Theater
  PO Box 771
  Norton, VA 24273
  roadsidetheater@verizon.net
  www.roadside.org

3 Values and Mission Statement, Community Arts and Higher Education Partnership

Grassroots Performance Project in the Lower East Side – spring 2007

Mission and values

The Grassroots Performance Project is a New York University/Tisch School of the Arts training studio for theatre artists committed to justice. As affiliates of NYU and, in many cases, residents of the Lower East Side, we feel we are responsible for understanding and addressing, through the work that we do, the issues that face our communities and neighborhoods. Because the arts have the unique ability to open up lines of communication within and across communities, we believe the arts are a viable tool for addressing social, economic, and cultural inequality. Correlating with a theory of change that posits those with the problem must be the generative base for the solution, as NYU affiliates and/or local residents, we are committed to issues that involve NYU and its Lower East Side community. In the spring 2006 Grassroots Performance Project, students were introduced to the concerns on the minds and in the hearts of their neighbors. In 2007, we wish to further investigate one of the leading critical issues identified by students and residents alike: the intersection of real estate, gentrification, and displacement, and the importance of home and community.

To pursue this critical issue, students and faculty will collaborate with local residents with the goal of using the skills of theatre arts and community organizing to collectively problem solve. We seek to develop equitable partnerships that are reciprocal and mutually beneficial. For example, over the course of the semester, students will leave the university's walls to learn from local organizations, and NYU students and faculty will open their studio and classroom doors to community members.

The project will include an ongoing series of public events, large and small, which will be structured in such a way as to be welcoming and open to the entire community. This may include performance pieces which would involve community members as well as students. In all public interactions, a respect and a desire for a diversity of opinions and a dedication to improving everyone's listening and analytical skills will be valued.

Specific project goals of the partners

- Increase the Lower East Side's capacity to act in its own collective self-interest, by supporting diverse local leadership.
- Further establish NYU as a reliable ally and resource for inclusive citizen participation in shaping the Lower East Side's future. Foster expanded opportunities for students to gain a greater sense of community responsibility and social justice.
- Through collectively designing the Grassroots Performance Project, begin to develop a widely applicable interdisciplinary model for training artists enrolled in professional arts schools for whom advancing social justice is at the core of their artistic practice.
- Through NYU's participation in a grassroots sister project in spring 2007 with Xavier, Dillard, and Tulane universities, develop a partnership model for universities to pursue social justice projects that are community-based.
- Participate in regional and national forums about the role of the arts in sustainable community development based on the principles of equity and justice.

Key questions

The Grassroots Performance Project seeks to pursue the following key questions:

How can a powerful university, such as NYU, take responsibility for generating solutions to seemingly intractable problems – on both a local and global scale – that threaten us all? Examples include neighborhood preservation, gentrification, the rising cost of real estate, stark economic inequality including the increasingly prohibitive cost of higher education, environmental degradation, racism, pandemic disease, and global terrorism. How can faculty encourage NYU to take on a leadership role in meeting these responsibilities? How can students be empowered to be leaders in this effort? At Tisch, specifically, how do we triangulate artist training, scholarship, and community engagement methodology to help solve community problems? How can Tisch effectively collaborate with other schools and grassroots organizations to further the public good of justice?

Responsibilities

All partners, both at NYU and in the community, will play an active role in furthering the project's goals and pursuing the project's key questions. Some specific responsibilities for all participants include:

- Articulate the mission and values of the project often, holding ourselves and each other accountable.
- Facilitate and participate in regular critical assessment of the project's progress, reflecting about successes and failures encountered.
- Candidly communicate with the project collective should problems arise.
- Through an iterative process of doing and reflecting, continue to define the current compelling issues of the Lower East Side and the NYU communities.

Grassroots interpersonal goals

The additional statement was devised on February 2, 2007 by the spring 2007 Grassroots Performance Project collective to help guide our processes for communicating with each other.

- We will approach each other with mutual respect.
- We will enter into discussions and disagreements with trust in each other so that we may realize our shared mission.
- We will treat all projects as a joint effort. Everyone is responsible for driving and shaping what we do.
- We are all teachers. Knowledge does not trickle down from the top, rather it is shared between us horizontally in a process of mutual mentorship.
- We will agree collectively when to lead and when to follow.
- We are committed to maintaining the lines of communication between each individual or group open and continuous (so as to keep everyone updated and aware).

4 Criteria, Syracuse Public Art Commission

Applications will be evaluated based on the following criteria, with the understanding that individual factors may be more germane to a particular proposal than others and therefore weighted accordingly.

- *Artistic merit and quality*, as substantiated by an artist's past history of exhibitions or sales, awards or other recognition, or an outstanding first work, as well as the inherent quality in terms of timelessness of vision, design, aesthetics and excellence;
- *Intentionality of the artist* concerning the meaning and proposed or desired effect of the work as public art upon the viewing public, as rationalized and elaborated upon in the project description;
- *Sense of place*, creating a sense of excitement in public spaces and fresh ways of seeing ourselves and our city reflected;
- *Representation of styles and tastes within the public art collection*, acknowledging existing works in the public art collection and striving for diversity of style, scale and media;
- *Safety and durability*, including the ability of the artwork to withstand weather conditions, as well as structural and surface integrity;
- *Unrestricted public viewing*, primarily the opportunity for public access, but also suitability for public participation, social and political attitudes, and functional considerations; and
- *Installation and maintenance of the work*, from practicality of fabrication and transport, to installation and long-term care.

5 Resources from The Curriculum Project Research

The following resources were recommended by survey respondents:

Organizations (in alphabetical order): Alternate ROOTS; Americans for the Arts and its program, Animating Democracy; ArtServe Michigan; Association of Performing Arts Presenters; Association of Theatre in Higher Education; College Art Association; Community Arts Network; Community Arts Partnership; Imagining America; National Alliance of Media Arts and Culture; National Guild of Community Schools of The Arts; National Performance Network; Network of Ensemble Theatres; Pedagogy and Theatre of the Oppressed; and Theatre Communications Group.

Books (in alphabetical order according to author): Augusto Boal, *Games for Actors and Non-Actors* and *Theatre of the Oppressed*; William Cleveland, *Art in Other Places, Artists at Work in America's Community and Social Institutions* and *Making Exact Change* (a report published by the Community Arts Network); Jan Cohen-Cruz, *Local Acts: Community-based Performance in* *the United States* and, co-edited with Mady Schutzman, *A Boal Companion: Dialogues on Theatre and Cultural Politics*; Paulo Freire, *Pedagogy of The Oppressed*; Robert Gard, *Grassroots Theater: A Search for Regional Arts in America*; James Bau Graves, *Cultural Democracy: The Arts, Community, and the Public Purpose*; Arlene Goldbard, *New Creative Community: The Art of Cultural Development*; Arlene Goldbard and Don Adams, *Creative Community: The Art of Cultural Development* and *Community, Culture and Globalization*; Suzanne Lacy, *Mapping The Terrain: New Genre Public Art*; and Michael Rohd, *Theatre for Community, Conflict, and Dialogue*.

In addition to noting the Community Arts Network (CAN) website as a rich source, participants mentioned two anthologies published by Art in The Public Interest, CAN's parent organization: *Performing Communities: The Grassroots Ensemble Theater Research Project*; and *The Citizen Artist: 20 Years of Art in the Public Arena*. The Animating Democracy series published by Americans for the Arts was also frequently mentioned.

Institutions and programs mentioned (in alphabetical order): California College of the Arts, including its Center for Art and Public Life, Oakland, CA; Columbia College Chicago, Master of Arts Management Degree in Youth and Community Development and the Center for Community Arts Partnerships, Chicago, IL; Cornerstone Theater, The Cornerstone Institute Summer Residency, Los Angeles, CA; Maryland Institute College of Art, Master of Arts in Community Arts, Baltimore, MD; Virginia Tech, Master of Fine Arts in Directing and Public Dialogue, Blacksburg, VA; California State University, Monterey Bay, Bachelor of Arts in Visual and Public Art, Seaside, CA; City University of New York, Creative Arts Team, located in the School of Professional Studies, New York, NY; Otis College of Art and Design, Master of Fine Arts in Public Practice, Los Angeles, CA; Tisch School of The Arts, New York University, Minor in Applied Theatre and the Interactive Telecommunications Program, New York, NY; Intermedia Arts Institute for Community Cultural Development, Minneapolis, MN; Liz Lerman Dance Exchange, Summer Institute, Takoma Park, MD; Tyler College of Arts, Temple University, Cross-Disciplinary Arts in Community Program, Philadelphia, PA; Sojourn Theatre Summer Institute, Portland, OR; Urban Bush Women Summer Institute, Brooklyn, NY.

In addition to the above programs, which received three or more mentions, 105 other academic or community-based initiatives were listed, from specific degree programs such as the Cultural Policy Program at The Ohio State University; to programs focused on a small number of courses or a unifying project, such as PCAP: Prison Creative Arts Project at the University of Michigan; to non-academic programs such as Alternate ROOTS' Resources for Social Change training initiative. Many individual mentions were made of training elements within particular community-based organizations, either those devised for their own staff members and volunteers or those they conduct as part of community residencies.

NOTES

INTRODUCTION

1 See Richard Schechner (1985) on the phases of performance.
2 From 1978 to 1998, Linda Burnham and Steven Durland edited *High Performance*, which shifted from a journal about performance art to one about community-based art. In 1999, the metamorphosis was complete and *High Performance* was reborn as the Community Arts Network (www.communityarts. net), a website dedicated to community arts.
3 What we in the USA typically call *community-based theatre* is a collaboration of artists and a coherent grouping of others whose lives directly inform the subject matter, expressing collective meaning. Community-based art may or may not include an overt political agenda, but it is premised on broad participation in the actual making of art, and a commitment to taking on subject matter that is meaningful to those participating. Because I have discussed the term community at length in my book *Local Acts*, let me just repeat here that community refers to people who share not only geographical proximity, but any fundamental aspect of identity, as likely to be a shared tradition or spirit. (See deNobriga 1993: 13.)
4 I am grateful to Mary Langer, an engaged theatre-maker in South Africa, for this turn of phrase.
5 I thank Tom Leabhart for these insights, shared over *café au lait* in Paris on July 4, 2009.
6 As James Thompson and Richard Schechner pithily note, what's called applied theatre in the UK and Australia – and I would add, increasingly in US higher education – is known as community-based theatre in the USA, theatre for development in certain Asian and African countries, popular theatre in Canada, and social theatre in Italy (Thompson and Schechner 2004: 11).
7 Pedagogy and Theatre of the Oppressed (PTO) is an organization that builds on the work of educator Paulo Freire and theatre-maker Augusto Boal. It features an annual meeting that brings together liberatory educators, activists, and artists. Cocke and I made that particular presentation at the 12th Annual PTO Conference, in Chapel Hill, North Carolina, May 19–21, 2006.

1 PLAYWRIGHTING: PUTTING PLAYS TO USE

1 See especially Bertolt Brecht's writings in *Brecht on Theatre* (Willett 1957; 1964).
2 Aristotle's *Poetics*, the foundational text of western dramatic art, identifies the audience's emotional release at the end of a tragedy as one of its core characteristics and greatest values. In order to achieve catharsis, Aristotle examines

Oedipus Rex and identifies the five most important elements of serious dramatic art. See Butcher's translation (Aristotle 1961).

3 Leni Riefenstahl's film *Triumph of the Will*, about the Nuremberg rallies, while made at Hitler's behest, is a grim document of how coercive, mystifying, and overwhelming spectacle can be.

4 We see the character Grusha make a choice at the moment in *Caucasian Chalk Circle* when she picks up the baby the royal family has forgotten in their haste to flee the palace uprising (Brecht 1966).

5 A variation of this paradigm is more recent "radical ridicule", activists in the late 20th/early 21st century who include larger-than-life satirical performative modes in the context of that period's social movement activism. See Larry Bogad (2005).

6 The Stonewall riots, marking the first widespread resistance against police raids at a gay bar, took place in New York City, June 28, 1969. They are taken as the beginning of the gay rights movement in the United States.

7 For more on the utopian impulse in theatrical performances, see Jill Dolan (2005).

8 Dinner theatre is the practice of including dinner and a play for the price of admission. It tends to be rather light fare intellectually.

9 See Harry Elam, Jr (2001) for a well-articulated argument concerning political theatre as ritual, with "the cause" greater than the individual and able to unify people in a social struggle.

10 For a full account of Grotowski's work at the point I encountered it, see his *Towards a Poor Theatre* (Grotowski 1968).

2 SPECTA(C)TING

1 Among critics who appreciate Boal's use of theatre for political ends are those who see some of his techniques as over-simplified (see Taussig and Schechner 1994). Yet the simplified, embodiable nature of that work is probably why it is so accessible to diverse audiences.

2 For an introduction to Boal's work see his first book, *Theatre of the Oppressed* (Boal 1974).

3 See Boal's very useful *Games for Actors and Non-Actors* (Boal 1992).

4 These are described at length in *Theatre of the Oppressed* (Boal 1974).

5 For more detailed descriptions of the philosophies and techniques of The Joker System, see Boal (1974: 159–97).

6 As stated on its website, "Circus Amok is a New York City based circus-theater company whose mission is to provide free public art addressing contemporary issues of social justice to the people of New York City." For more information visit www.circusamok.org.

7 My description of *Upset!* is based on viewing the production both live and, subsequently, on DVD (Schutzman 2006).

8 All Aviles's quotes come from interviews I conducted and emails I exchanged with him in 2005.

9 Christo, and his collaborator Jean Claude, are artists known for the enormous scale of their projects, which interact with urban and rural landscapes. Works include wrapping such as Pont Neuf in Paris, erecting 24 miles of white nylon fence through California's Sonoma and Marin counties, and, erecting 15-foot-tall "gates" of orange fabric over the pathways of New York City's Central Park. One of the world's best-selling artists, the biggest obstacle to realizing his work is obtaining permission from the authorities.

10 "Nuyoricans" refers to Puerto Ricans brought up in New York City.

11 See Antonin Artaud (1958).

3 SELF-REPRESENTING

1 Living Newspaper is a theatrical genre that dramatizes current events. Gaining popularity during the Great Depression, when people's hunger for the news was great, a number of living newspapers were produced by the Federal Theatre Project. See Hallie Flanagan (1940;1985) for more.

4 CULTURAL ORGANIZING

1 While this chapter is not an examination of the many ways in which the arts are used *within* prisons, with inmate participation, I refer you to work that does – the Theatre in Prisons and Probation Research and Development Centre (www. tipp.org.uk); *Theatre in Prison: Theory and Practice* by Michael Balfour (2006, Intellect Books, Bristol, UK); Buzz Alexander through the Prison Creative Arts Practice (www.lsa.umich.edu/english/pcap); Grady Hillman (e.g. "Working through Walls", *Movement Research Journal #15, Moving Communities*, fall/winter 1997–98); *Art in Other Places* by Bill Cleveland (2000, Arts Extension Service Press, University of Massachusetts); *Theatre behind Bars: Can the Arts Rehabilitate?* by Philip Taylor (2010, Trentham Books, Stoke-on-Trent, UK).
2 Information about the development of *Thousand Kites* comes from intermittent phone conversations with Kirby and Szuberla throughout 2007.
3 The Citizen Engagement Lab (CEL) uses new media and technology to inform and activate issue-based communities, with a focus on amplifying the voices of African Americans, Latinos, and young people. Their mission is "to create a network of overlapping constituencies that act as distribution channels for key progressive messages and calls-to-action. CEL serves as an infrastructure umbrella for our current projects (ColorOfChange, Video the Vote, and GNN. tv), an incubator for launching new initiatives, and a strategic new media and technology resource center to strengthen the progressive infrastructure." CEL's process entails organizing communities online using digital media and targeted calls to action; facilitating ongoing activity among community members while identifying influencers who seek a deeper level of engagement; and providing tools to those influencers to help them assume leadership and facilitate the engagement of others.
4 Cocke remarked that the Czechs found theatre to be the most subversive art during communism because it is the hardest to control. Playwrights would describe new plays to the censors and make changes as required. But in performance, some of the offending language could find its way back in, although actors and playwright could deny ever veering from the approved script.

5 GATHERING ASSETS

1 Doubting that the storm would be of a great magnitude, many people did not evacuate. So when it proved to be very bad indeed, the city opened the Superdome, the major sports arena. Conditions were chaotic, without proper or sufficient bathroom facilities, pillows and blankets, food, and support. Evacuee accounts noted the sense that no-one was in charge, the overwhelming smell of excrement, the piercing sound level, and the stifling lack of air conditioning as thousands packed the arena after harrowing experiences getting there in the first place.
2 Minshall had helped design the opening awards ceremonies for the 1987 Pan-American Games, the 1992 Barcelona Olympics, the 1996 Atlanta Olympics, the 1994 Football World Cup, and the 2002 Salt Lake City Winter Olympics.
3 An account of one such disagreement around the neighborhood's racial identity – a desire among some Porch leaders to reflect a largely black constituency and

among others to display its inter-racial makeup – is the subject of an essay by Rachael Breunlin and Helen Regis (2009).

4 According to folk legend, bottle trees originated in the Congo or perhaps northern Africa, and were brought to the Americas during the slave trade. Slaves hung blue bottles from trees and huts as talismans to ward off evil spirits. Such spirits were thought to be drawn into the bottle by the lovely colors, only to be destroyed the next day by the sunlight.

5 See anthropologist Helen Regis's insightful development of this idea in the work cited above and her other writings on second line.

6 PARTICULARIZING PLACE

1 Unless otherwise noted, all Higgins's quotes come from the interview I conducted with her on October 21, 2008 in Syracuse, New York.

2 These included reports by F.O.C.U.S. Greater Syracuse, the CNY Speaks Initiative, and Onondaga Citizens League (2006).

3 See Appendix for Syracuse Public Art Commission criteria.

4 This figure comes from a report entitled "Syracuse, NY – The Near West Side" (draft, 2009), a Near West Side Analysis created through the Atlantic States Legal Foundation.

5 City governments can set conditions for property redevelopment. In New York City, "80/20" arrangements were standard in the 1980s, meaning 80% of new housing could cost what the market would bear, and 20% needed to be reserved for low-income renters. Two ways in which developers got around that rule were: adding the provision of a time limit for such a policy, as little as ten or 20 years; and making a deal so that they provided the requisite number of low-income units per high-cost units, but in other neighborhoods.

7 TRAINING

1 We undertook The Curriculum Project research in 2007–08, thanks to funding from the Nathan Cummings Foundation. Project advisors included Jamie Haft, a former applied theatre student of mine at New York University; Sonia BasSheva Majnon, vice-president for diversity and strategic partnerships at Wesleyan University; and community organizer Ludovic Blain III. We conducted 28 interviews, posted a survey, and analyzed the 231 responses from community cultural development artists and the staff of partnering community organizations, students, and teachers. We examined several dozen syllabuses and descriptions of minors and majors in fields related to engaged art offered in US colleges and universities, as well as workshops and courses offered by nationally-regarded independent artists.

2 All quotes from The Curriculum Project interviews were conducted under conditions of anonymity and are thus unattributed. A list of the interviewees appears at the end of this chapter.

3 Paulo Freire is a Brazilian known for the pedagogy of the oppressed, encouraging dialogic education rather than "the banking method." Theatre-maker Augusto Boal translated Freire's principles to a highly participatory and efficacious set of techniques known as theatre of the oppressed (see chapter two).

4 For specific syllabi visit www.communityarts.net as well as the appendix to The Curriculum Project on the Imagining America website (www.curriculumproject. net/report.html).

5 Bruce Burgett directs Interdisciplinary Studies at the University of Washington Bothell. The program is grounded not in a discipline, but in a set of skills that

students learn, described on the website as to take intellectual risks, write and think critically, communicate clearly, read closely, research effectively, and work collaboratively.

6 In cultural mapping, typically a group of people just beginning a project respond to various prompts from a facilitator by standing in the space accordingly, "mapping," as it were, where they are each situated in relationship to those questions. Once in place, they take a few moments to discuss how it affected who they are today. The exercise often begins by imagining that the room is a map, and identifying north, south, etc. The facilitator asks people to stand where they were born. This requires conversation, so that someone born in Bosnia is not standing to the west of someone born in Philadelphia. The next prompt might be, stand where you consider home. Then the configuration moves to a continuum line. If you have no siblings, stand way left; if you have many siblings, far right. People with the same number of siblings stand in a vertical line intersecting the horizontal continuum. Or people may form clusters around the room based on religious identity, etc. The facilitator asks people to notice who they are often standing near to – which can be unexpected.

7 Art often reflects the relationship between a society's cultural values and political system. Leni Riefenstahl's film of the Nazi Party Nuremberg rallies in the early 1930s, *Triumph of the Will*, evidences that large-scale, carefully-orchestrated-from-above spectacle as a cultural expression of totalitarianism. The choral singing and collective playwriting typical of left-leaning workers' theatres in the former Soviet Union, and even the USA of the 1930s, displayed an effort to collectivize the means of production and to portray an idealized worker in culture and politics alike. And the US counter-culture of the 1960s, the root of many of the values in the contemporary US socially-engaged art field, tries to hold the USA accountable to its rhetoric of democracy featuring pluralism, equity, and broad-based inclusion.

8 Many curricular initiatives are organized as "service learning courses," whereas some faculty prefer to think of their courses as engaged scholarship and typically part of a several-year project. While some faculty and staff use the two terms interchangeably, service learning tends to be identified as focused more on the student than the relationship between campus and community partners; more limited to one term and structured strictly within class time; and more infused with an attitude of higher education as the asset contributing to the needy community.

9 Burgett is part of a team of scholars, affiliated with Imagining America, who initiated the Assessing the Practices of Public Scholarship effort. For his introduction of this initiative to our constituents at our national conference in 2009 in New Orleans, and the remarks of other participants on the same plenary panel, see http://curriculumproject.net/2009.plenary.html.

BIBLIOGRAPHY

Ackroyd, Judith (2007) *Applied Theatre: An Exclusionary Discourse?* Applied Theatre Researcher #8. Brisbane, Australia: Centre for Applied Theatre Research at Griffith University.

Albright, Charlotte (2004) *Border Control*, Maine Public Radio archive: 1/27. Animating Democracy Initiative. Online. Available HTTP: www.artsusa.org/animatingdemocracy/about.

American Society of Civil Engineers (2007) *External Review of IPET New Orleans Analysis Notes Progress, Yet Risks Remain.* Online. Available HTTP: www.asce.org/static/hurricane/whitehouse.cfm.

Arce, Elia and Malpede, John (2002) "LAPD, Skid Row & the Real Deal". Community Arts Network: Reading Room. Online. Available HTTP: www.communityarts.net/readingroom/archivefiles/2002/09/lapd_skid_row_t.php.

Aristotle (1961) *The Poetics*, trans. S.H. Butcher; Introduction, Francis Fergusson. New York: Hill & Wang.

Artaud, Antonin (1958) *The Theatre and Its Double*, trans. M.C. Richards. New York: Grove Press.

Atlas, Caron and Richardson, R. Lena (2008) *Bridge Conversations: People Who Live and Work in Multiple Worlds.* Community Arts Network: Reading Room. Online. Available HTTP: www.communityarts.net/readingroom/archivefiles/bridge_conversations_all2/index.php.

Baiocchi, Gianpaolo (2006) "Performing Democracy in the Streets: Participatory Budgeting and Legislative Theatre in Brazil", in Jan Cohen-Cruz and Mady Schutzman (eds) *A Boal Companion.* New York and London: Routledge.

Bechet, Ron and Koritz, Amy (2008) "The New Hybridity: HOME, New Orleans and Emerging Forms of Community/University/Arts Collaboration", *Community Arts Perspectives* I (4), September, Community Arts Network: Reading Room. Online. Available HTTP: www.communityarts.net/readingroom/archivefiles/2008/09/the_new_hybridi.php.

Boal, Augusto (1974; trans. 1979) *Theatre of the Oppressed*, trans. Charles A. and Maria-Odilla Leal McBride. New York: Urizen.

——(1992) *Games for Actors and Non-Actors*, trans. Adrian Jackson. New York and London: Routledge.

——(1995) *The Rainbow of Desire*, trans. Adrian Jackson. London and New York: Routledge.

214

——(1998) *Legislative Theatre*, trans. Adrian Jackson. New York and London: Routledge.

——(2006) *The Aesthetics of the Oppressed*, trans. Adrian Jackson. New York and London: Routledge.

——(2009) "today is world theatre day". World Theatre Day message: March 27. Scrappy Jack's World-Wide Theatricals and Dime Museum. Online. Available HTTP: http://clancyproductions.blogspot.com/2009_03_01_archive.html.

Bogad, Larry (2005) *Electoral Guerrilla Theatre: Radical Ridicule and Social Movement*. London: Routledge.

Borrup, Tom (2005) "What's Revolutionary About Valuing Assets as a Strategy in Cultural Work?". Community Arts Network: Reading Room. Online. Available HTTP: www.communityarts.net/readingroom/archivefiles/2005/09/radical_whats_r.php.

——(2006) *The Creative Community Builder's Handbook: How to Transform Communities Using Local Assets, Arts, and Culture*. Saint Paul, MN: Fieldstone Alliance.

Boyer, Ernest L. (1990) *Scholarship Reconsidered: Priorities of the Professoriate*. New York: The Carnegie Foundation for the Advancement of Teaching.

Brecht, Bertolt (1937; 1965) *The Exception and the Rule*, English version by Eric Bentley. New York: Grove Press.

——(1966) *Caucasian Chalk Circle*, revised English version by Eric Bentley. New York: Grove Press.

Breunlin, Rachael and Regis, Helen (2009) "Can There Be a Critical Collaborative Ethnography? Creativity and Activism in the Seventh Ward, New Orleans." *Collaborative Anthropologies* 2: 115–46.

Burnham, Linda Frye, Durland, Steve and Ewell, Maryo Gard (2004) *The CAN Report. The State of the Field of Community Cultural Development: Something New Emerges*. A Report from the CAN Gathering, May 2004. Community Arts Network: Reading Room. Online. Available HTTP: www.communityarts.net/readingroom/archive/canreport/index.php.

Calhoun, Craig J. (1988) "Populist Politics, Communications Media, and Large Scale Societal Integration", *Sociological Theory* 6: 219–41.

Case, Dick (2007) "Spitzer Dangles Some Candy at Downtown Ghost Town", *Post–Standard*, Syracuse, New York, October 30: B1.

Charlesworth, Max (1975) *The Existentialists and Jean Paul Sartre*. St Lucia, Queensland: University of Queensland Press.

Clark, Mary Marshall (2002) "Oral History", in Don Adams and Arlene Goldbard (eds) *Community, Culture and Globalization*. New York: Rockefeller Foundation.

Clifford, James (1988) *The Predicament of Culture*. Cambridge, MA and London: Harvard University Press.

Cohen-Cruz, Jan (2004) *Local Acts: Community-Based Performance in the United States*. New Brunswick, NJ and London: Rutgers University Press.

Conquergood, Dwight (2006) "Rethinking Ethnography: Towards a Critical Cultural Politics", in D.S. Madison and J. Hamera (eds) *The Sage Handbook of Performance Studies*. Thousand Oaks, CA: Sage.

Cook, Alice and Kirk, Gwen (1983) "Taking Direct Action", in *Greenham Women Everywhere: Dreams, Ideas and Actions from the Women's Peace Movement*. London: Pluto Press.

215

deNobriga, Kathie (1993) "An Introduction to Alternate ROOTS", *High Performance* 16 (4): 11.

Dietsch, Deborah K. (2002) *The Washington Post*, October 10: H01.

Dolan, Jill (2005) *Utopia in Performance*. Ann Arbor: University of Michigan Press.

Du Bois, W.E.B. (1926) "Criteria for Negro Art", *The Crisis*, 32, October: 290–97.

——(1946) "On the Drama", speech 7 October, Du Bois Papers, Box 381, University of Massachusetts/Amherst.

Elam, Harry J., Jr (2001) *Taking It to the Streets: The Social Protest Theater of Luis Valdez and Amiri Baraka*. Ann Arbor: University of Michigan Press.

Ellison, Julie and Eatman, Timothy K. (2008) *Scholarship in Public: Knowledge Creation and Tenure Policy in the Engaged University. A Resource on Promotion and Tenure in the Arts, Humanities, and Design*. Syracuse, NY: Imagining America. Online. Available HTTP: www.imaginingamerica.org/TTI/TTI_FINAL.pdf.

Flanagan, Hallie (1940; 1985) *Arena*. New York: Limelight Editions.

Florida, Richard (2002) *The Rise of the Creative Class*. New York: Basic Books.

Freire, Paulo (1970) *Pedagogy of the Oppressed*, trans. Myra Bergman Ramos. New York: Continuum.

Friedman, Debra and McAdam, Doug (1992) "Identity Incentives and Activism: Networks, Choices and the Life of a Social Movement", in Carol Mueller and Aldon Morris (eds) *Frontiers in Social Movement Theory*. New Haven, CT: Yale University Press.

Fung, Archon and Wright, Erik O. (2003) *Deepening Democracy*. London and New York: Verso.

Gielgud, John (1936; 1948) "Introduction" to Stanislavski, Constantin, *An Actor Prepares*, trans. Elizabeth Reynolds Hapgood. New York: Theatre Arts Books/ Methuen.

Goldbard, Arlene (2008) "The Curriculum Project Report". Online. Available HTTP: http://curriculumproject.net/report.html.

——(2008) "The Path of Stories: Artists and The Thousand Kites Project". Online. Available HTTP: www.communityarts.net/readingroom/archivefiles/2008/05/the_-path_of_sto.php.

Graves, James Bau (2005) *Cultural Democracy*. Urbana and Chicago, IL: University of Illinois Press.

Graves, James Bau and O'Neill, Phyllis M. (2004) "20 Years and Counting". Portland, ME: Center for Cultural Exchange.

Greig, Noël (2005) *Playwriting: A Practical Guide*. London and New York: Routledge.

Grotowski, Jerzy (1968) *Towards a Poor Theatre*. New York: Simon & Schuster.

Guinier, Lani and Torres, Gerard (2002) *The Miner's Canary*. Cambridge, MA: Harvard University Press.

Handke, Peter (1998) "Theater-in-the-Street and Theater-in-Theaters", in Jan Cohen-Cruz (ed.) *Radical Street Performance*. New York and London: Routledge.

Hoagland, Edward (1979) "Americana, etc.", in Geoffrey Wolff (ed.) *The Edward Hoagland Reader*. New York: Random House.

Holcomb, H. Briavel and Beauregard, Robert A. (1981) *Revitalizing Cities*. Washington, DC: Resource Publications in Geography.

Horton, Myles and Freire, Paulo (1990) *We Make the Road by Walking*. Philadelphia, PA: Temple University Press.

216

Jackson, Bruce (1987) "Interviewing", *Fieldwork*. Urbana, IL: University of Illinois Press, pp. 79–102.

Jackson, Maria Rosario (2008) "Art and Cultural Participation at the Heart of Community Life", in Joni Maya Cherbo, Ruth Ann Stewart and Margaret Jane Wyszomirski (eds) *Understanding the Arts and the Creative Sector in the United States*. New Brunswick, NJ and London: Rutgers University Press, pp. 92–104.

Jay, Gregory (2009) "What (Public) Good Are the (Engaged) Humanities?" Online. Available HTTP: http://curriculumproject.net/materials.html.

Johnstone, Keith (1979) *Impro: Improvisation and the Theatre*. London: Faber & Faber.

Kaufman, Michael T. (1999) Obituary for William H. Whyte. *New York Times*, January 13.

Kester, Grant H. (2004) *Conversation Pieces: Community + Communication in Modern Art*. Berkeley, Los Angeles, London: University of California Press.

King, Martin Luther, Jr (1963) "Letter from a Birmingham Jail." Online. Available HTTP: www.africa.upenn.edu/Articles_Gen/Letter_Birmingham.html.

Kuftinec, Sonja (2003) *Staging America: Cornerstone and Community-Based Theater*. Carbondale, IL: Southern Illinois University Press.

Kushner, Tony (1992) *Angels in America: A Gay Fantasia on National Themes. Part I: Millennium Approaches*. New York: Theatre Communications Group.

——(1994) *Angels in America: A Gay Fantasia on National Themes. Part II: Perestroika*. New York: Theatre Communications Group.

Laub, Dori (1992) "Bearing Witness or the Vicissitudes of Listening", in Shoshana Felman and Dori Laub (eds) *Testimony*. New York and London: Routledge.

Lewis, David Levering (2000) *W.E.B. Du Bois*. New York: Henry Holt & Co.

Lind, Levy (1972) Aeschylus: *Prometheus Bound*, in *Ten Greek Plays in Contemporary Translation*. Belmont, CA: Wadsworth Publishing.

Markusen, Ann and Johnson, Amanda (2006) *Artists' Centers: Evolution and Impact on Careers, Neighborhoods and Economies*. Minneapolis: University of Minnesota, Humphrey Institute of Public Affairs.

Martin, Randy (2006) "Staging the Political", in Jan Cohen-Cruz and Mady Schutzman (eds) *A Boal Companion*. New York and London: Routledge, pp. 23–32.

Massey, Doreen (1994) *Space, Place and Gender*. Minneapolis: University of Minnesota Press.

McCall, Anthony (2009) "Lawrence Weiner & Anthony McCall", *The Creative Times*. Online. Available HTTP: www.creativetime.org/programs/archive/2009/ctimes/P1.html.

McKnight, John and Kretzmann, John (1993) *Building Communities from the Inside Out: A Path Toward Finding and Mobilizing Community Assets*. Evanston, IL: Institute for Policy Research, Northwestern University.

Mill, John Stuart (1859; 1956) *On Liberty*. New York: Bobbs-Merrill Co.

Murray, Paul (2009) "Playing with Mental Health: Pathologizing Peter to Play Paul", unpublished dissertation. Winchester, UK: University of Winchester.

Mutz, Diana C. (2006) *Hearing the Other Side*. New York: Cambridge University Press.

Nicholson, Helen (2005) *Applied Drama*. New York: Palgrave Macmillan.

Onondaga Citizens League (2006) "Leveraging Better Outcomes for Downtown". Online. Available HTTP: http://onondagacitizensleague.org/ocl_studies/2006/pdfs/OCLRevDowtownrev2.pdf.

Prentki, Tim and Preston, Sheila (2009) *The Applied Theatre Reader*. London and New York: Routledge.

Putnam, Robert (2000) "The Arts and Social Capital", in *Better Together: The Report*, Saguaro Seminar, Kennedy School of Government, Harvard University. Online. Available HTTP: www.bettertogether.org/pdfs/Arts.pdf.

——(2003) *Bowling Alone: The Collapse and Revival of American Community*. New York: Simon & Schuster.

Putnam, Robert and Feldstein, Lewis (2003) *Better Together: Restoring the American Community*. New York: Simon & Schuster.

Rawls, John (1971; 1999) *A Theory of Justice*. Cambridge, MA: Harvard University Press.

Regis, Helen (2010) "Second-Line Parades, Citizenship and the Future of Public Space in New Orleans after Katrina", in Adelaide Russo and Simon Harel (eds) *Espaces Precaires: Enonciation des lieux/Le lieu de L'énonciation dans les contextes francophones interculturels*. Saint Nicholas, Quebec: Presses de l'Université Laval. (In press.)

Reinelt, Janelle (1997) "Notes on *Angels in America* as American Epic Theater", in Deborah R. Geis and Steven F. Kruger (eds) *Approaching the Millennium*. Ann Arbor: University of Michigan, pp. 234–44.

Rohd, Michael (1998) *Theatre for Community, Conflict & Dialogue: The Hope is Vital Training Manual*. Portsmouth, NH: Heinemann.

Roman, David (1997) "November 1, 1992: AIDS/*Angels in America*", in Deborah R. Geis and Steven F. Kruger (eds) *Approaching the Millennium*. Ann Arbor: University of Michigan, pp. 40–55.

Romano, Carlin (2009) "Amartya Sen Shakes up Justice Theory", *The Chronicle of Higher Education*, September 18: B4.

Schechner, Richard (1985) *Between Theater and Anthropology*. Philadelphia, PA: University of Pennsylvania Press.

Schutzman, Mady (2006) *Upset!* Live performance and subsequent DVD produced by CalArts Community Arts Partnership and Plaza de la Raza at REDCAT, Los Angeles, 27 May.

——(2009) "What a Riot!" in Sue Jennings (ed.) *Dramatherapy and Social Theatre: Necessary Dialogues*. London: Routledge.

Scriven, Michael (1999) *Jean-Paul Sartre: Politics and Culture in Postwar France*. New York: St Martin's Press.

Sen, Rinku (2003) *Stir It Up*. San Francisco, CA: Jossey-Bass.

Shulan, Michael *et al.* (2004) "Introduction", in *Here is New York*. Zurich: Scalo Publishers.

Smith, Linda Tuhiwai (1999) *Decolonizing Methodologies: Research and Indigenous Peoples*. London: Zed Books.

Smitherman, Geneva (1977) *Talkin and Testifyin*. Detroit, MI: Wayne State University Press.

Spinrad, Diana (1991) "Address Unknown", *Chicago Reader*, April 11.

Spolin, Viola (1999) *Improvisation for the Theater*, 3rd edn. Evanston, IL: Northwestern University Press.

Stewart, Ruth Ann (2008) "The Arts and Artist in Urban Revitalization", in Joni Maya Cherbo, Ruth Ann Stewart and Margaret Jane Wyszomirski (eds)

Understanding the Arts and the Creative Sector in the United States. New Brunswick, NJ and London: Rutgers University Press, pp. 105–28.

Stockton Rush Bartol Foundation (undated) *Culture Builds Community: The Power of Arts and Culture in Community Building*. Philadelphia, PA: Stockton Rush Bartol Foundation.

Strom, Elizabeth (2002) "Converting Pork into Porcelain: Cultural Institutions and Downtown Development", *Urban Affairs Review* 38 (1), September 3–21: 5.

Tarrow, Sidney (1998) *Power in Movement: Social Movements and Contentious Politics*. Cambridge, UK: Cambridge University Press.

Taussig, Michael and Schechner, Richard (1994) "Boal in Brazil, France, the USA", in Mady Schutzman and Jan Cohen-Cruz (eds) *Playing Boal: Theatre, Therapy, Activism*. London and New York: Routledge, pp. 17–32.

Taylor, Diana (1997) "Making a Spectacle: the Mothers of the Plaza de Mayo", in Alexis Jetter, Annelise Orleck and Diana Taylor (eds) *The Politics of Motherhood*. Hanover, NH: University Press of New England.

Thompson, James (2003) *Applied Theater: Bewilderment and Beyond*. Oxford: Peter Lang.

——(2005) *Digging Up Stories: Applied Theatre, Performance and War*. Manchester, UK: Manchester University Press.

——(2009) *Performance Affects: Applied Theatre and the End of Effect*. London and New York: Palgrave Macmillan.

Thompson, James and Schechner, Richard (2004) "Why 'Social Theatre'?", *TDR: The Journal of Performance Studies* T181: 11–16.

Thompson, Nato (2009) *Introduction to The Creative Time Summit: Revolutions in Public Practice*, program, New York Public Library, New York, October 23–24.

Vorlicky, Robert, ed. (1998) *Kushner in Conversation*. Ann Arbor, MI: University of Michigan.

Warren, Jenifer (2008) *One in 100: Behind Bars in America 2008*. Washington, DC: Pew Charitable Trusts.

Whyte, William H. (2001) *The Social Life of Small Urban Places*. New York: Project for Public Spaces.

Willett, John, ed. (1957; 1964) *Brecht on Theatre*. New York: Hill & Wang.

INDEX